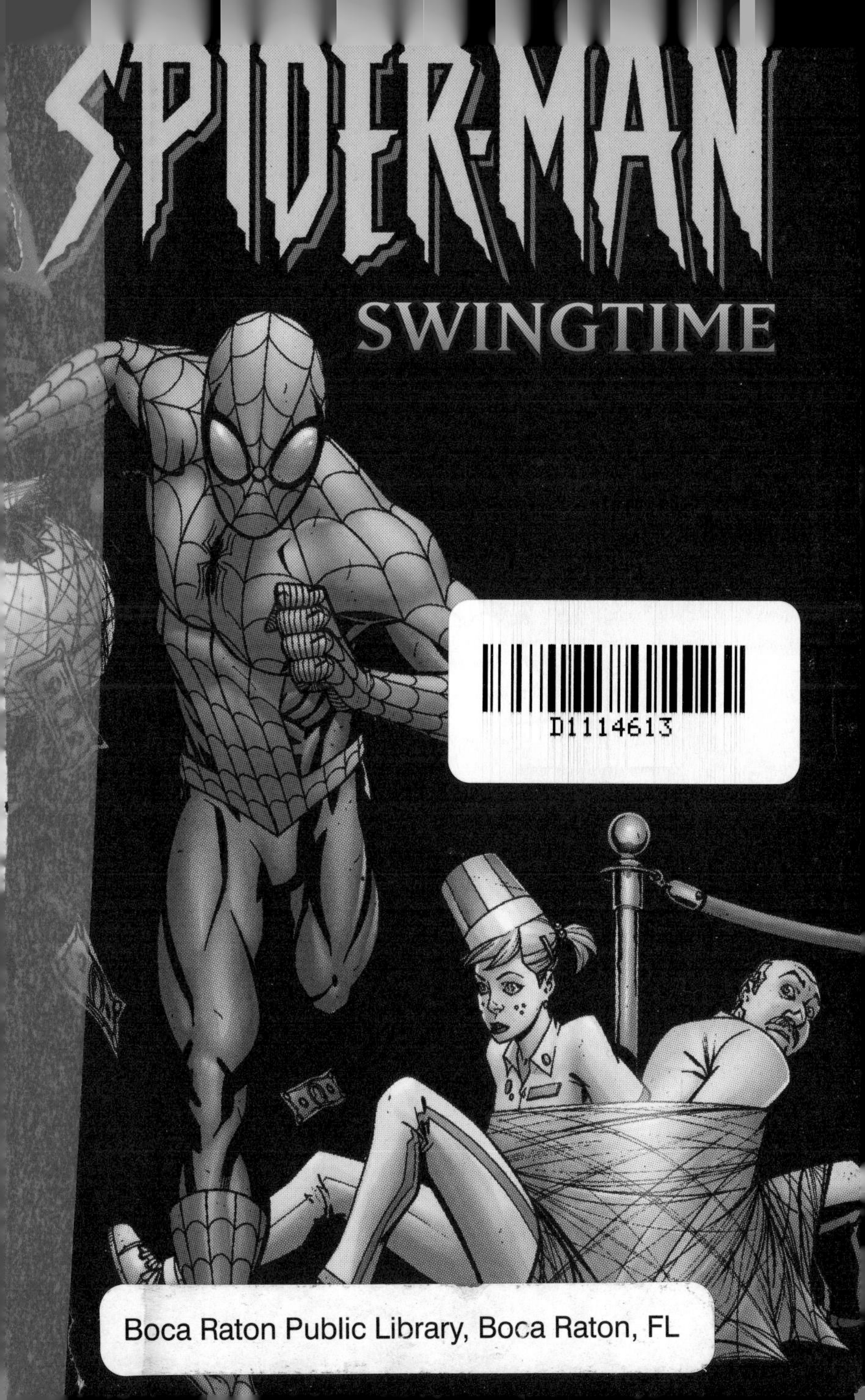
SPIDER-MAN
SWINGTIME

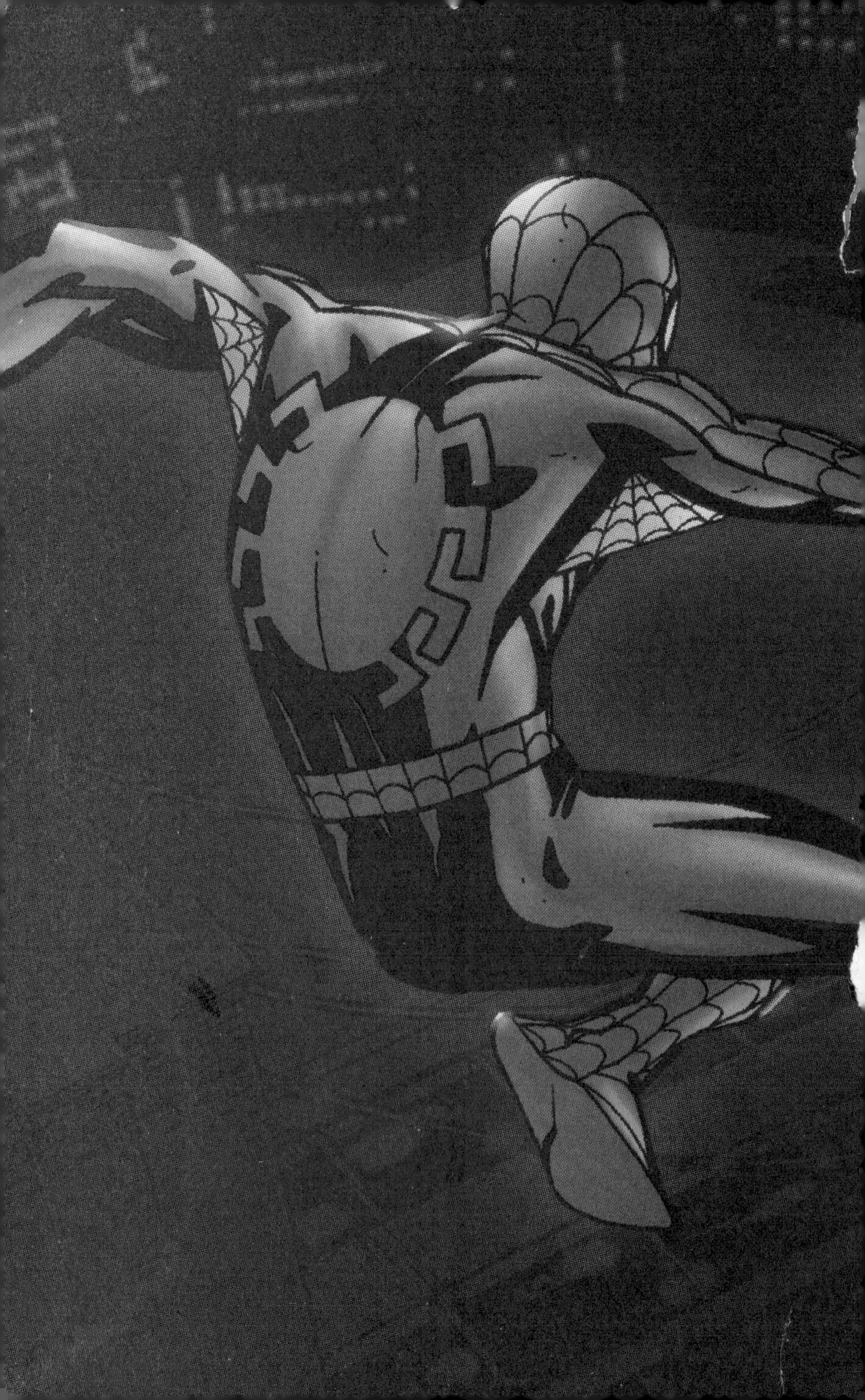

SPIDER-MAN

SWINGTIME

Writers: **Todd Dezago & Mike Raicht**

Pencils: **Patrick Scherberger, Logan Lubera, Valentine De Landro & Derec Aucoin**

Inks: **Rob Campanella, Craig Yeung, Norman Lee & Derec Aucoin**

Colors: **UDON's Lary Molinar with Christina Strain, Lisa Lubera, Guru eFX & Avalon's Dave Kemp**

Letters: **Virtual Calligraphy's Randy Gentile, Rus Wooton & Cory Petit**

Assistant Editor: **MacKenzie Cadenhead**

Editor: **C.B. Cebulski**

Consulting Editor: **Ralph Macchio**

Collections Editor: **Jeff Youngquist**

Assistant Editor: **Jennifer Grünwald**

Book Designer: **Carrie Beadle**

Editor in Chief: **Joe Quesada**

Publisher: **Dan Buckley**

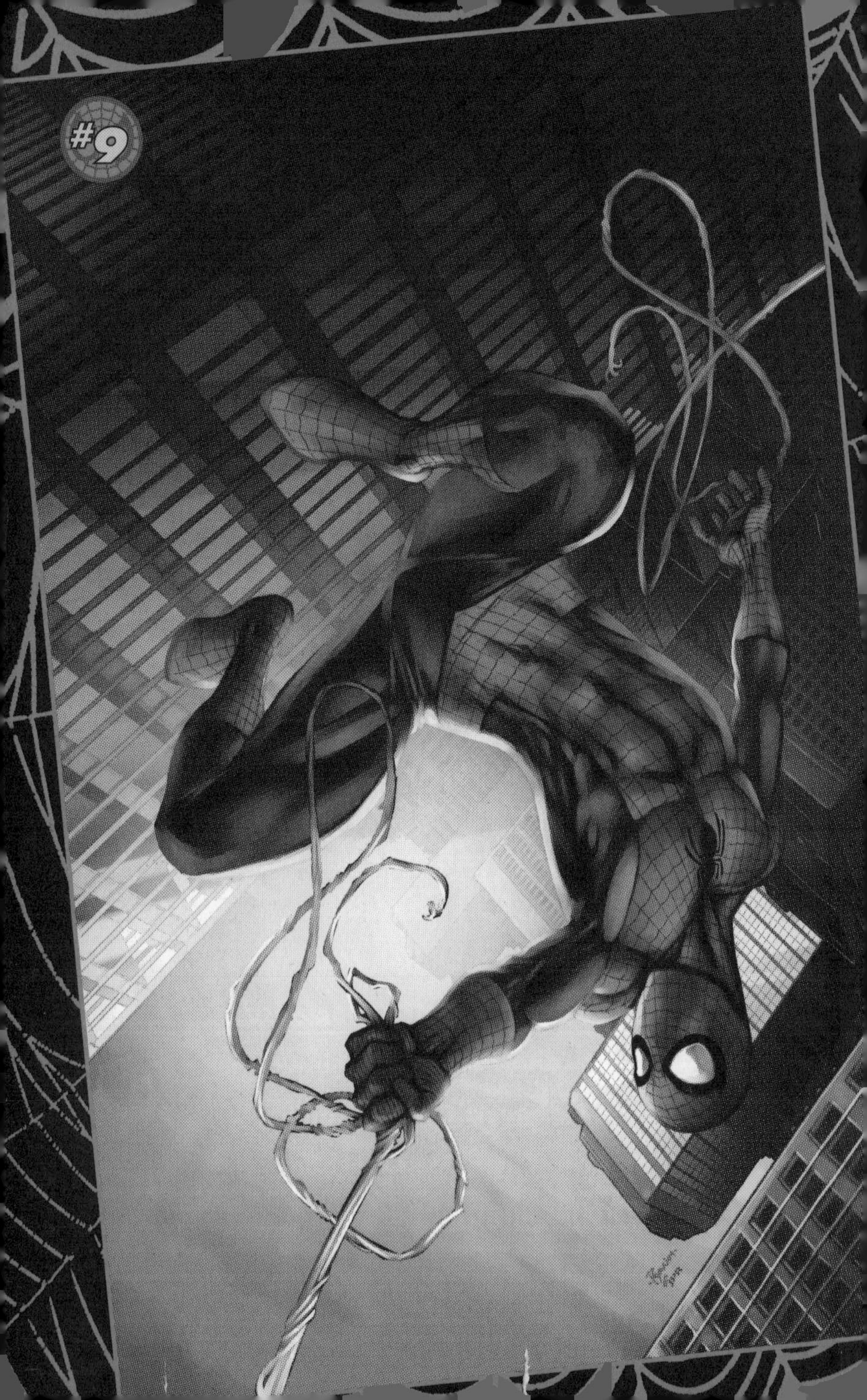
#9

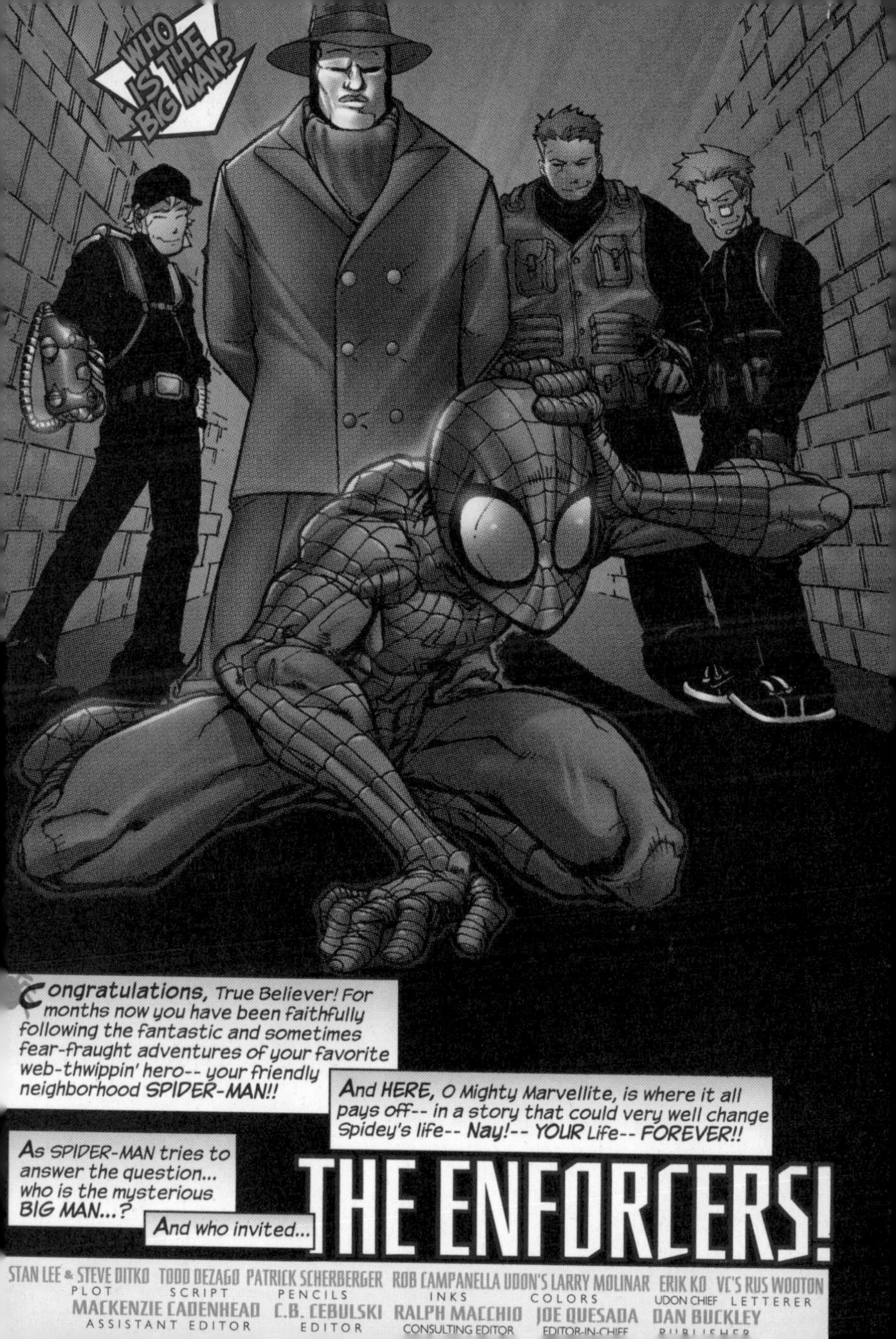
WHO IS THE BIG MAN?
Congratulations, True Believer! For months now you have been faithfully following the fantastic and sometimes fear-fraught adventures of your favorite web-thwippin' hero-- your friendly neighborhood SPIDER-MAN!!
And HERE, O Mighty Marvellite, is where it all pays off-- in a story that could very well change Spidey's life-- Nay!-- YOUR Life-- FOREVER!!
As SPIDER-MAN tries to answer the question... who is the mysterious BIG MAN...?
And who invited...
THE ENFORCERS!
STAN LEE & STEVE DITKO PLOT
TODD DEZAGO SCRIPT
PATRICK SCHERBERGER PENCILS
ROB CAMPANELLA INKS
UDON'S LARRY MOLINAR COLORS
ERIK KO UDON CHIEF
VC'S RUS WOOTON LETTERER
MACKENZIE CADENHEAD ASSISTANT EDITOR
C.B. CEBULSKI EDITOR
RALPH MACCHIO CONSULTING EDITOR
JOE QUESADA EDITOR-IN-CHIEF
DAN BUCKLEY

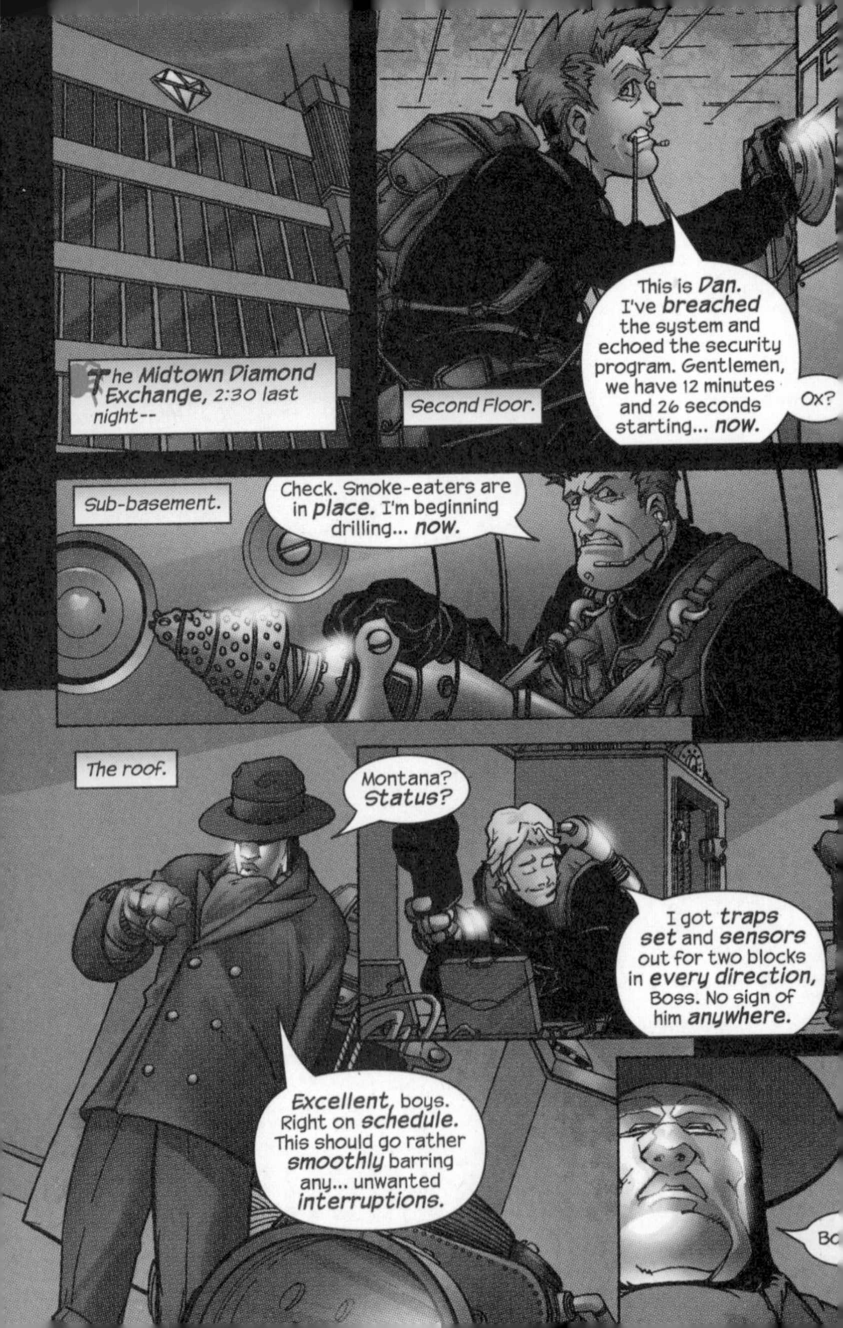

The Midtown Diamond Exchange, 2:30 last night--
Second Floor.
This is Dan. I've breached the system and echoed the security program. Gentlemen, we have 12 minutes and 26 seconds starting... now.
Ox?
Sub-basement.
Check. Smoke-eaters are in place. I'm beginning drilling... now.
The roof.
Montana? Status?
I got traps set and sensors out for two blocks in every direction, Boss. No sign of him anywhere.
Excellent, boys. Right on schedule. This should go rather smoothly barring any... unwanted interruptions.

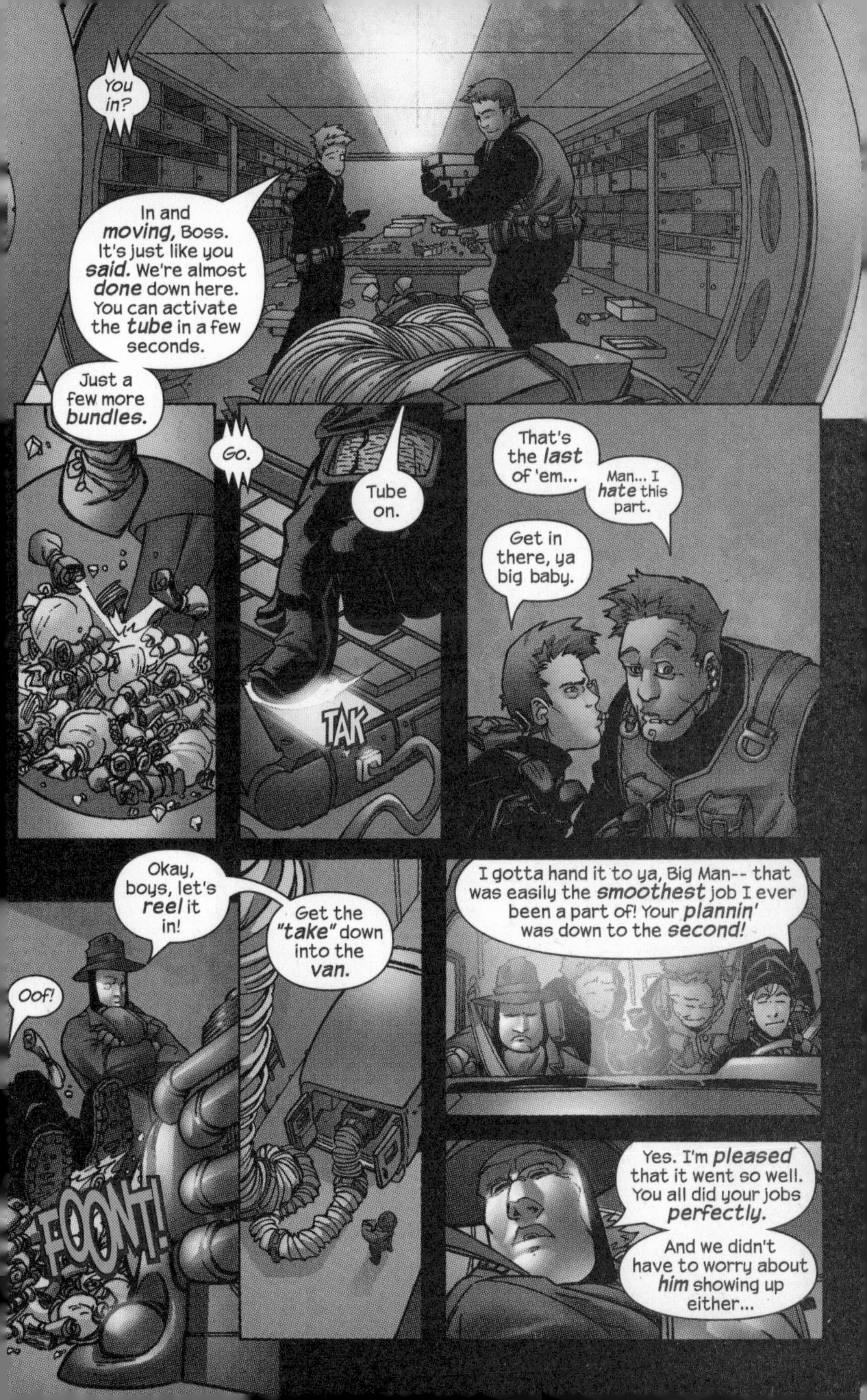
You in?
In and moving, Boss. It's just like you said. We're almost done down here. You can activate the tube in a few seconds.
Just a few more bundles.
Go.
Tube on.
TAK
That's the last of 'em...
Man... I hate this part.
Get in there, ya big baby.
Okay, boys, let's reel it in!
Get the "take" down into the van.
Oof!
FOONT!
I gotta hand it to ya, Big Man-- that was easily the smoothest job I ever been a part of! Your plannin' was down to the second!
Yes. I'm pleased that it went so well. You all did your jobs perfectly.
And we didn't have to worry about him showing up either...

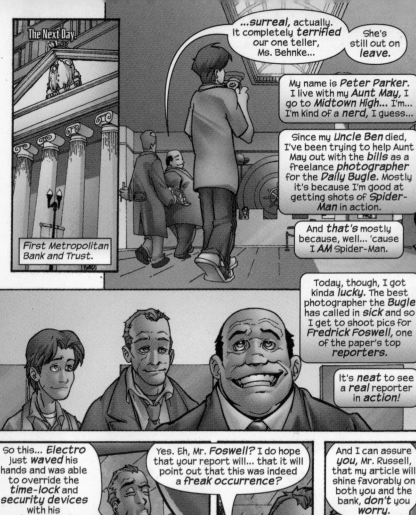

The Next Day.

First Metropolitan Bank and Trust.

...*surreal*, actually. It completely *terrified* our one teller, Ms. Behnke...

She's still out on *leave*.

My name is *Peter Parker*. I live with my *Aunt May*, I go to *Midtown High*... I'm... I'm kind of a *nerd*, I guess...

Since my *Uncle Ben* died, I've been trying to help Aunt May out with the *bills* as a freelance *photographer* for the *Daily Bugle*. Mostly it's because I'm good at getting shots of *Spider-Man* in action.

And *that's* mostly because, well... 'cause I *AM* Spider-Man.

Today, though, I got kinda *lucky*. The best photographer the *Bugle* has called in *sick* and so I get to shoot pics for *Fredrick Foswell*, one of the paper's top *reporters*.

It's *neat* to see a *real* reporter in *action!*

So this... *Electro* just *waved* his hands and was able to override the *time-lock* and *security devices* with his *electricity?*

Yes. Eh, Mr. *Foswell?* I do hope that your report will... that it will point out that this was indeed a *freak occurrence?*

And I can assure *you*, Mr. Russell, that my article will shine favorably on both you and the bank, *don't* you *worry.*

We *pride* ourselves on having never been *robbed* before. We'd like to *reassure* our patrons that something like this will *never* happen *again.*

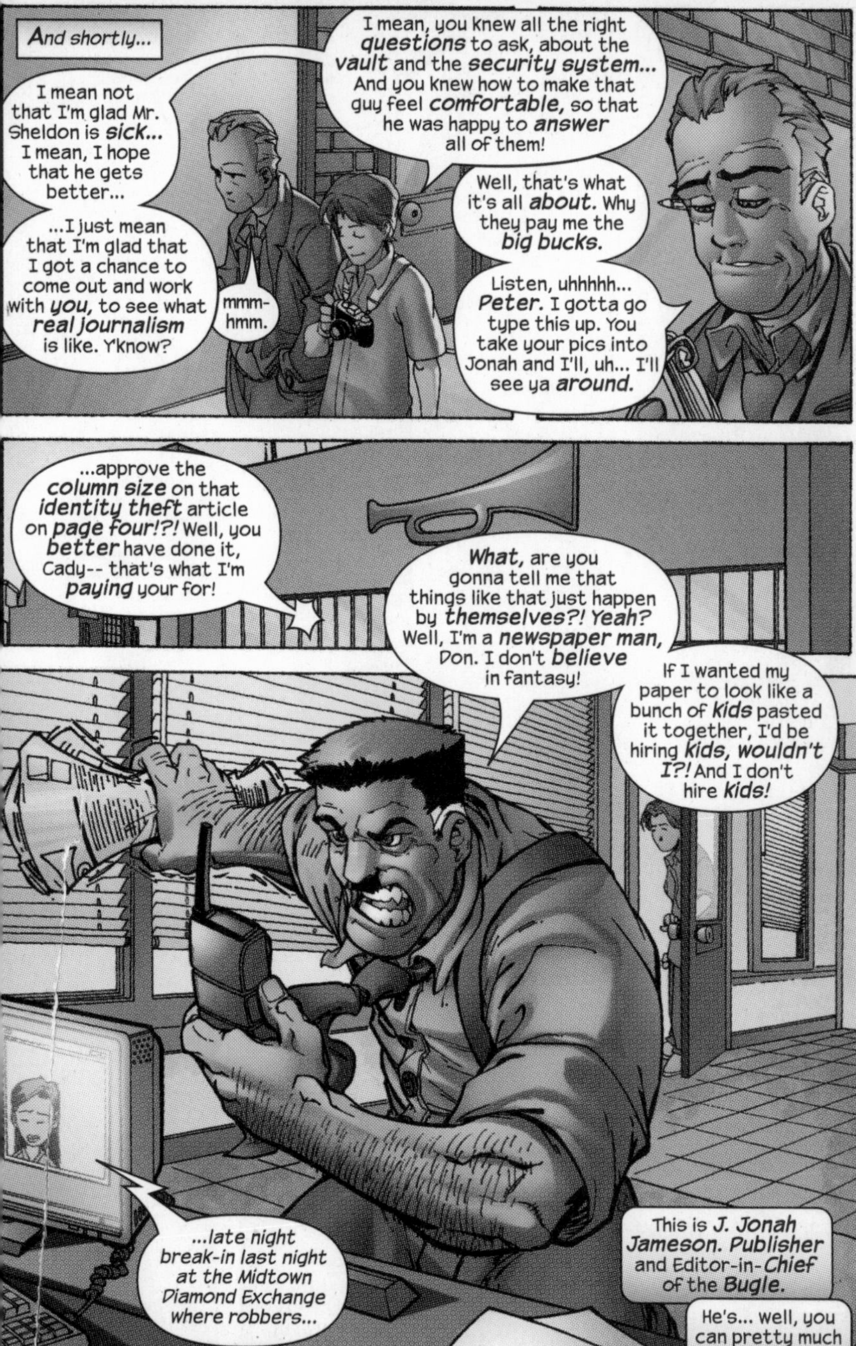
And shortly...
I mean not that I'm glad Mr. Sheldon is sick... I mean, I hope that he gets better...
...I just mean that I'm glad that I got a chance to come out and work with you, to see what real journalism is like. Y'know?
mmm-hmm.
I mean, you knew all the right questions to ask, about the vault and the security system... And you knew how to make that guy feel comfortable, so that he was happy to answer all of them!
Well, that's what it's all about. Why they pay me the big bucks.
Listen, uhhhhh... Peter. I gotta go type this up. You take your pics into Jonah and I'll, uh... I'll see ya around.
...approve the column size on that identity theft article on page four!?! Well, you better have done it, Cady-- that's what I'm paying your for!
What, are you gonna tell me that things like that just happen by themselves?! Yeah? Well, I'm a newspaper man, Don. I don't believe in fantasy!
If I wanted my paper to look like a bunch of kids pasted it together, I'd be hiring kids, wouldn't I?! And I don't hire kids!
...late night break-in last night at the Midtown Diamond Exchange where robbers...
This is J. Jonah Jameson. Publisher and Editor-in-Chief of the Bugle.
He's... well, you can pretty much see how he is.

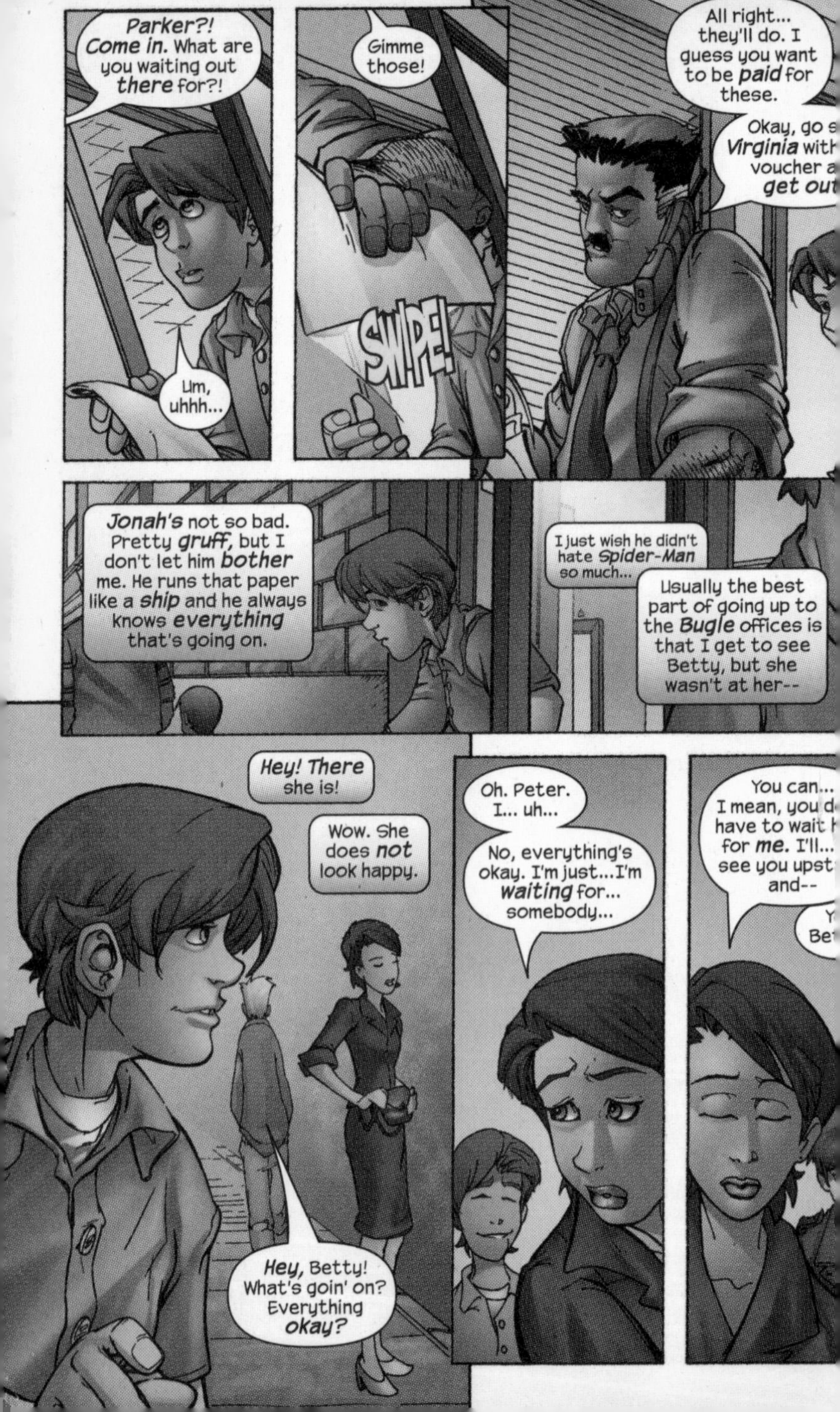
Parker?! Come in. What are you waiting out there for?!
Um, uhhh...
Gimme those!
SWIPE!
All right... they'll do. I guess you want to be paid for these.
Okay, go s
Virginia wit
voucher a
get out
Jonah's not so bad. Pretty gruff, but I don't let him bother me. He runs that paper like a ship and he always knows everything that's going on.
I just wish he didn't hate Spider-Man so much...
Usually the best part of going up to the Bugle offices is that I get to see Betty, but she wasn't at her--
Hey! There she is!
Wow. She does not look happy.
Hey, Betty! What's goin' on? Everything okay?
Oh. Peter. I... uh...
No, everything's okay. I'm just...I'm waiting for... somebody...
You can...
I mean, you d
have to wait
for me. I'll...
see you upst
and--

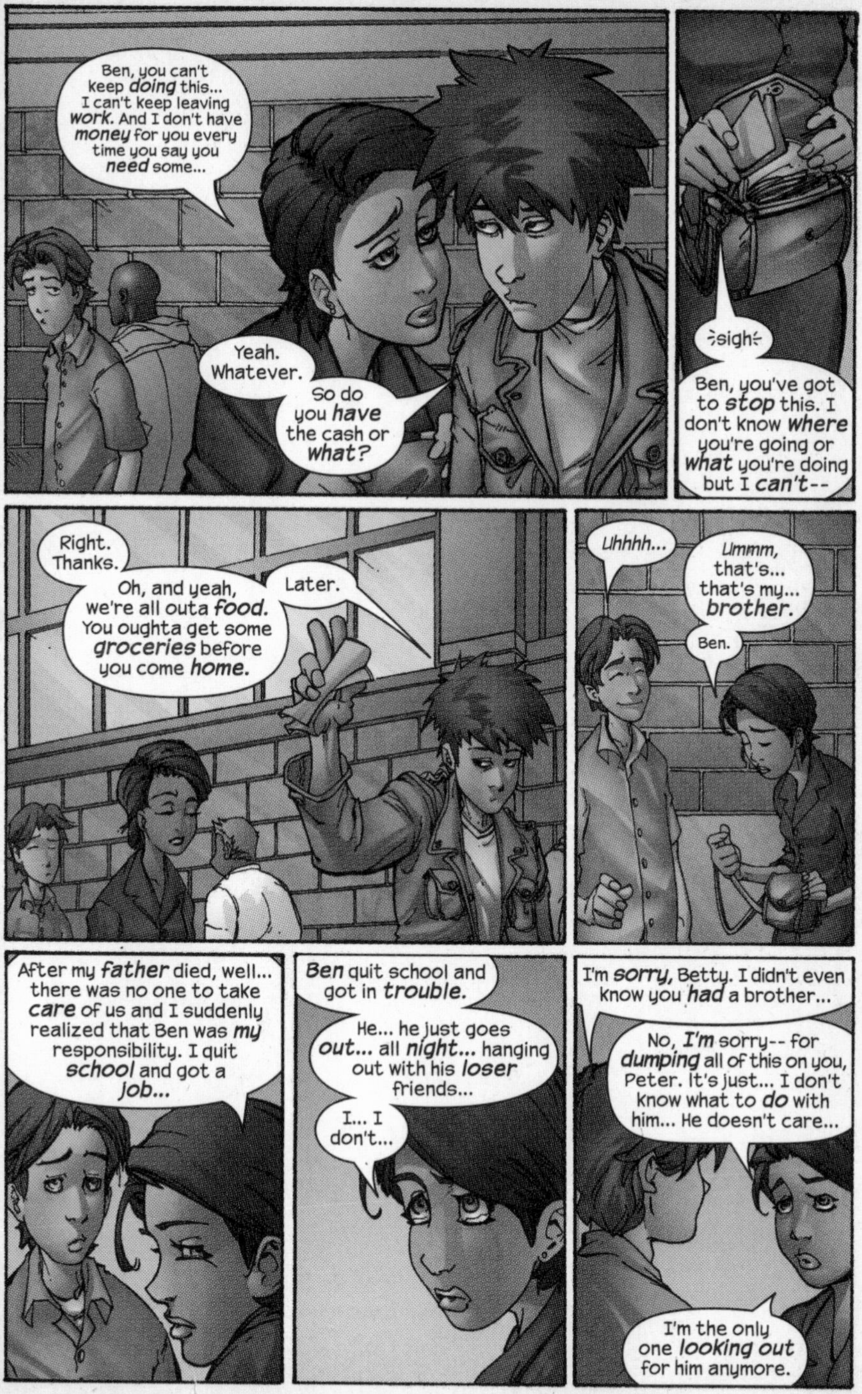
Ben, you can't keep doing this... I can't keep leaving work. And I don't have money for you every time you say you need some...
Yeah. Whatever.
So do you have the cash or what?
sigh
Ben, you've got to stop this. I don't know where you're going or what you're doing but I can't--
Right. Thanks.
Oh, and yeah, we're all outa food. You oughta get some groceries before you come home.
Later.
Uhhhh...
Ummm, that's... that's my... brother.
Ben.
After my father died, well... there was no one to take care of us and I suddenly realized that Ben was my responsibility. I quit school and got a job...
Ben quit school and got in trouble.
He... he just goes out... all night... hanging out with his loser friends...
I... I don't...
I'm sorry, Betty. I didn't even know you had a brother...
No, I'm sorry-- for dumping all of this on you, Peter. It's just... I don't know what to do with him... He doesn't care...
I'm the only one looking out for him anymore.

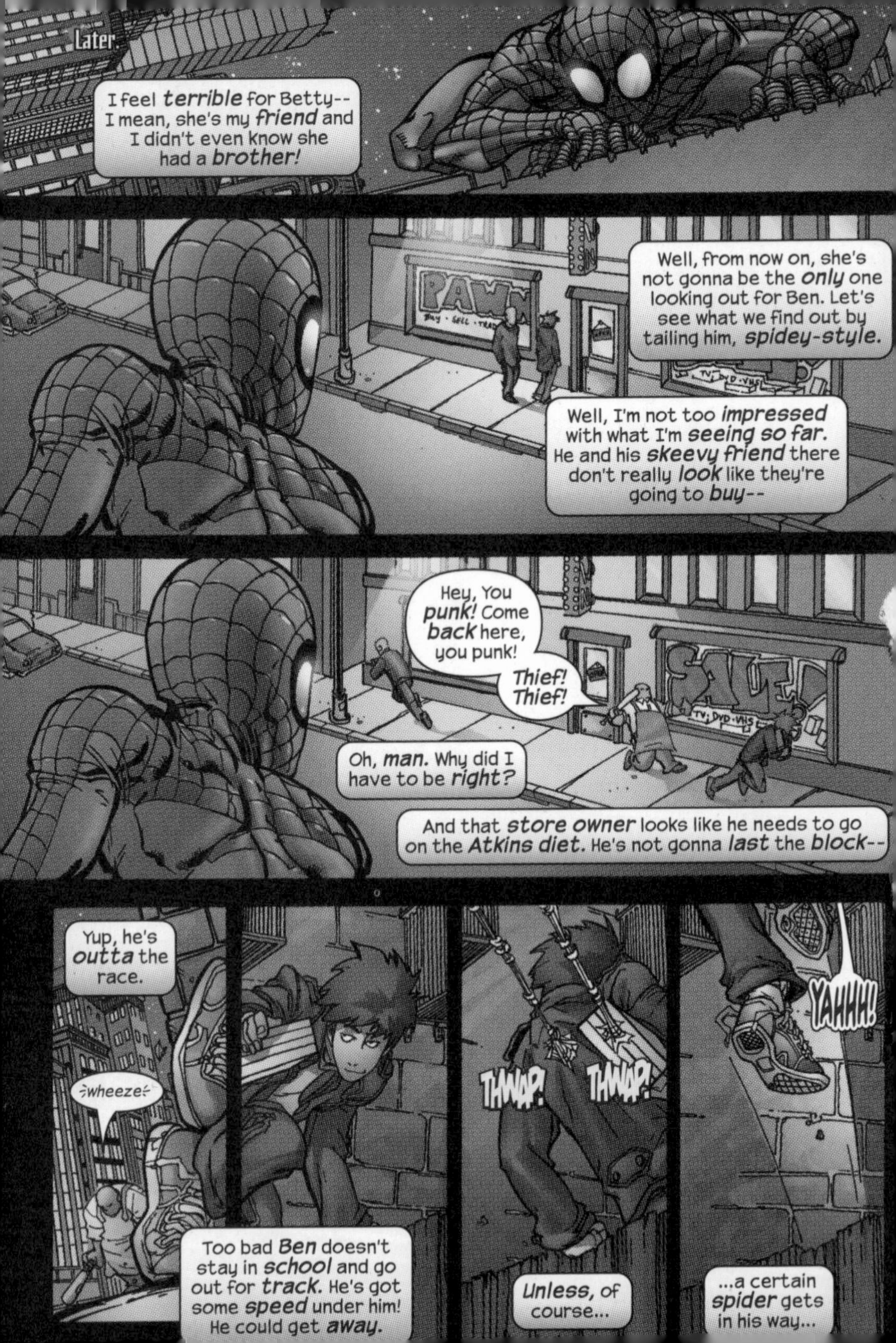
Later.
I feel terrible for Betty-- I mean, she's my friend and I didn't even know she had a brother!
Well, from now on, she's not gonna be the only one looking out for Ben. Let's see what we find out by tailing him, spidey-style.
Well, I'm not too impressed with what I'm seeing so far. He and his skeevy friend there don't really look like they're going to buy--
Hey, You punk! Come back here, you punk!
Thief! Thief!
Oh, man. Why did I have to be right?
And that store owner looks like he needs to go on the Atkins diet. He's not gonna last the block--
Yup, he's outta the race.
wheeze
Too bad Ben doesn't stay in school and go out for track. He's got some speed under him! He could get away.
THWAP! THWAP!
Unless, of course...
...a certain spider gets in his way...
YAHHH!

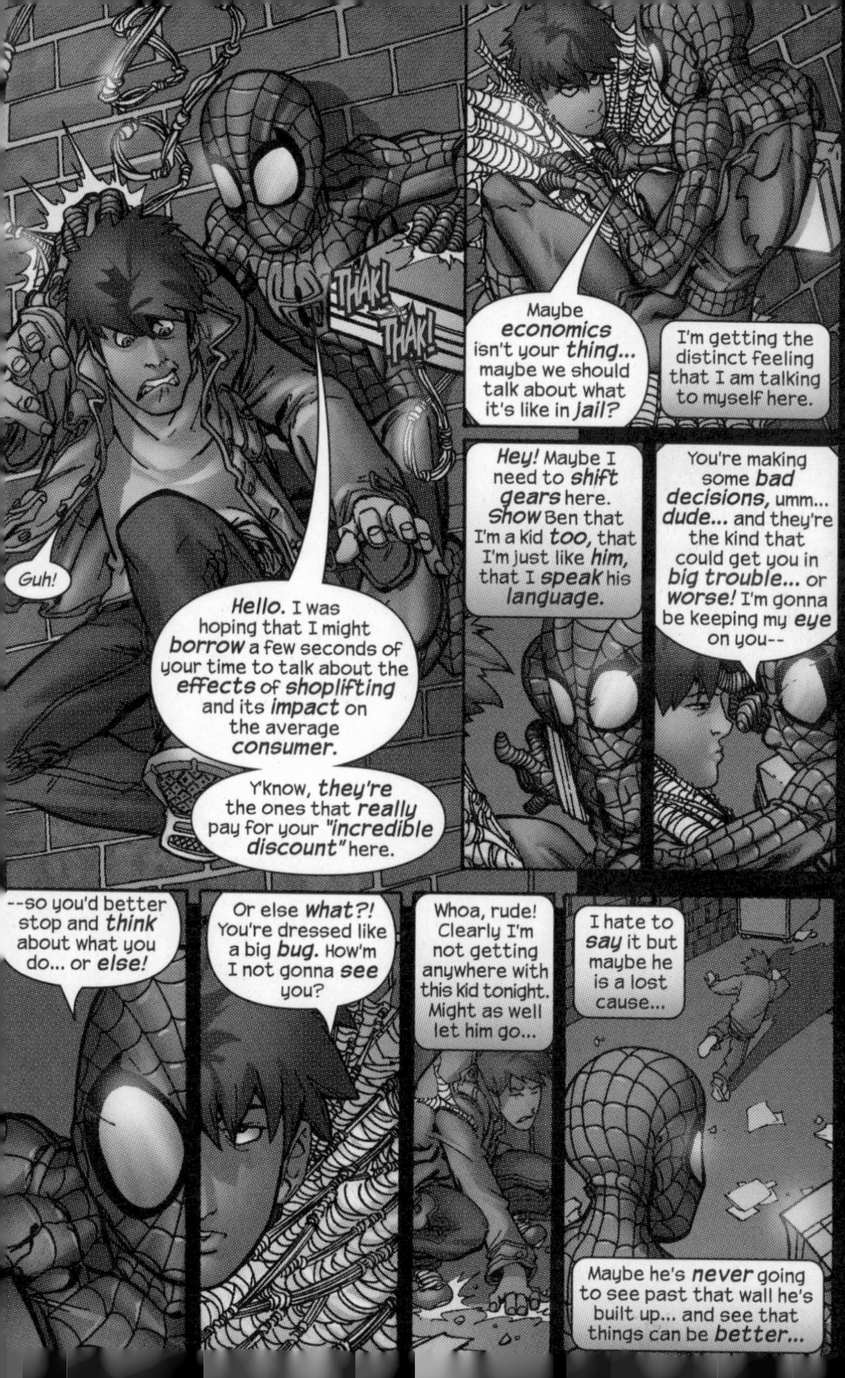

THAK!
THAK!
Guh!
Hello. I was hoping that I might borrow a few seconds of your time to talk about the effects of shoplifting and its impact on the average consumer.
Y'know, they're the ones that really pay for your "incredible discount" here.
Maybe economics isn't your thing... maybe we should talk about what it's like in jail?
I'm getting the distinct feeling that I am talking to myself here.
Hey! Maybe I need to shift gears here. Show Ben that I'm a kid too, that I'm just like him, that I speak his language.
You're making some bad decisions, umm... dude... and they're the kind that could get you in big trouble... or worse! I'm gonna be keeping my eye on you--
--so you'd better stop and think about what you do... or else!
Or else what?! You're dressed like a big bug. How'm I not gonna see you?
Whoa, rude! Clearly I'm not getting anywhere with this kid tonight. Might as well let him go...
I hate to say it but maybe he is a lost cause...
Maybe he's never going to see past that wall he's built up... and see that things can be better...

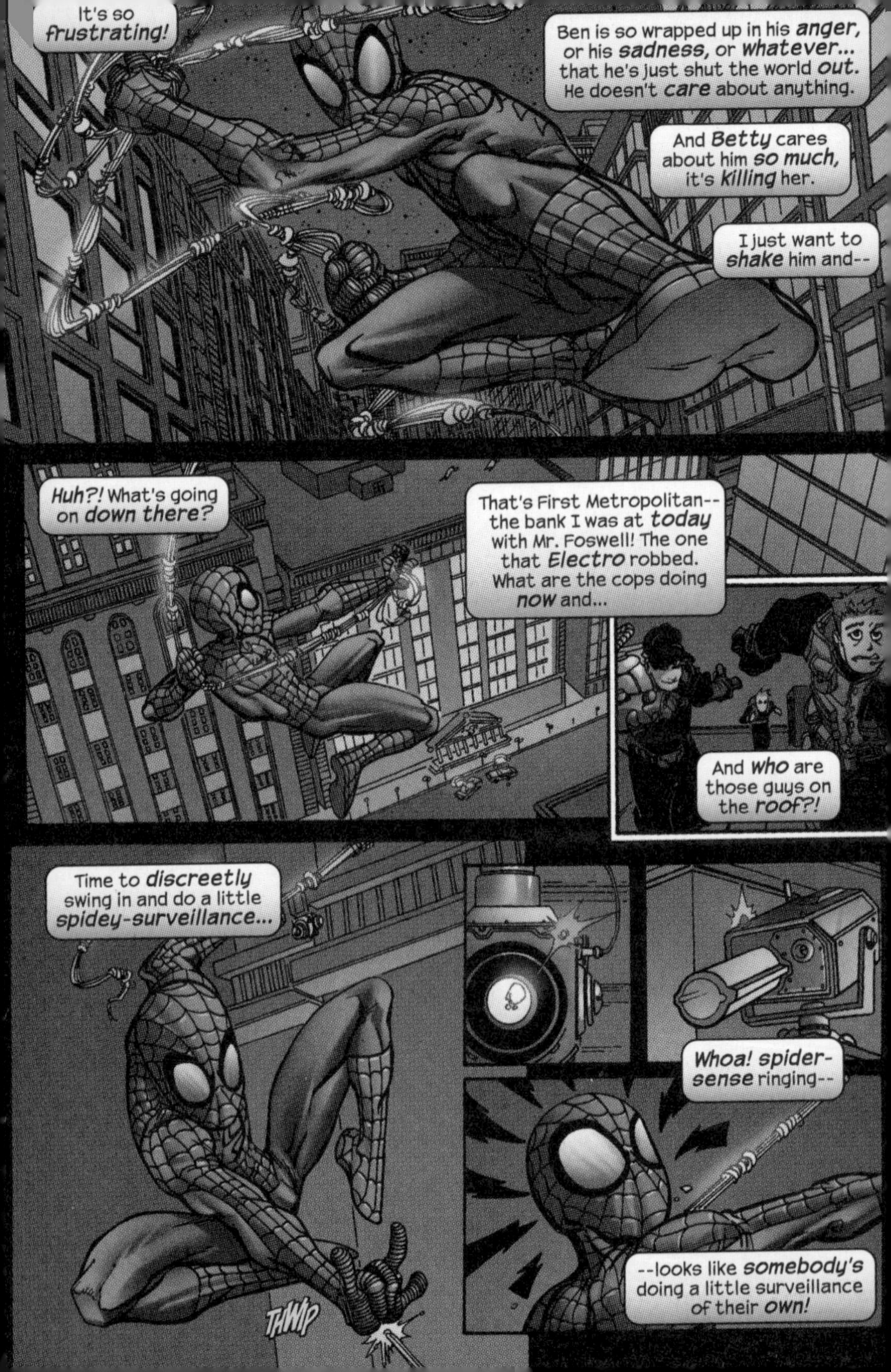
It's so frustrating!
Ben is so wrapped up in his anger, or his sadness, or whatever... that he's just shut the world out. He doesn't care about anything.
And Betty cares about him so much, it's killing her.
I just want to shake him and--
Huh?! What's going on down there?
That's First Metropolitan-- the bank I was at today with Mr. Foswell! The one that Electro robbed. What are the cops doing now and...
And who are those guys on the roof?!
Time to discreetly swing in and do a little spidey-surveillance...
THWIP
Whoa! spider-sense ringing--
--looks like somebody's doing a little surveillance of their own!

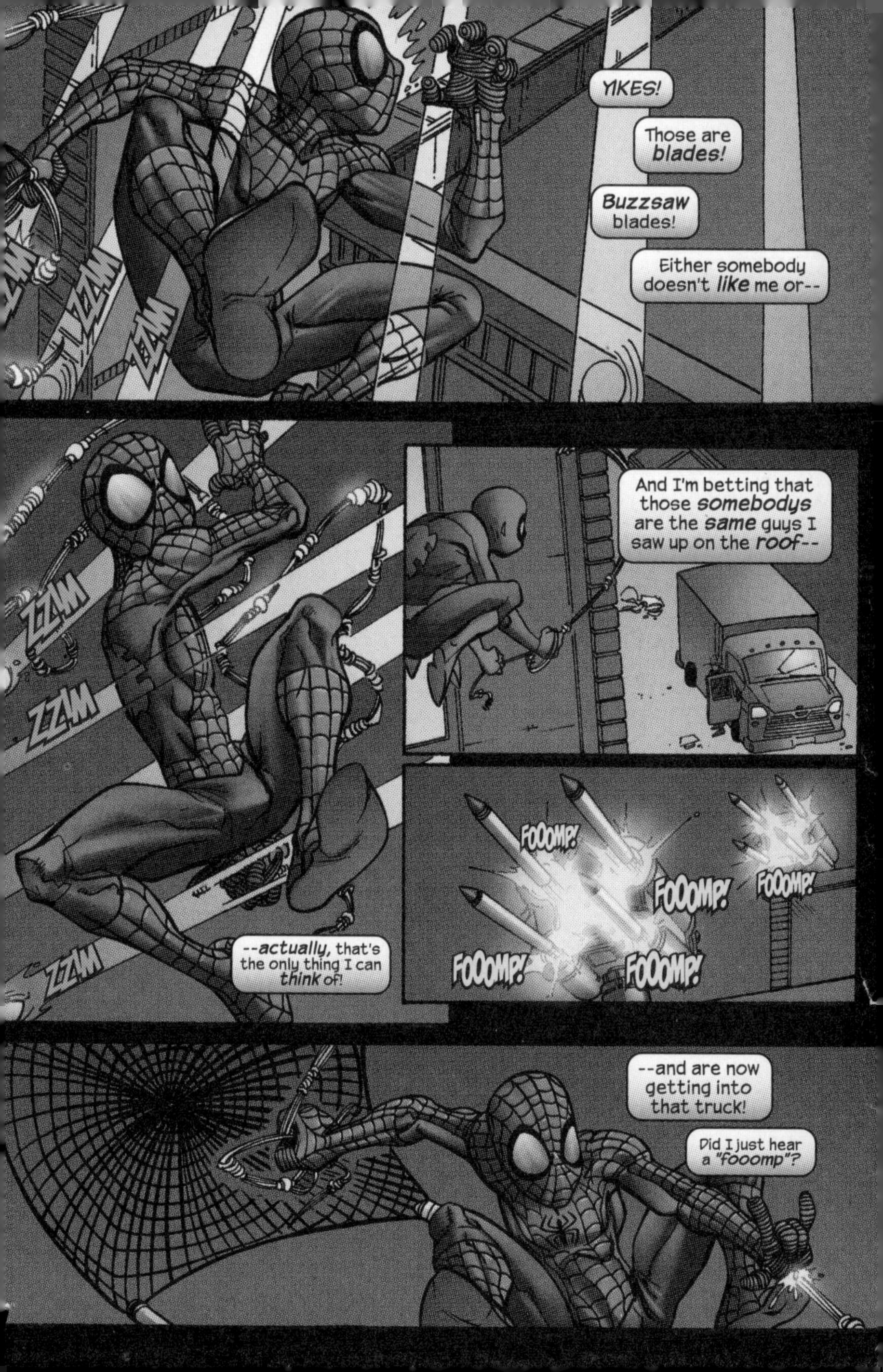

YIKES!
Those are blades!
Buzzsaw blades!
Either somebody doesn't like me or--
ZZAM
ZZAM
ZZAM
And I'm betting that those somebodys are the same guys I saw up on the roof--
ZZZAM
ZZAM
ZZAM
--actually, that's the only thing I can think of!
FOOOMP!
FOOOMP!
FOOOMP!
FOOOMP!
FOOOMP!
--and are now getting into that truck!
Did I just hear a "fooomp"?

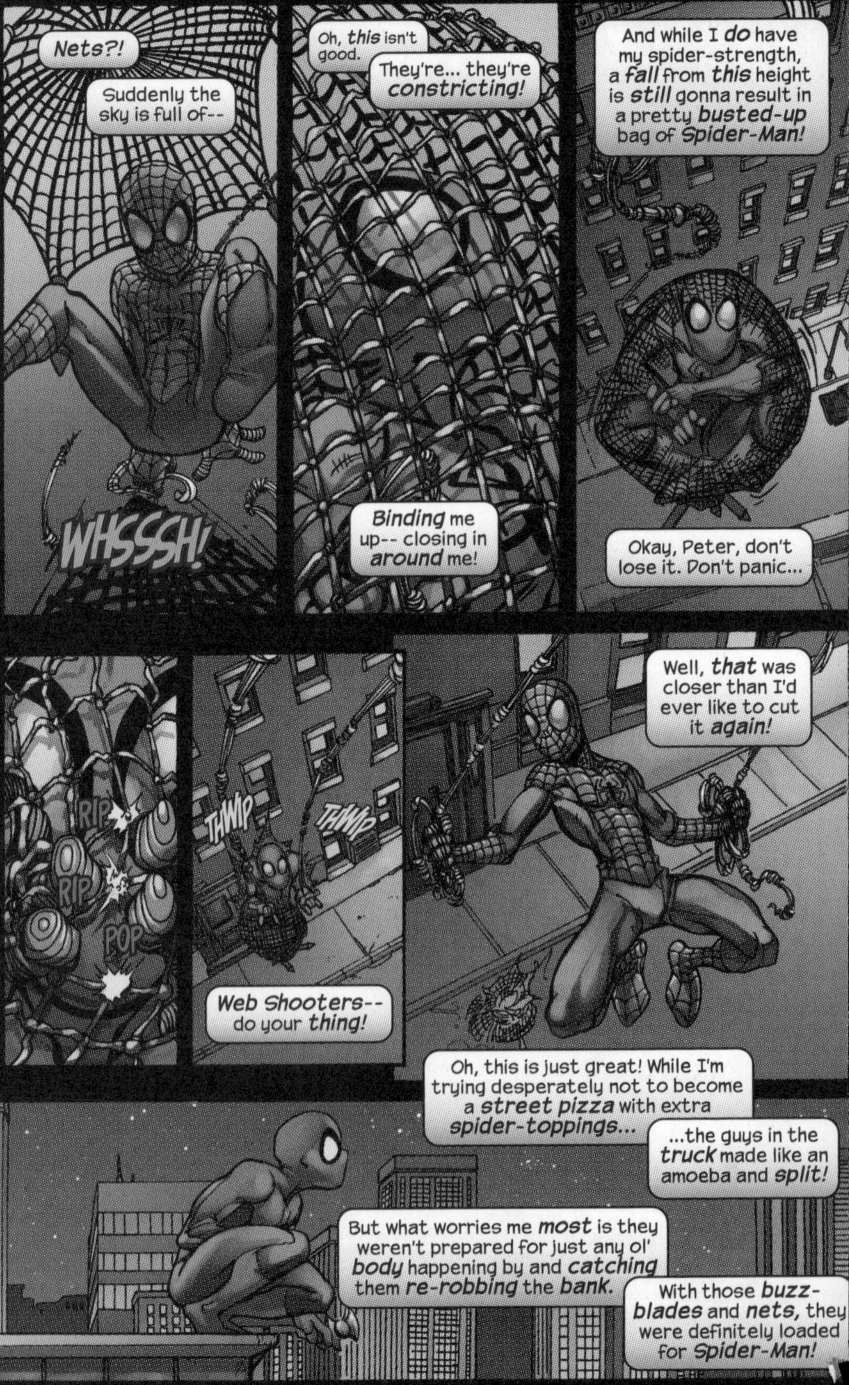
Nets?!
Suddenly the sky is full of--
WHSSSH!
Oh, this isn't good.
They're... they're constricting!
Binding me up-- closing in around me!
And while I do have my spider-strength, a fall from this height is still gonna result in a pretty busted-up bag of Spider-Man!
Okay, Peter, don't lose it. Don't panic...
RIP
RIP
POP
THWIP
THWIP
Web Shooters-- do your thing!
Well, that was closer than I'd ever like to cut it again!
Oh, this is just great! While I'm trying desperately not to become a street pizza with extra spider-toppings...
...the guys in the truck made like an amoeba and split!
But what worries me most is they weren't prepared for just any ol' body happening by and catching them re-robbing the bank.
With those buzz-blades and nets, they were definitely loaded for Spider-Man!

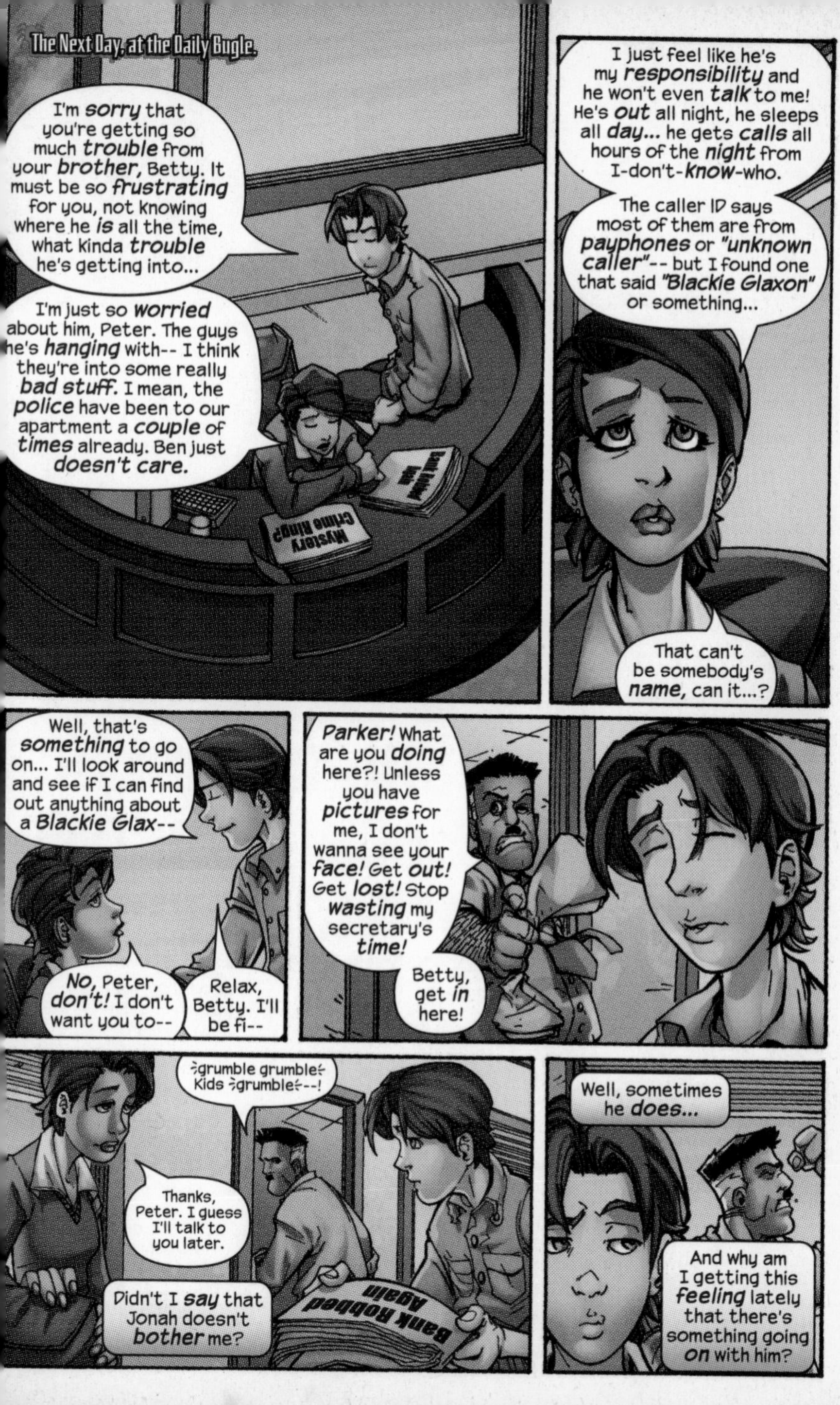

The Next Day, at the Daily Bugle.
I'm sorry that you're getting so much trouble from your brother, Betty. It must be so frustrating for you, not knowing where he is all the time, what kinda trouble he's getting into...
I'm just so worried about him, Peter. The guys he's hanging with-- I think they're into some really bad stuff. I mean, the police have been to our apartment a couple of times already. Ben just doesn't care.
Mystery Crime Ring?
I just feel like he's my responsibility and he won't even talk to me! He's out all night, he sleeps all day... he gets calls all hours of the night from I-don't-know-who.
The caller ID says most of them are from payphones or "unknown caller"-- but I found one that said "Blackie Glaxon" or something...
That can't be somebody's name, can it...?
Well, that's something to go on... I'll look around and see if I can find out anything about a Blackie Glax--
No, Peter, don't! I don't want you to--
Relax, Betty. I'll be fi--
Parker! What are you doing here?! Unless you have pictures for me, I don't wanna see your face! Get out! Get lost! Stop wasting my secretary's time!
Betty, get in here!
Thanks, Peter. I guess I'll talk to you later.
grumble grumble Kids grumble--!
Didn't I say that Jonah doesn't bother me?
Bank Robbed Again
Well, sometimes he does...
And why am I getting this feeling lately that there's something going on with him?

Over the next few *days*, things go pretty much the *same*.

I try to keep my eye on *Ben*, hoping to find some way to keep him out of *trouble*.

The mysterious *crime ring* continues to make *headlines* with their seemingly *erratic* robberies.

ight Break-In ransportation Commission

Ben seemed to be Blackie's new *favorite*. He gave him a *cell phone* to keep in touch. I saw them together a *lot*, but never doing anything I could *come down* on them for.

Spider-Menace Responsible Fo Rash Of Robberie

Not that you have to be doing anything wrong for someone to come down on you, though.

...won't be able to get within two city blocks of us, Big Man.

I want him out of the picture... for good.

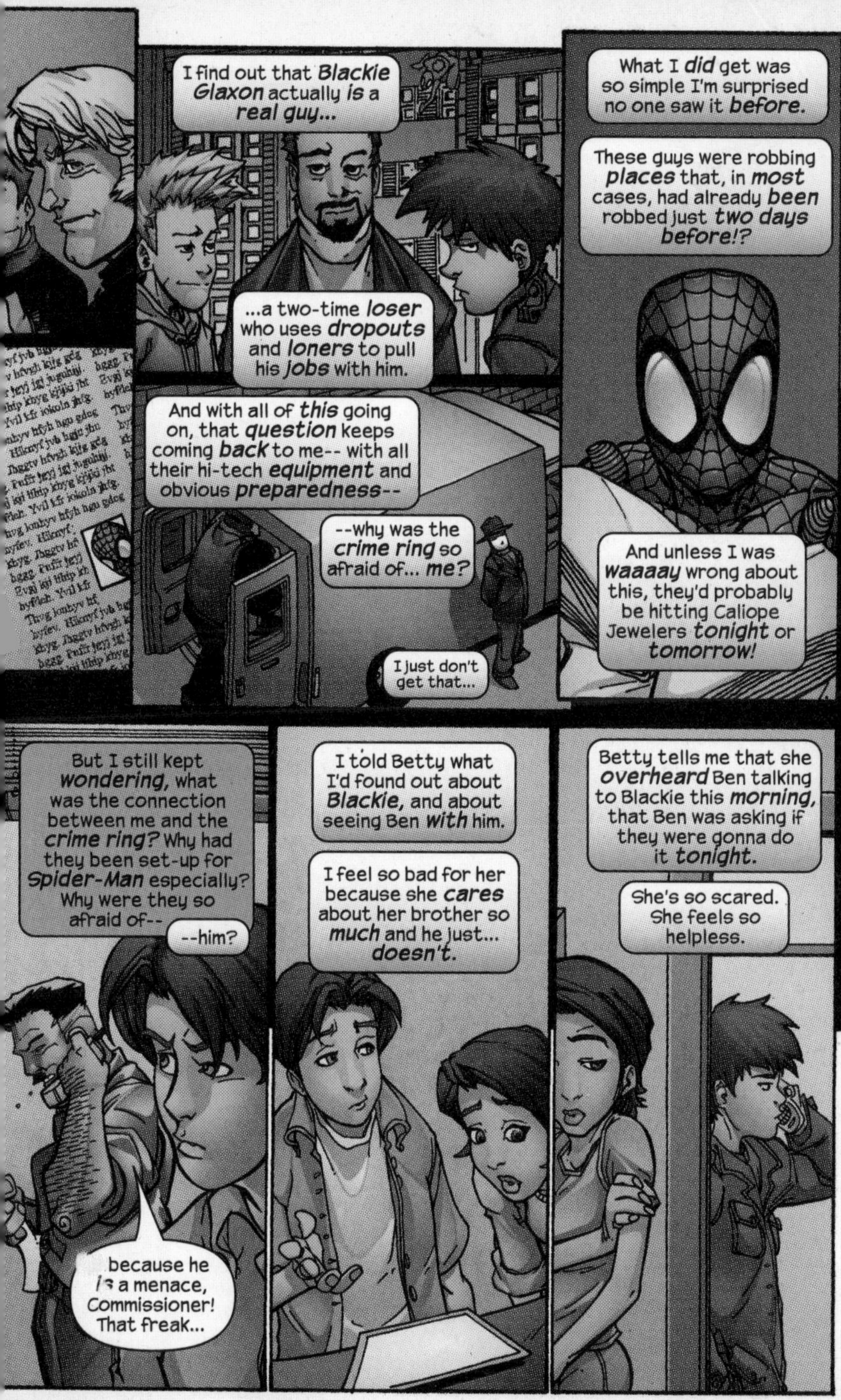
I find out that Blackie Glaxon actually is a real guy...
...a two-time loser who uses dropouts and loners to pull his jobs with him.
What I did get was so simple I'm surprised no one saw it before.
These guys were robbing places that, in most cases, had already been robbed just two days before!?
And with all of this going on, that question keeps coming back to me-- with all their hi-tech equipment and obvious preparedness--
--why was the crime ring so afraid of... me?
I just don't get that...
And unless I was waaaay wrong about this, they'd probably be hitting Caliope Jewelers tonight or tomorrow!
But I still kept wondering, what was the connection between me and the crime ring? Why had they been set-up for Spider-Man especially? Why were they so afraid of--
--him?
because he is a menace, Commissioner! That freak...
I told Betty what I'd found out about Blackie, and about seeing Ben with him.
I feel so bad for her because she cares about her brother so much and he just... doesn't.
Betty tells me that she overheard Ben talking to Blackie this morning, that Ben was asking if they were gonna do it tonight.
She's so scared. She feels so helpless.

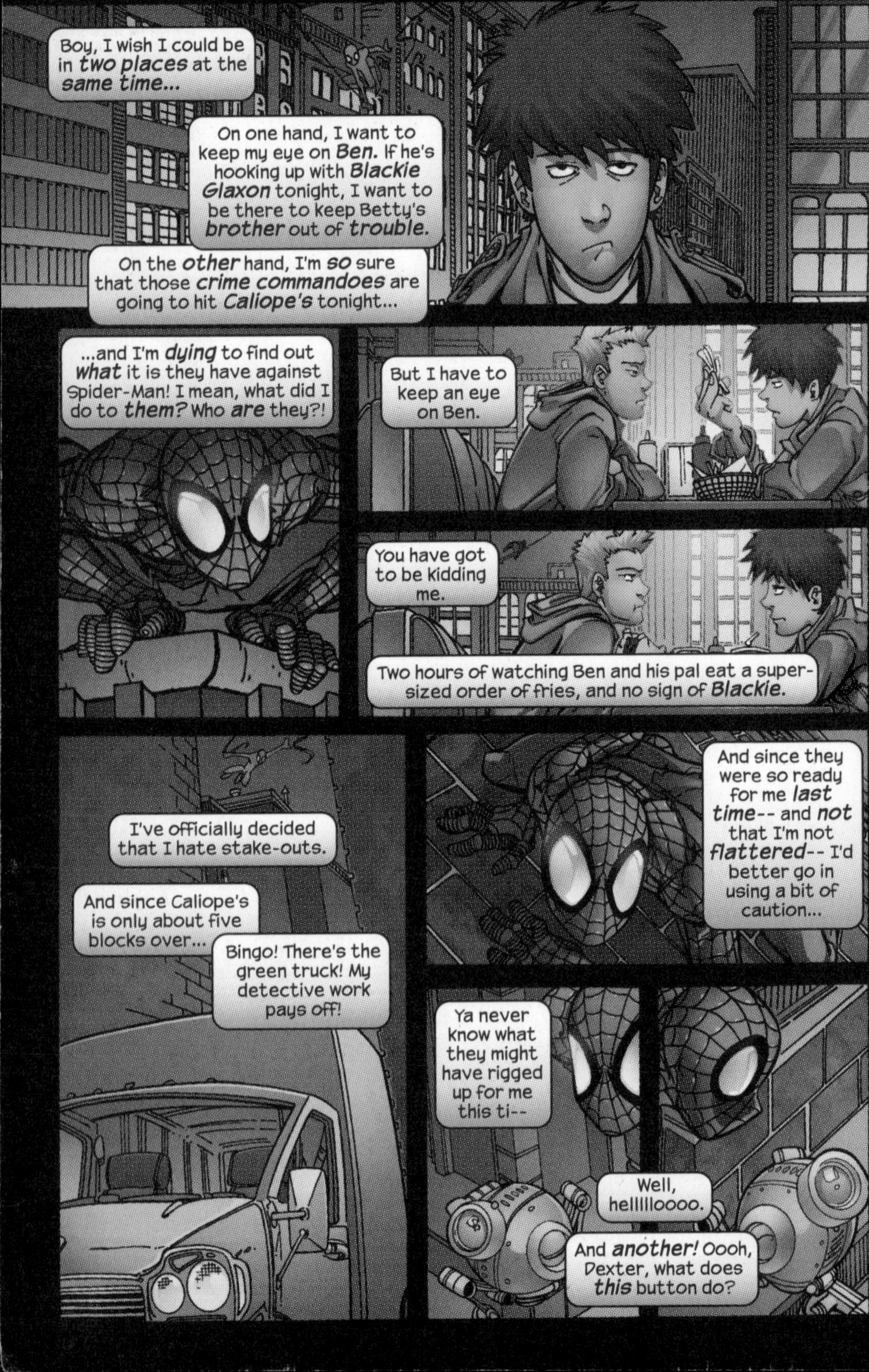

Boy, I wish I could be in two places at the same time...
On one hand, I want to keep my eye on Ben. If he's hooking up with Blackie Glaxon tonight, I want to be there to keep Betty's brother out of trouble.
On the other hand, I'm so sure that those crime commandoes are going to hit Caliope's tonight...
...and I'm dying to find out what it is they have against Spider-Man! I mean, what did I do to them? Who are they?!
But I have to keep an eye on Ben.
You have got to be kidding me.
Two hours of watching Ben and his pal eat a super-sized order of fries, and no sign of Blackie.
I've officially decided that I hate stake-outs.
And since Caliope's is only about five blocks over...
Bingo! There's the green truck! My detective work pays off!
And since they were so ready for me last time-- and not that I'm not flattered-- I'd better go in using a bit of caution...
Ya never know what they might have rigged up for me this ti--
Well, helllllloooo.
And another! Oooh, Dexter, what does this button do?

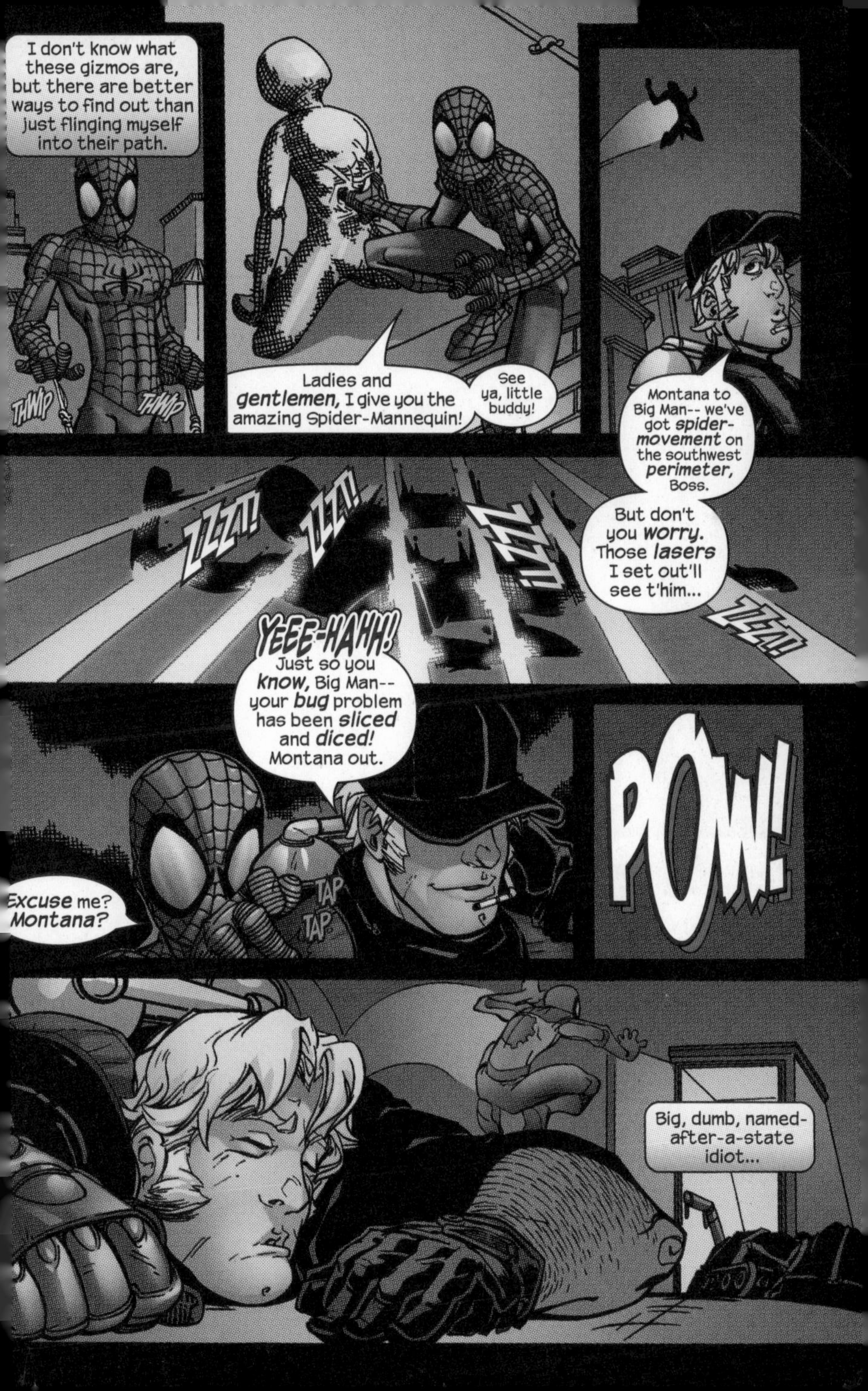
I don't know what these gizmos are, but there are better ways to find out than just flinging myself into their path.
THWIP
THWIP
Ladies and gentlemen, I give you the amazing Spider-Mannequin!
See ya, little buddy!
Montana to Big Man-- we've got spider-movement on the southwest perimeter, Boss.
But don't you worry. Those lasers I set out'll see t'him...
ZZZT!
ZZZT!
ZZZT!
ZZZT!
YEEE-HAHH!
Just so you know, Big Man-- your bug problem has been sliced and diced! Montana out.
TAP
TAP
Excuse me? Montana?
POW!
Big, dumb, named-after-a-state idiot...

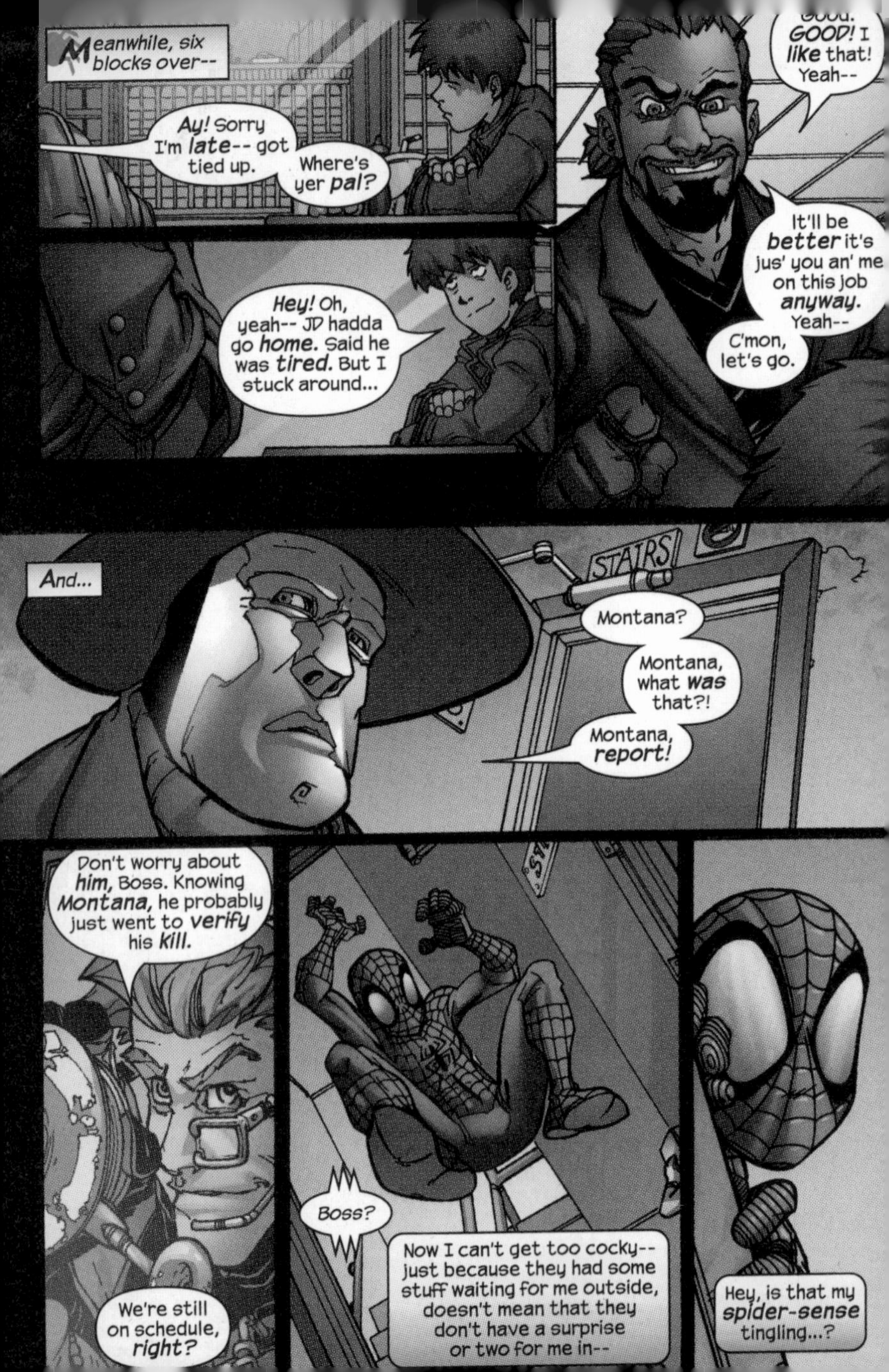

Meanwhile, six blocks over--
Ay! Sorry I'm late-- got tied up.
Where's yer pal?
Hey! Oh, yeah-- JD hadda go home. Said he was tired. But I stuck around...
GOOD! I like that! Yeah--
It'll be better it's jus' you an' me on this job anyway. Yeah--
C'mon, let's go.
And...
STAIRS
Montana?
Montana, what was that?!
Montana, report!
Don't worry about him, Boss. Knowing Montana, he probably just went to verify his kill.
We're still on schedule, right?
Boss?
Now I can't get too cocky-- just because they had some stuff waiting for me outside, doesn't mean that they don't have a surprise or two for me in--
Hey, is that my spider-sense tingling...?

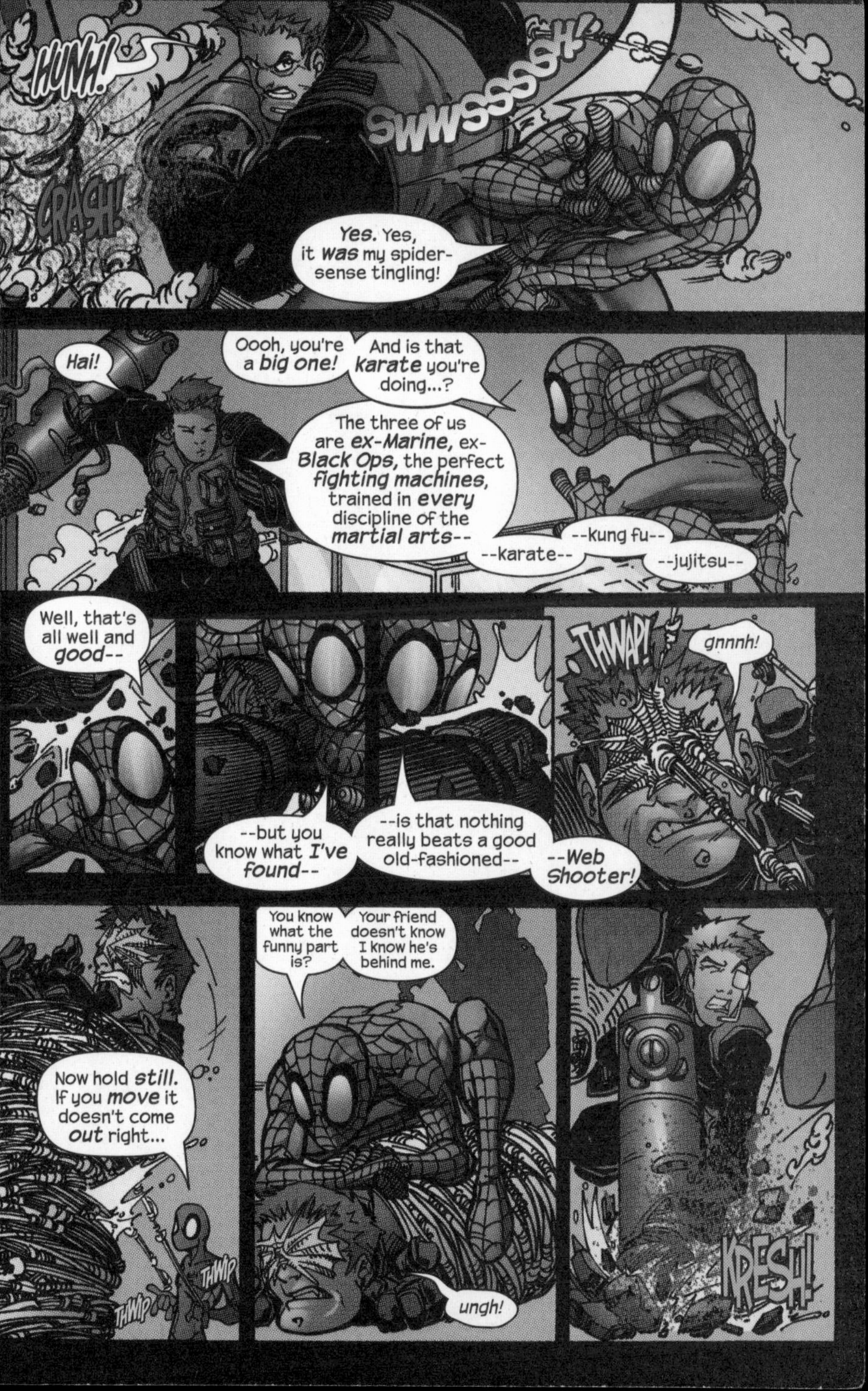
HUNH!
SWWSSSSSH!
CRASH!
Yes. Yes, it was my spider-sense tingling!
Hai!
Oooh, you're a big one!
And is that karate you're doing...?
The three of us are ex-Marine, ex-Black Ops, the perfect fighting machines, trained in every discipline of the martial arts--
--karate--
--kung fu--
--jujitsu--
Well, that's all well and good--
--but you know what I've found--
--is that nothing really beats a good old-fashioned--
THWAP!
gnnnh!
--Web Shooter!
Now hold still. If you move it doesn't come out right...
THWIP
THWIP
You know what the funny part is?
Your friend doesn't know I know he's behind me.
ungh!
KRESH!

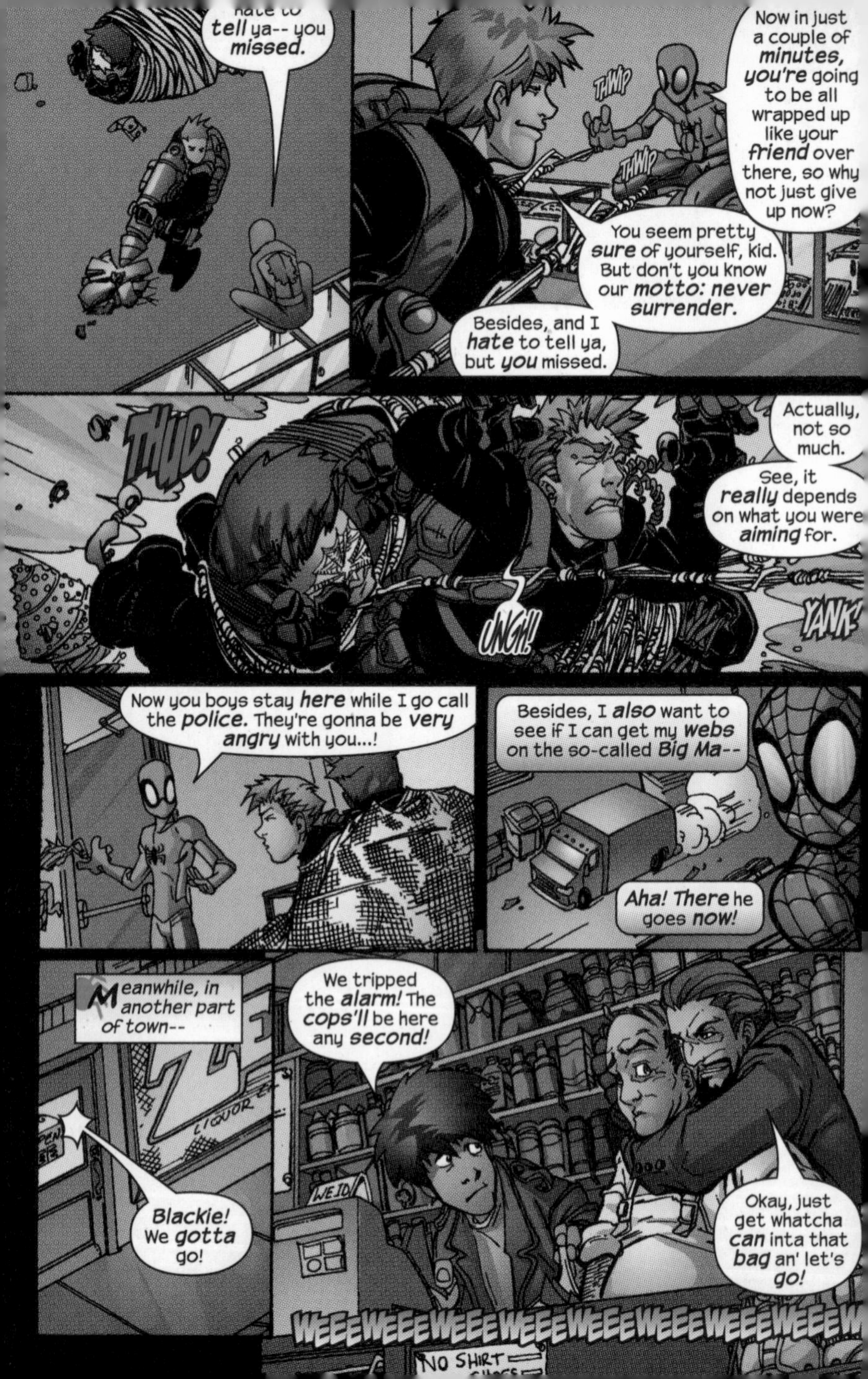

hate to tell ya-- you missed.
Now in just a couple of minutes, you're going to be all wrapped up like your friend over there, so why not just give up now?
THWIP
THWIP
You seem pretty sure of yourself, kid. But don't you know our motto: never surrender.
Besides, and I hate to tell ya, but you missed.
THUD!
Actually, not so much.
See, it really depends on what you were aiming for.
UNGH!
YANK!
Now you boys stay here while I go call the police. They're gonna be very angry with you...!
Besides, I also want to see if I can get my webs on the so-called Big Ma--
Aha! There he goes now!
Meanwhile, in another part of town--
We tripped the alarm! The cops'll be here any second!
Blackie! We gotta go!
Okay, just get whatcha can inta that bag an' let's go!
WEEEWEEEWEEEWEEEWEEEWEEEWEEEWEEEW
LIQUOR
NO SHIRT

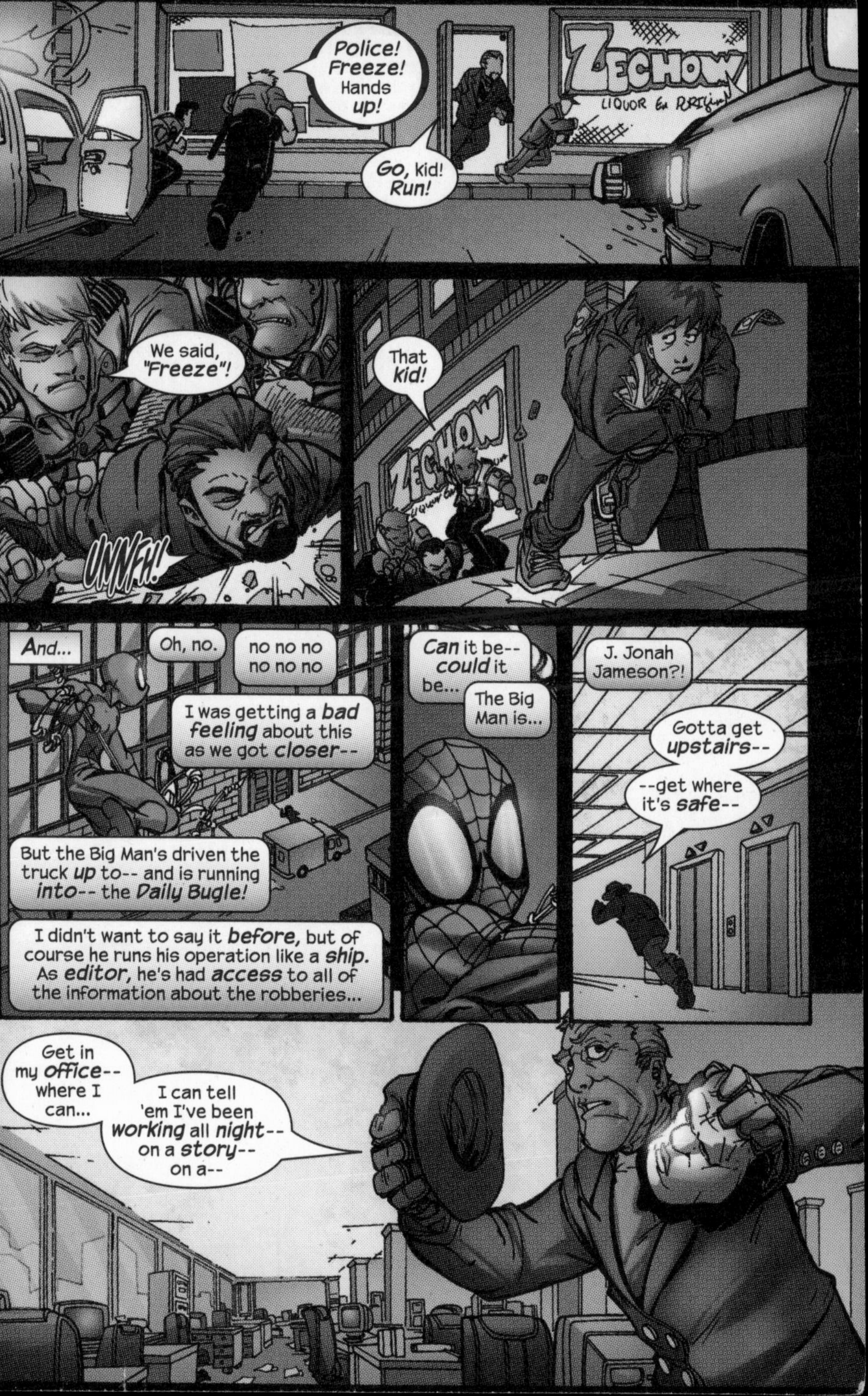
ZECHOW
LIQUOR EN PORTIÓN
Police! Freeze! Hands up!
Go, kid! Run!
We said, "Freeze"!
UNNFH!
That kid!
ZECHOW
And...
Oh, no.
no no no no no no
I was getting a bad feeling about this as we got closer--
But the Big Man's driven the truck up to-- and is running into-- the Daily Bugle!
I didn't want to say it before, but of course he runs his operation like a ship. As editor, he's had access to all of the information about the robberies...
Can it be-- could it be...
The Big Man is...
J. Jonah Jameson?!
Gotta get upstairs--
--get where it's safe--
Get in my office-- where I can...
I can tell 'em I've been working all night-- on a story-- on a--

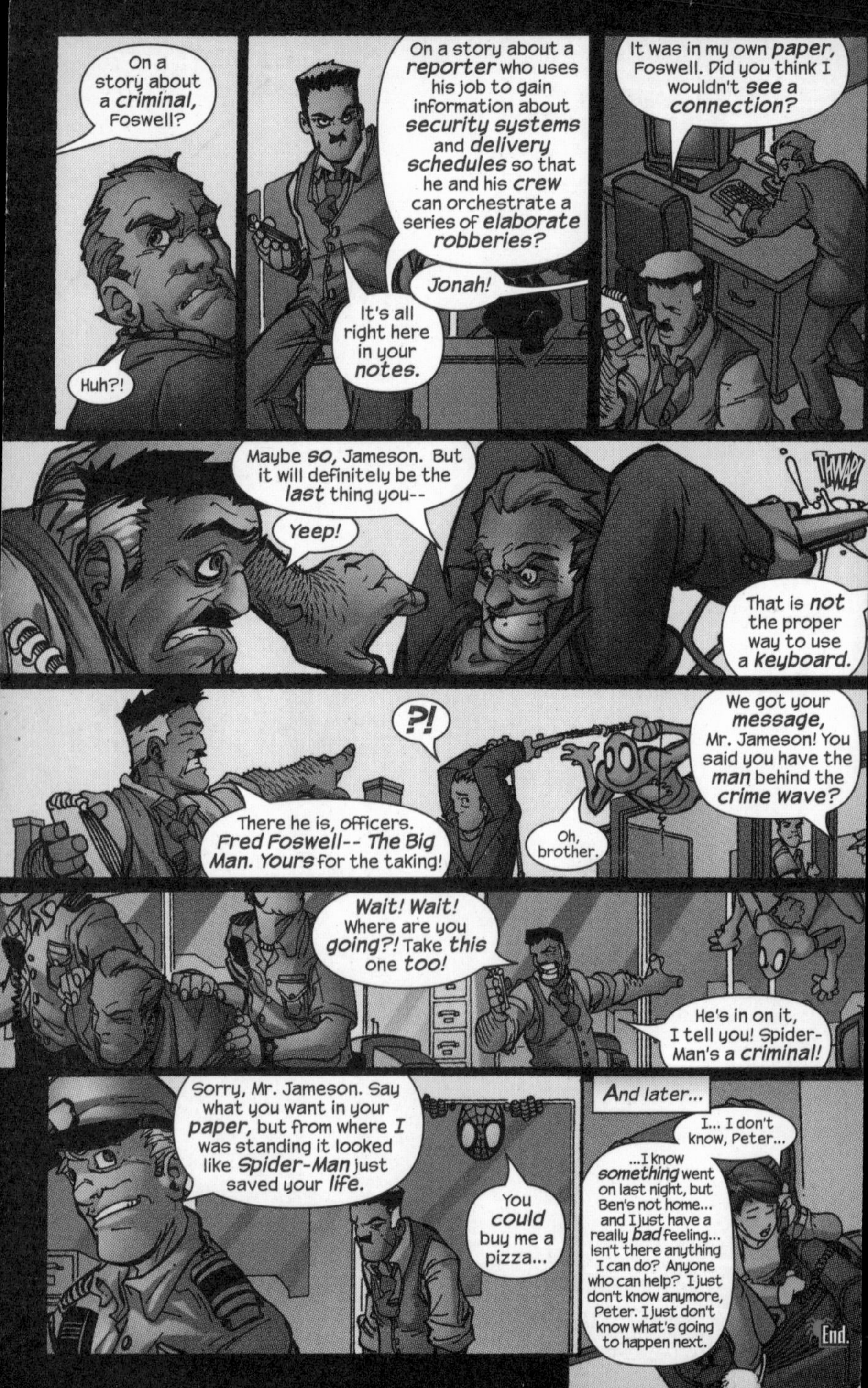
On a story about a criminal, Foswell?
Huh?!
On a story about a reporter who uses his job to gain information about security systems and delivery schedules so that he and his crew can orchestrate a series of elaborate robberies?
It's all right here in your notes.
Jonah!
It was in my own paper, Foswell. Did you think I wouldn't see a connection?
Maybe so, Jameson. But it will definitely be the last thing you--
Yeep!
THWAP!
That is not the proper way to use a keyboard.
?!
We got your message, Mr. Jameson! You said you have the man behind the crime wave?
There he is, officers. Fred Foswell-- The Big Man. Yours for the taking!
Oh, brother.
Wait! Wait! Where are you going?! Take this one too!
He's in on it, I tell you! Spider-Man's a criminal!
Sorry, Mr. Jameson. Say what you want in your paper, but from where I was standing it looked like Spider-Man just saved your life.
You could buy me a pizza...
And later...
I... I don't know, Peter...
...I know something went on last night, but Ben's not home... and I just have a really bad feeling... Isn't there anything I can do? Anyone who can help? I just don't know anymore, Peter. I just don't know what's going to happen next.
End.

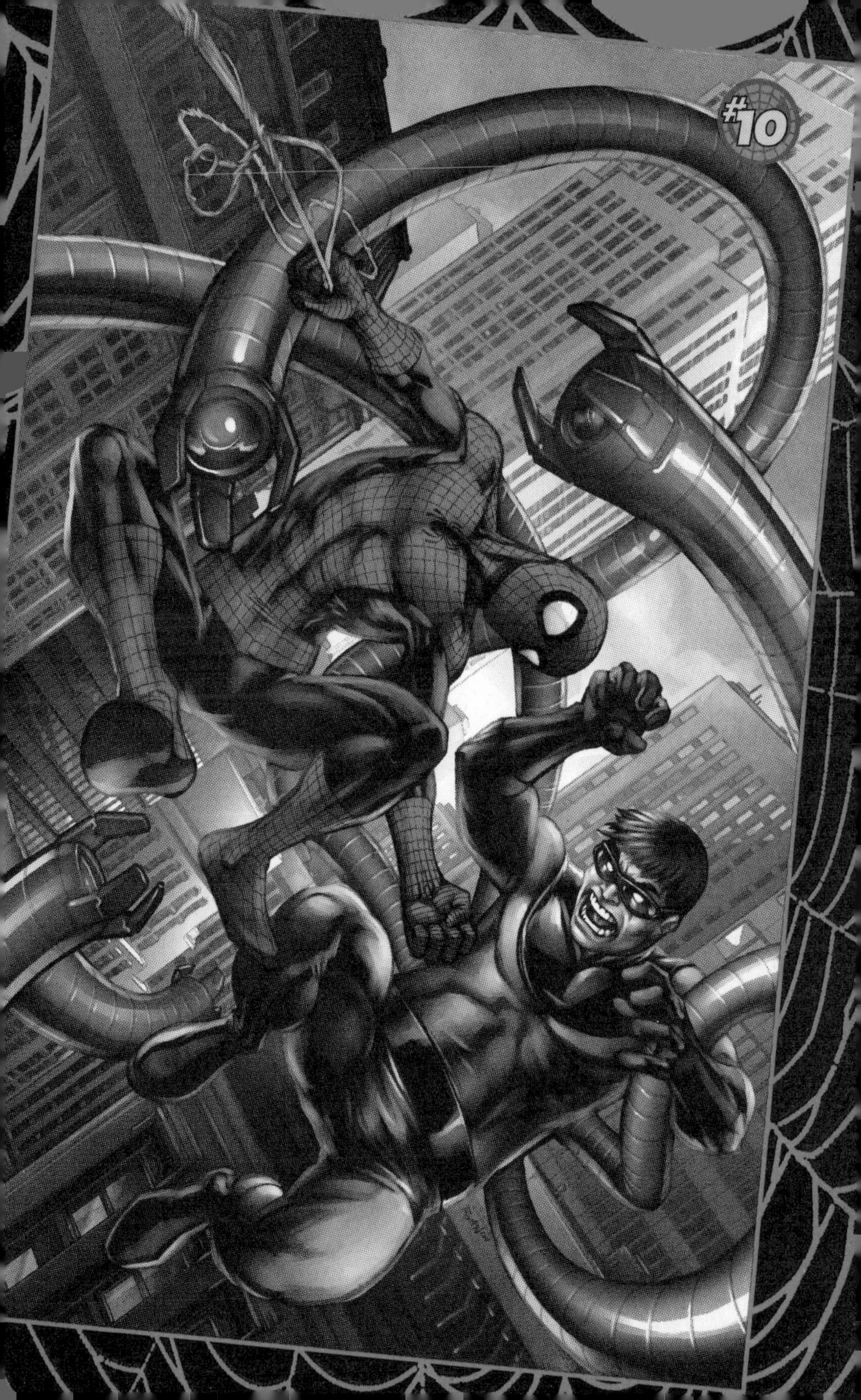
#10

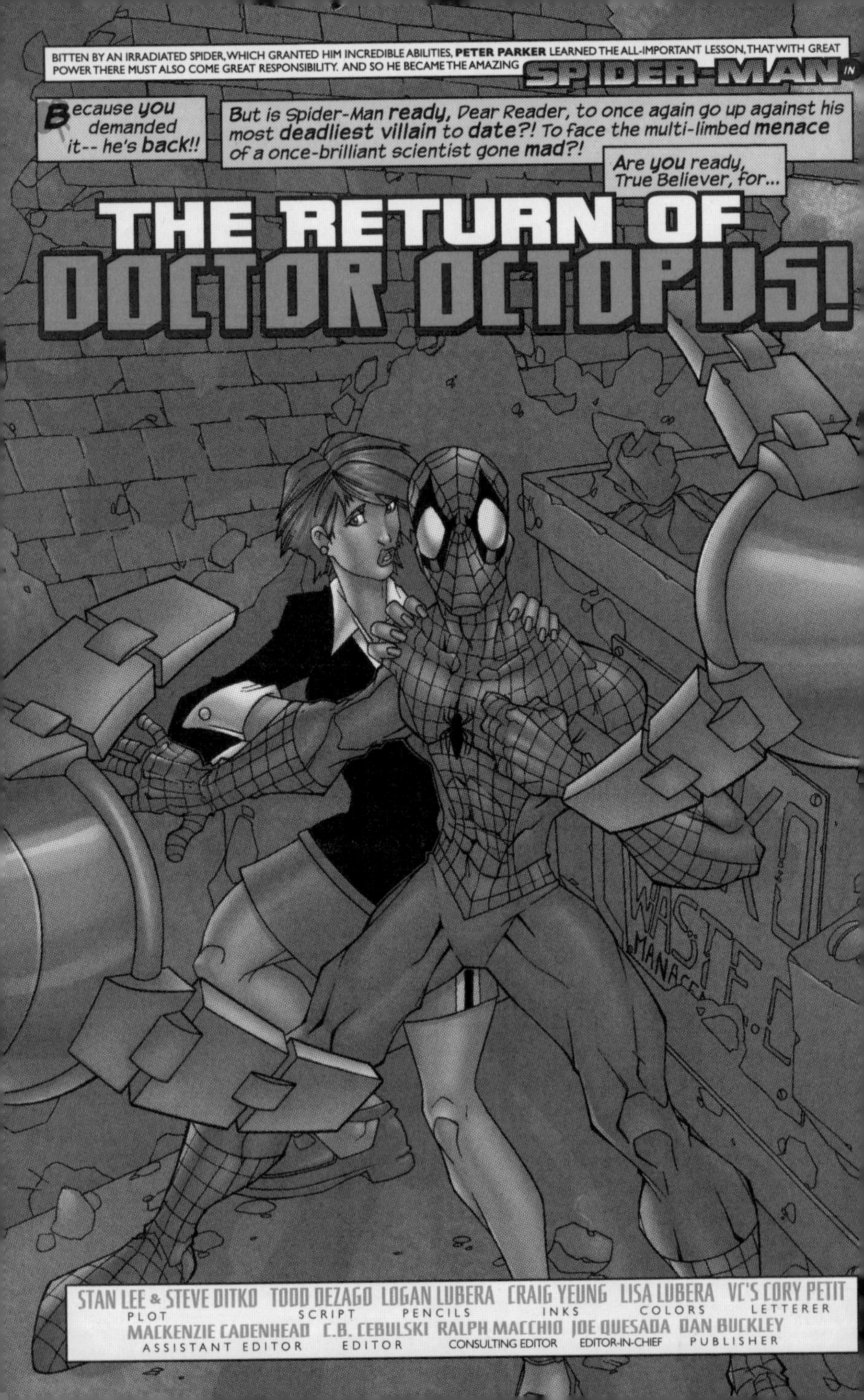
BITTEN BY AN IRRADIATED SPIDER, WHICH GRANTED HIM INCREDIBLE ABILITIES, PETER PARKER LEARNED THE ALL-IMPORTANT LESSON, THAT WITH GREAT POWER THERE MUST ALSO COME GREAT RESPONSIBILITY. AND SO HE BECAME THE AMAZING SPIDER-MAN IN
Because you demanded it-- he's back!!
But is Spider-Man ready, Dear Reader, to once again go up against his most deadliest villain to date?! To face the multi-limbed menace of a once-brilliant scientist gone mad?!
Are you ready, True Believer, for...
THE RETURN OF DOCTOR OCTOPUS!
W.A.S.T.E.
STAN LEE & STEVE DITKO PLOT
TODD DEZAGO SCRIPT
LOGAN LUBERA PENCILS
CRAIG YEUNG INKS
LISA LUBERA COLORS
VC'S CORY PETIT LETTERER
MACKENZIE CADENHEAD ASSISTANT EDITOR
C.B. CEBULSKI EDITOR
RALPH MACCHIO CONSULTING EDITOR
JOE QUESADA EDITOR-IN-CHIEF
DAN BUCKLEY PUBLISHER

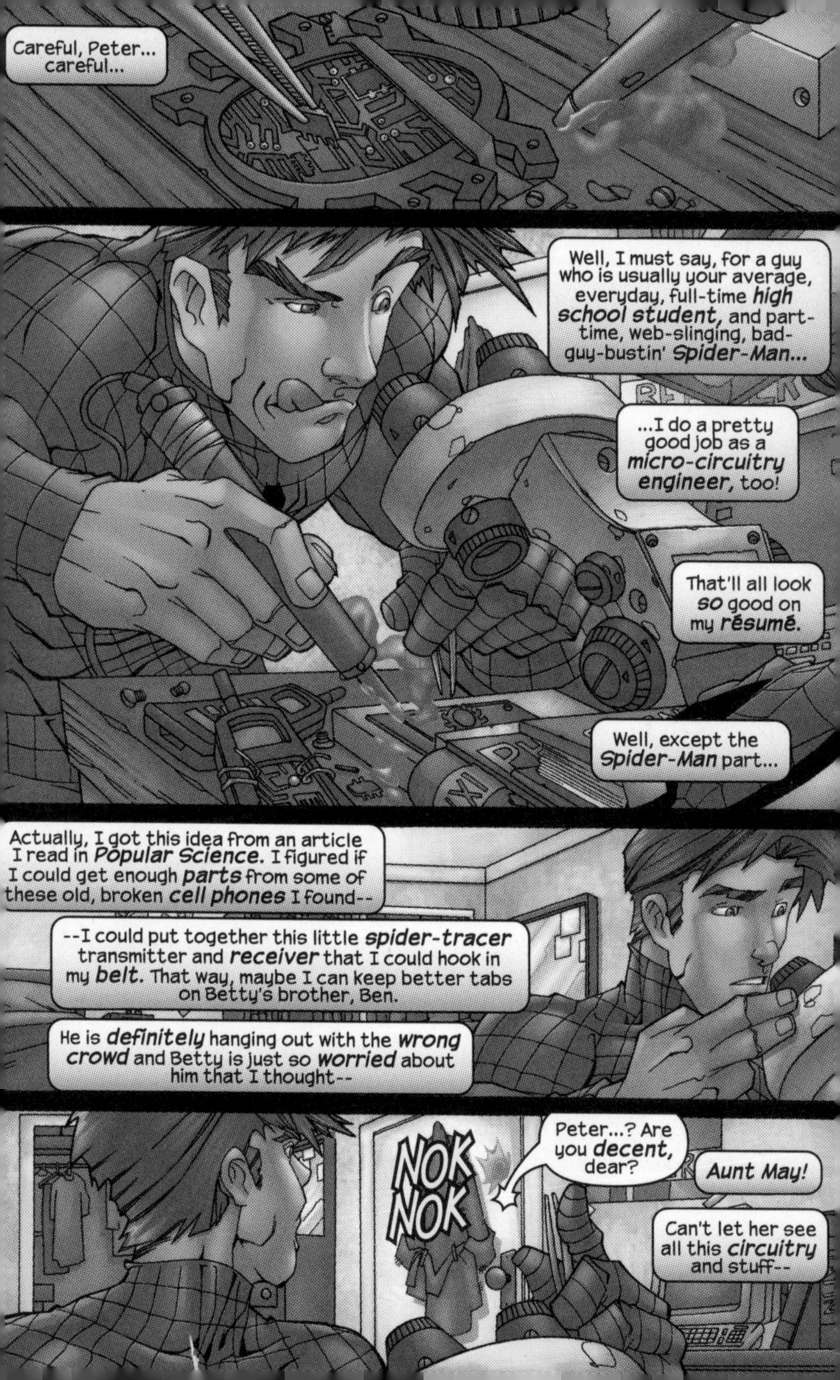
Careful, Peter... careful...
Well, I must say, for a guy who is usually your average, everyday, full-time high school student, and part-time, web-slinging, bad-guy-bustin' Spider-Man...
...I do a pretty good job as a micro-circuitry engineer, too!
That'll all look so good on my résumé.
Well, except the Spider-Man part...
Actually, I got this idea from an article I read in Popular Science. I figured if I could get enough parts from some of these old, broken cell phones I found--
--I could put together this little spider-tracer transmitter and receiver that I could hook in my belt. That way, maybe I can keep better tabs on Betty's brother, Ben.
He is definitely hanging out with the wrong crowd and Betty is just so worried about him that I thought--
NOK NOK
Peter...? Are you decent, dear?
Aunt May!
Can't let her see all this circuitry and stuff--

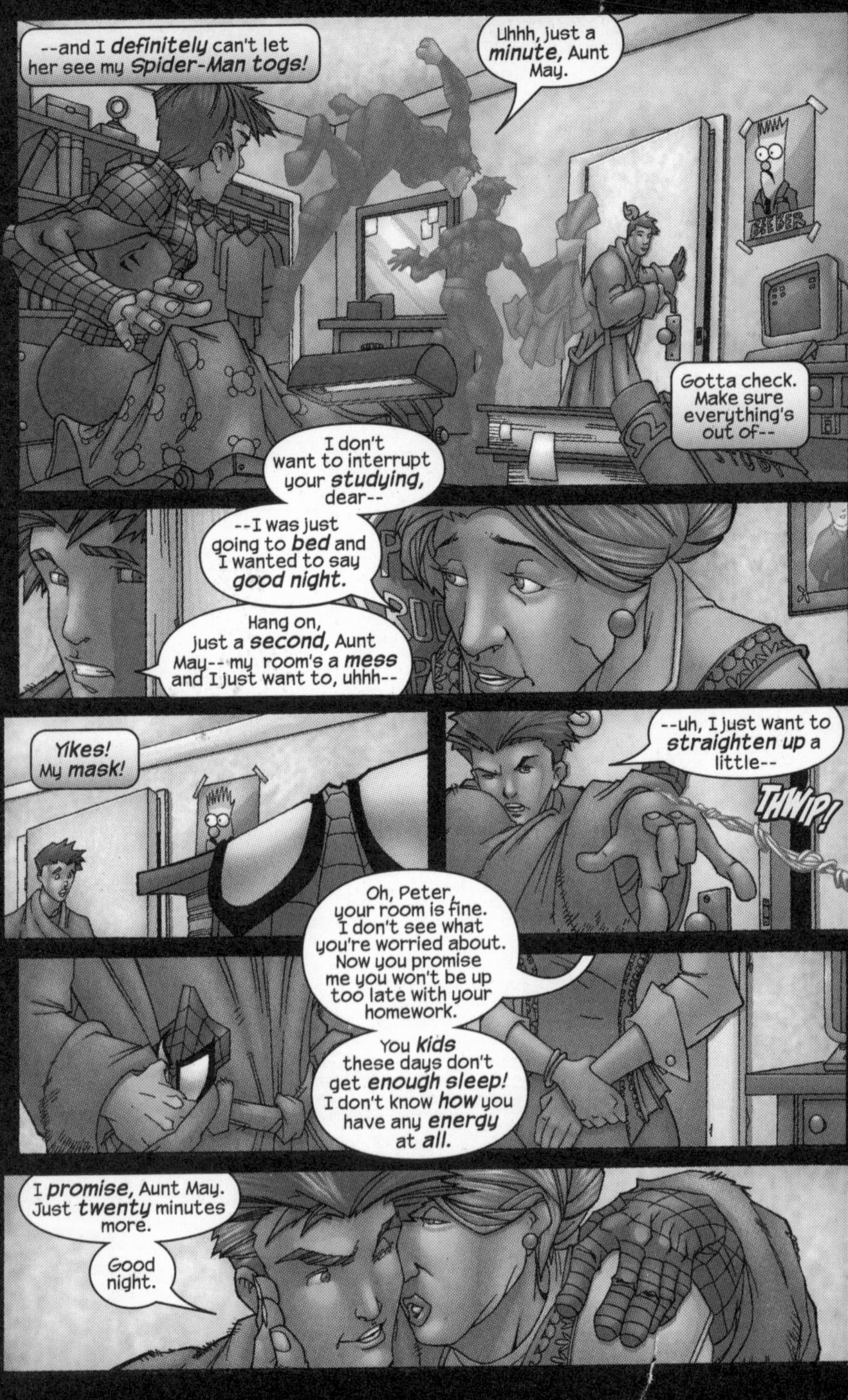
--and I definitely can't let her see my Spider-Man togs!
Uhhh, just a minute, Aunt May.
Gotta check. Make sure everything's out of--
I don't want to interrupt your studying, dear--
--I was just going to bed and I wanted to say good night.
Hang on, just a second, Aunt May-- my room's a mess and I just want to, uhhh--
Yikes! My mask!
--uh, I just want to straighten up a little--
THWIP!
Oh, Peter, your room is fine. I don't see what you're worried about. Now you promise me you won't be up too late with your homework.
You kids these days don't get enough sleep! I don't know how you have any energy at all.
I promise, Aunt May. Just twenty minutes more.
Good night.

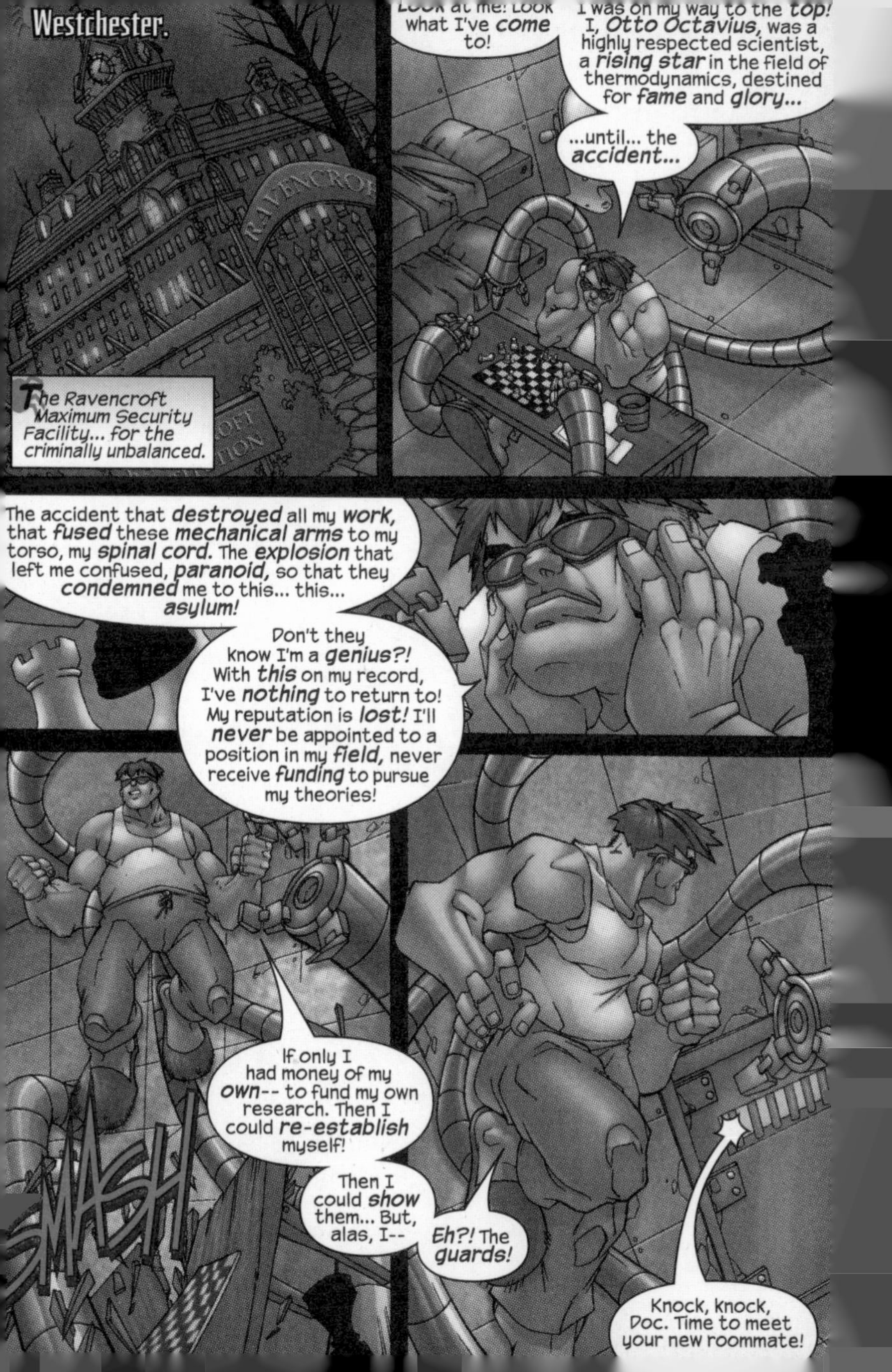
Westchester.
The Ravencroft Maximum Security Facility... for the criminally unbalanced.
RAVENCROFT
Look at me! Look what I've come to!
I was on my way to the top! I, Otto Octavius, was a highly respected scientist, a rising star in the field of thermodynamics, destined for fame and glory...
...until... the accident...
The accident that destroyed all my work, that fused these mechanical arms to my torso, my spinal cord. The explosion that left me confused, paranoid, so that they condemned me to this... this... asylum!
Don't they know I'm a genius?! With this on my record, I've nothing to return to! My reputation is lost! I'll never be appointed to a position in my field, never receive funding to pursue my theories!
If only I had money of my own-- to fund my own research. Then I could re-establish myself!
Then I could show them... But, alas, I--
SMASH
Eh?! The guards!
Knock, knock, Doc. Time to meet your new roommate!

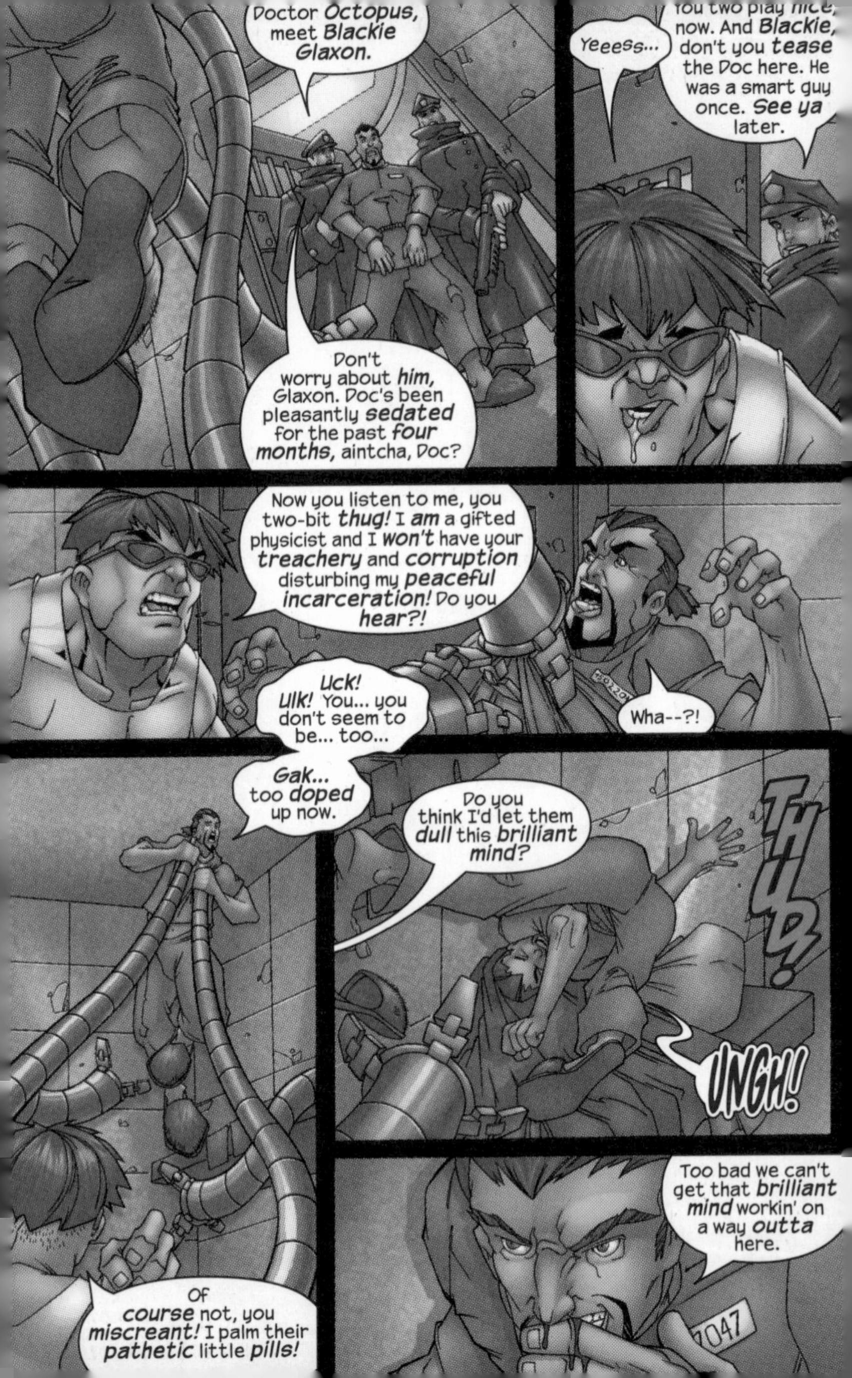
Doctor Octopus, meet Blackie Glaxon.
Don't worry about him, Glaxon. Doc's been pleasantly sedated for the past four months, aintcha, Doc?
Yeeess...
You two play nice, now. And Blackie, don't you tease the Doc here. He was a smart guy once. See ya later.
Now you listen to me, you two-bit thug! I am a gifted physicist and I won't have your treachery and corruption disturbing my peaceful incarceration! Do you hear?!
Wha--?!
Uck! Ulk! You... you don't seem to be... too...
Gak... too doped up now.
Do you think I'd let them dull this brilliant mind?
THUD!
UNGH!
Of course not, you miscreant! I palm their pathetic little pills!
Too bad we can't get that brilliant mind workin' on a way outta here.
7047

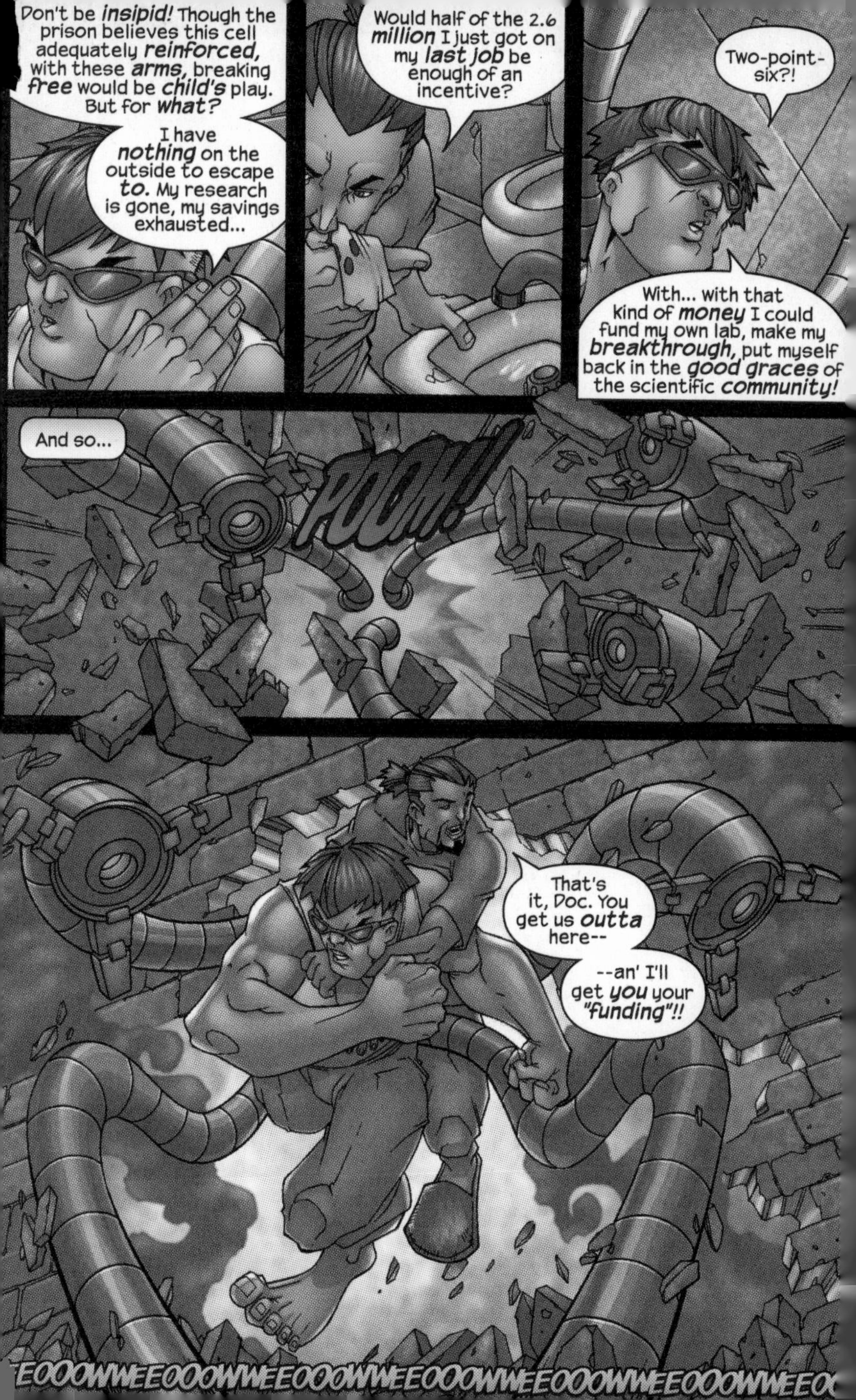
Don't be insipid! Though the prison believes this cell adequately reinforced, with these arms, breaking free would be child's play. But for what?
I have nothing on the outside to escape to. My research is gone, my savings exhausted...
Would half of the 2.6 million I just got on my last job be enough of an incentive?
Two-point-six?!
With... with that kind of money I could fund my own lab, make my breakthrough, put myself back in the good graces of the scientific community!
And so...
POOM!!
That's it, Doc. You get us outta here--
--an' I'll get you your "funding"!!
EEOOOWWEEOOOWWEEOOOWWEEOOOWWEEOOOWWEEOOOWWEEO

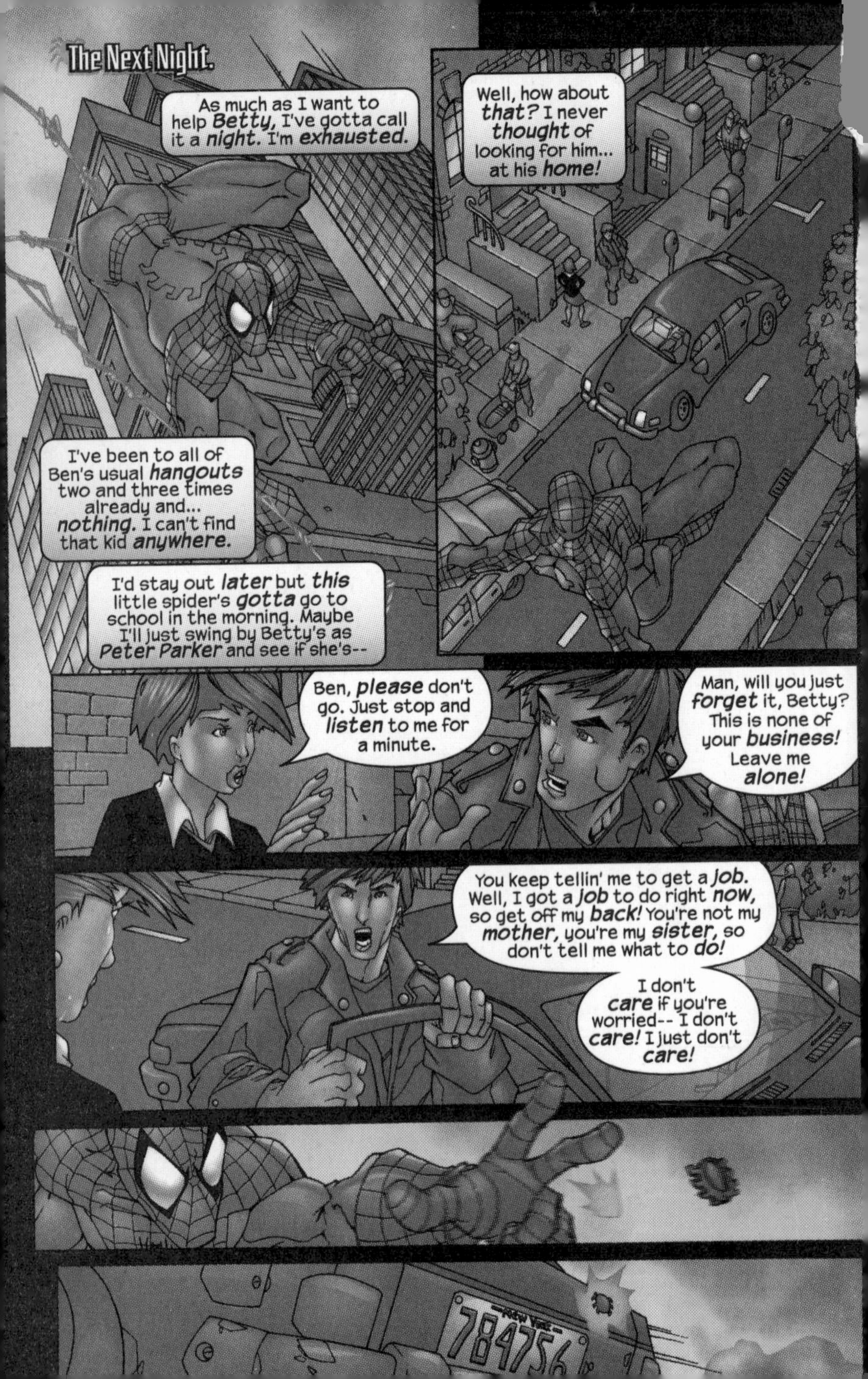
The Next Night.
As much as I want to help Betty, I've gotta call it a night. I'm exhausted.
I've been to all of Ben's usual hangouts two and three times already and... nothing. I can't find that kid anywhere.
I'd stay out later but this little spider's gotta go to school in the morning. Maybe I'll just swing by Betty's as Peter Parker and see if she's--
Well, how about that? I never thought of looking for him... at his home!
Ben, please don't go. Just stop and listen to me for a minute.
Man, will you just forget it, Betty? This is none of your business! Leave me alone!
You keep tellin' me to get a job. Well, I got a job to do right now, so get off my back! You're not my mother, you're my sister, so don't tell me what to do!
I don't care if you're worried-- I don't care! I just don't care!
NEW YORK
784756

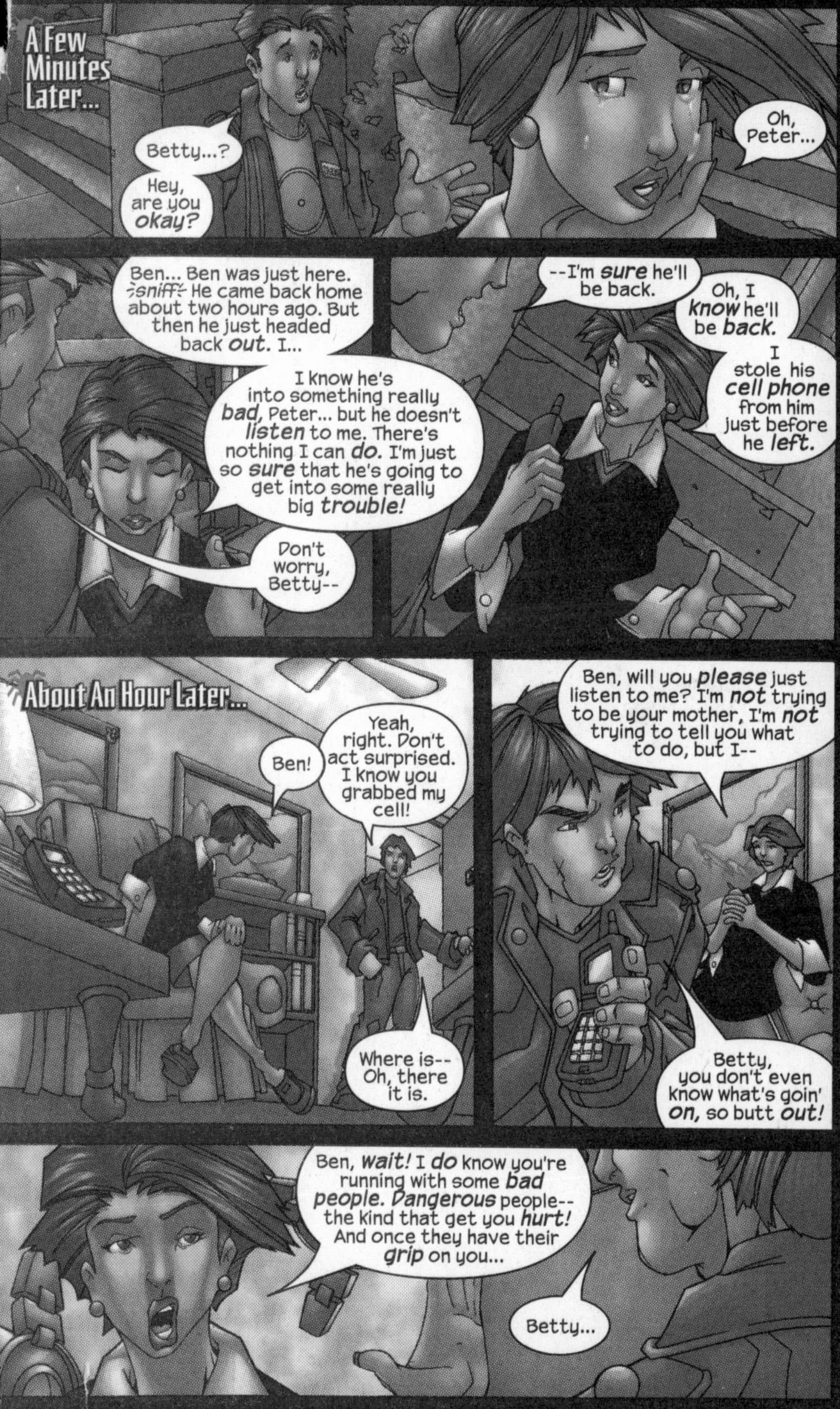
A Few Minutes Later...
Betty...?
Hey, are you okay?
Oh, Peter...
Ben... Ben was just here. ~sniff~ He came back home about two hours ago. But then he just headed back out. I...
I know he's into something really bad, Peter... but he doesn't listen to me. There's nothing I can do. I'm just so sure that he's going to get into some really big trouble!
Don't worry, Betty--
--I'm sure he'll be back.
Oh, I know he'll be back.
I stole his cell phone from him just before he left.
About An Hour Later...
Ben!
Yeah, right. Don't act surprised. I know you grabbed my cell!
Where is-- Oh, there it is.
Ben, will you please just listen to me? I'm not trying to be your mother, I'm not trying to tell you what to do, but I--
Betty, you don't even know what's goin' on, so butt out!
Ben, wait! I do know you're running with some bad people. Dangerous people-- the kind that get you hurt! And once they have their grip on you...
Betty...

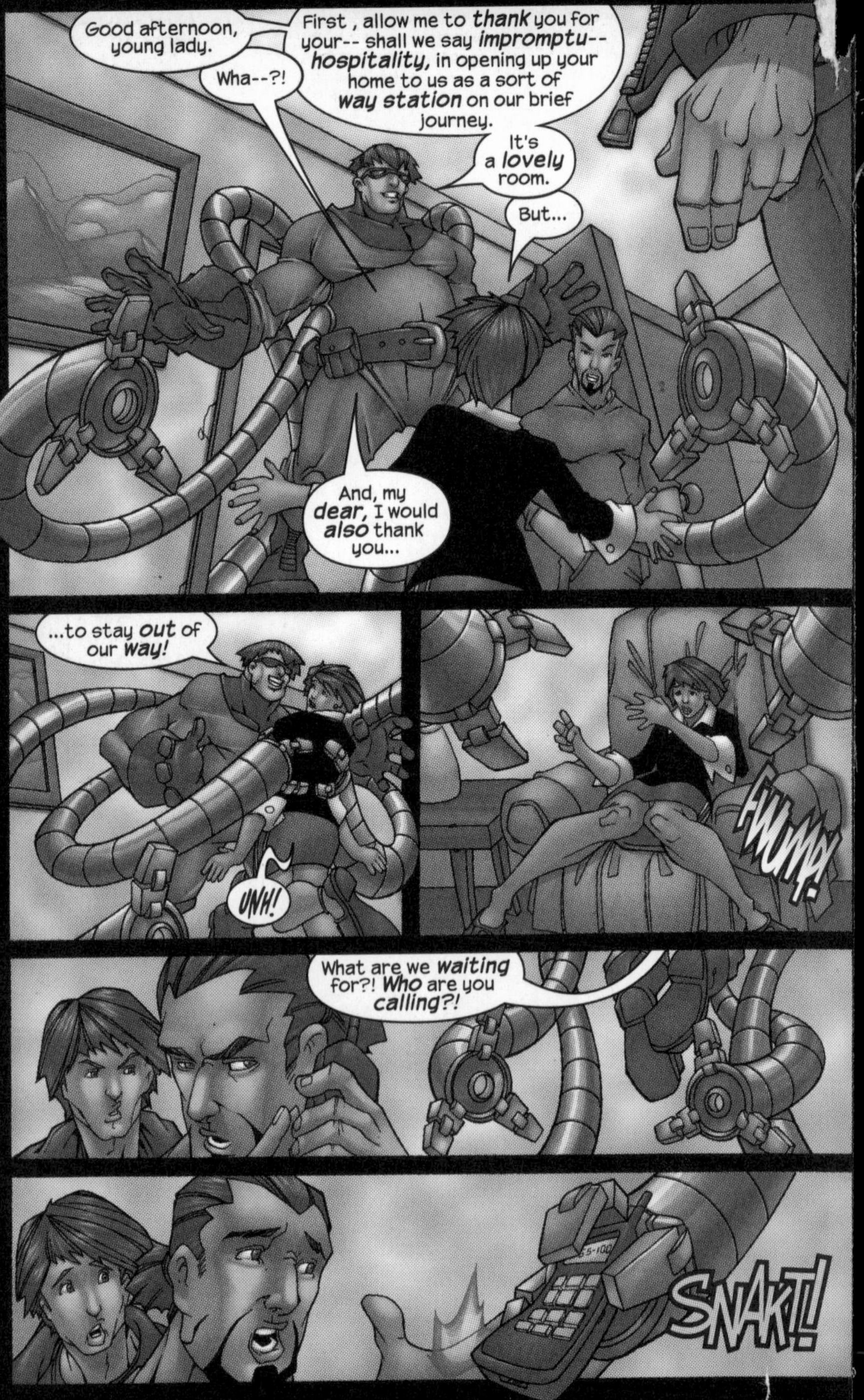
Good afternoon, young lady.
Wha--?!
First, allow me to thank you for your-- shall we say impromptu-- hospitality, in opening up your home to us as a sort of way station on our brief journey.
It's a lovely room.
But...
And, my dear, I would also thank you...
...to stay out of our way!
UNH!
FWUMP!
What are we waiting for?! Who are you calling?!
SNAKT!

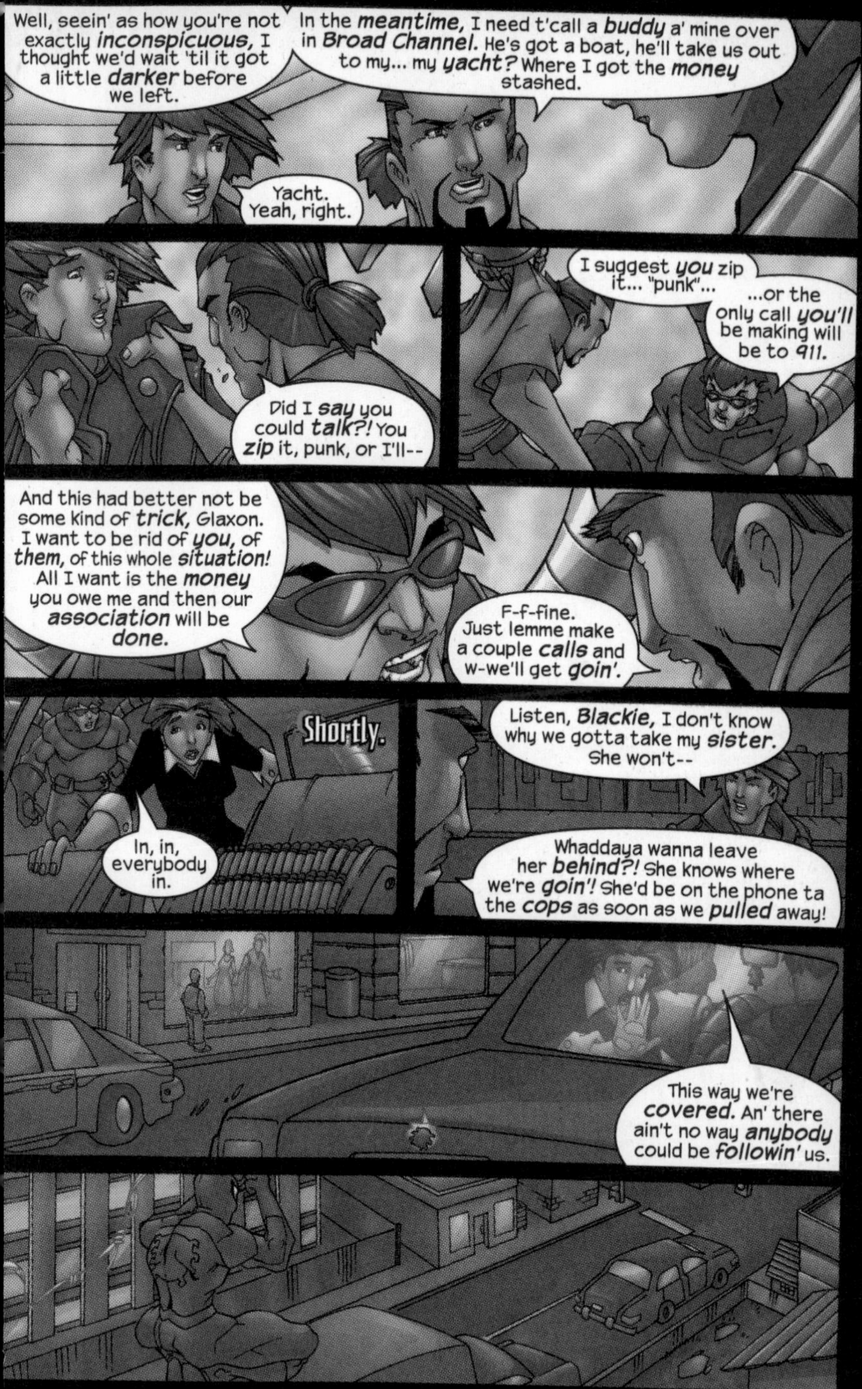
Well, seein' as how you're not exactly inconspicuous, I thought we'd wait 'til it got a little darker before we left.
In the meantime, I need t'call a buddy a' mine over in Broad Channel. He's got a boat, he'll take us out to my... my yacht? Where I got the money stashed.
Yacht. Yeah, right.
Did I say you could talk?! You zip it, punk, or I'll--
I suggest you zip it... "punk"...
...or the only call you'll be making will be to 911.
And this had better not be some kind of trick, Glaxon. I want to be rid of you, of them, of this whole situation! All I want is the money you owe me and then our association will be done.
F-f-fine. Just lemme make a couple calls and w-we'll get goin'.
Shortly.
In, in, everybody in.
Listen, Blackie, I don't know why we gotta take my sister. She won't--
Whaddaya wanna leave her behind?! She knows where we're goin'! She'd be on the phone ta the cops as soon as we pulled away!
This way we're covered. An' there ain't no way anybody could be followin' us.

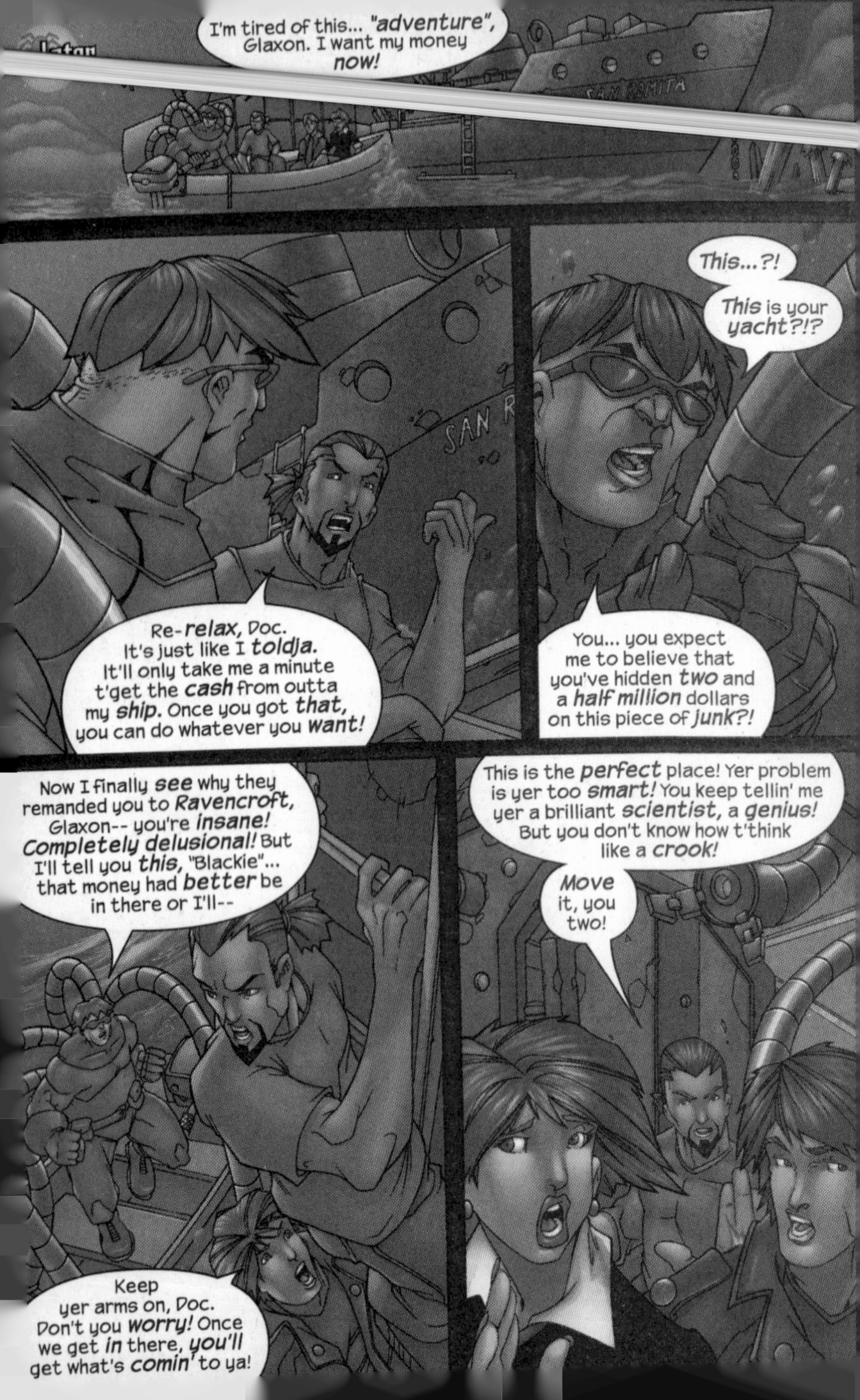

I'm tired of this... "adventure", Glaxon. I want my money now!
Re-relax, Doc. It's just like I toldja. It'll only take me a minute t'get the cash from outta my ship. Once you got that, you can do whatever you want!
This...?!
This is your yacht?!?
You... you expect me to believe that you've hidden two and a half million dollars on this piece of junk?!
Now I finally see why they remanded you to Ravencroft, Glaxon-- you're insane! Completely delusional! But I'll tell you this, "Blackie"... that money had better be in there or I'll--
Keep yer arms on, Doc. Don't you worry! Once we get in there, you'll get what's comin' to ya!
This is the perfect place! Yer problem is yer too smart! You keep tellin' me yer a brilliant scientist, a genius! But you don't know how t'think like a crook!
Move it, you two!

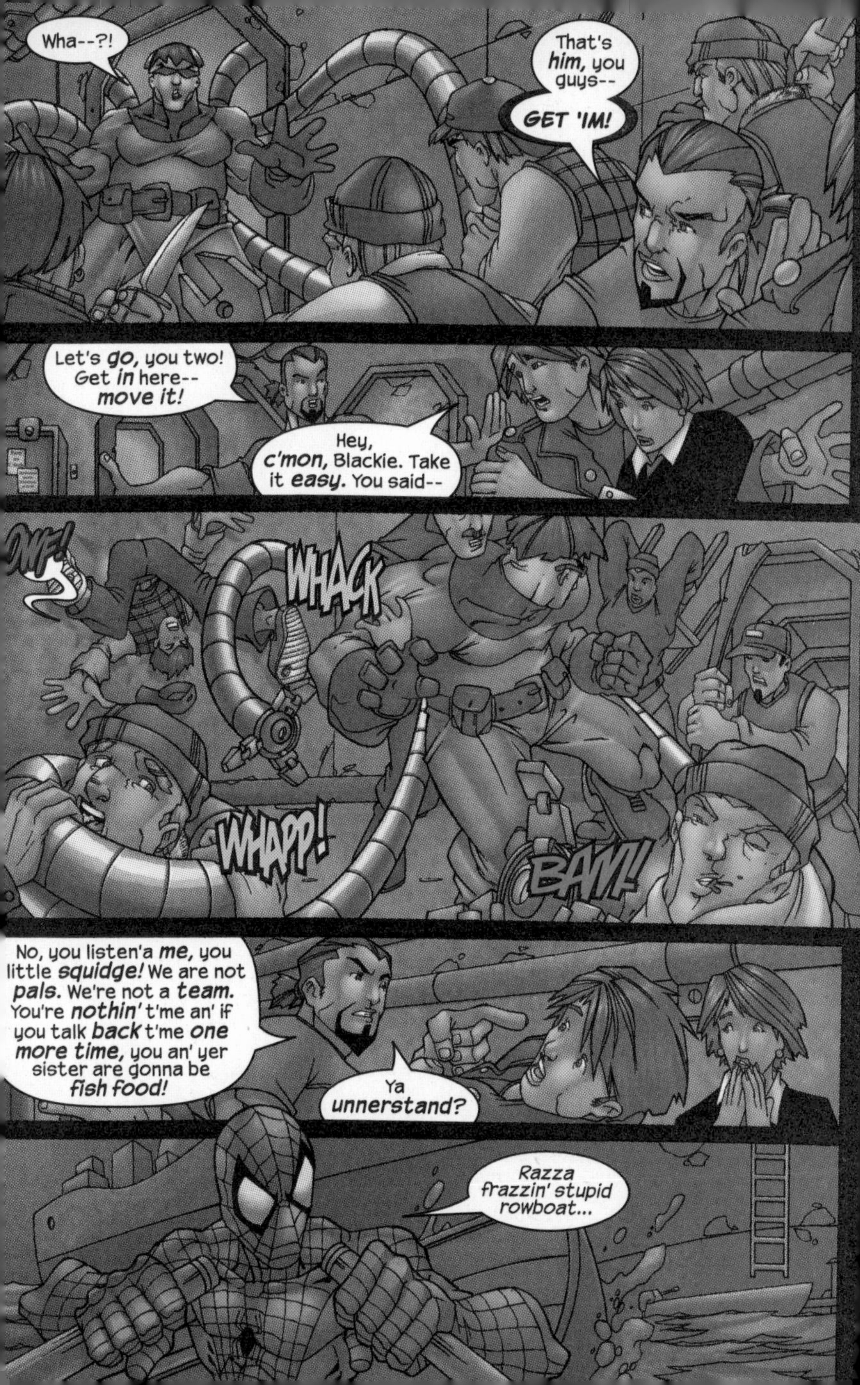
Wha--?!
That's him, you guys--
GET 'IM!
Let's go, you two! Get in here-- move it!
Hey, c'mon, Blackie. Take it easy. You said--
OOF!
WHACK
WHAPP!
BAM!
No, you listen'a me, you little squidge! We are not pals. We're not a team. You're nothin' t'me an' if you talk back t'me one more time, you an' yer sister are gonna be fish food!
Ya unnerstand?
Razza frazzin' stupid rowboat...

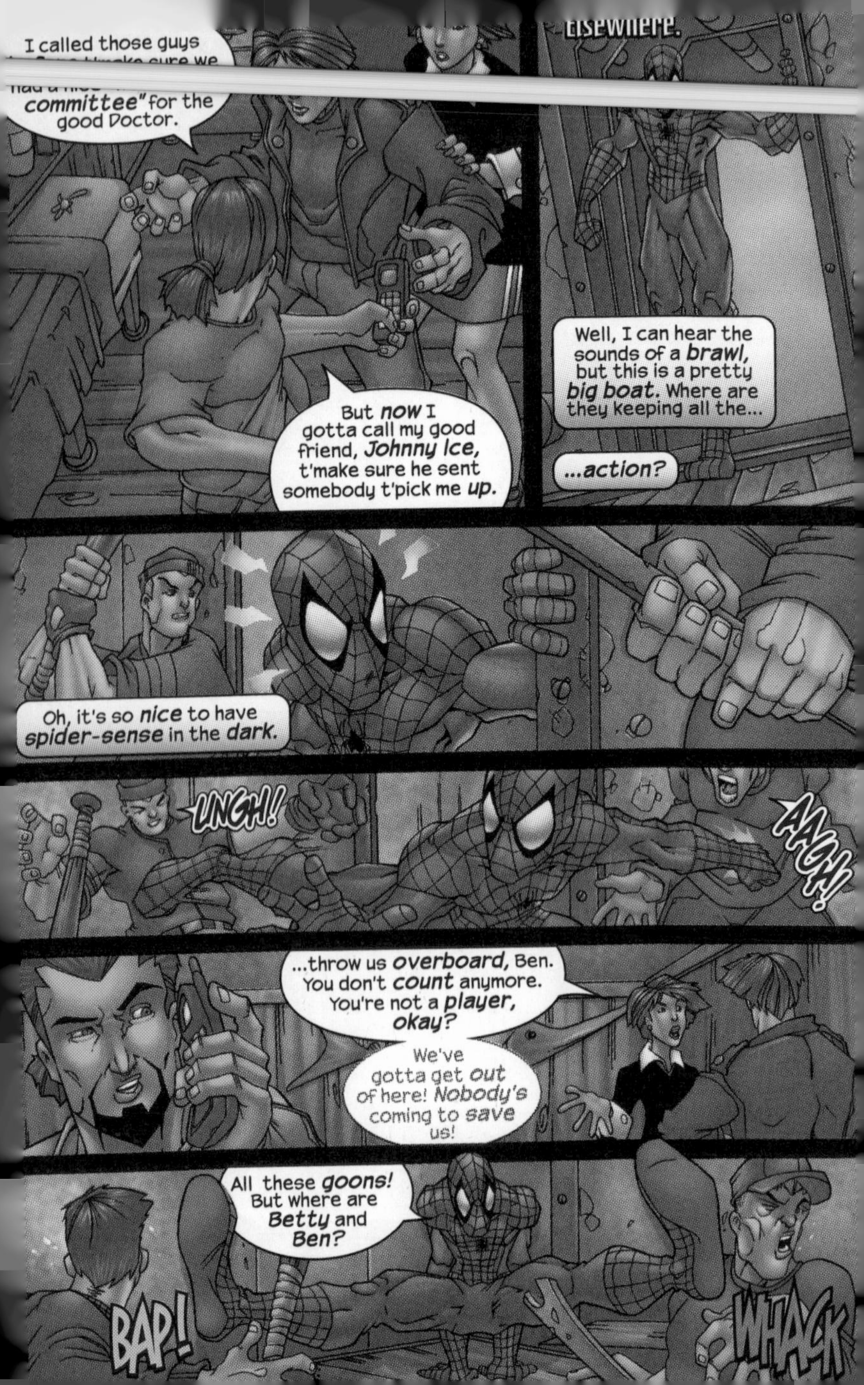

I called those guys
committee" for the good Doctor.
Elsewhere.
But now I gotta call my good friend, Johnny Ice, t'make sure he sent somebody t'pick me up.
Well, I can hear the sounds of a brawl, but this is a pretty big boat. Where are they keeping all the...
...action?
Oh, it's so nice to have spider-sense in the dark.
UNGH!
AAGH!
...throw us overboard, Ben. You don't count anymore. You're not a player, okay?
We've gotta get out of here! Nobody's coming to save us!
All these goons! But where are Betty and Ben?
BAP!
WHACK

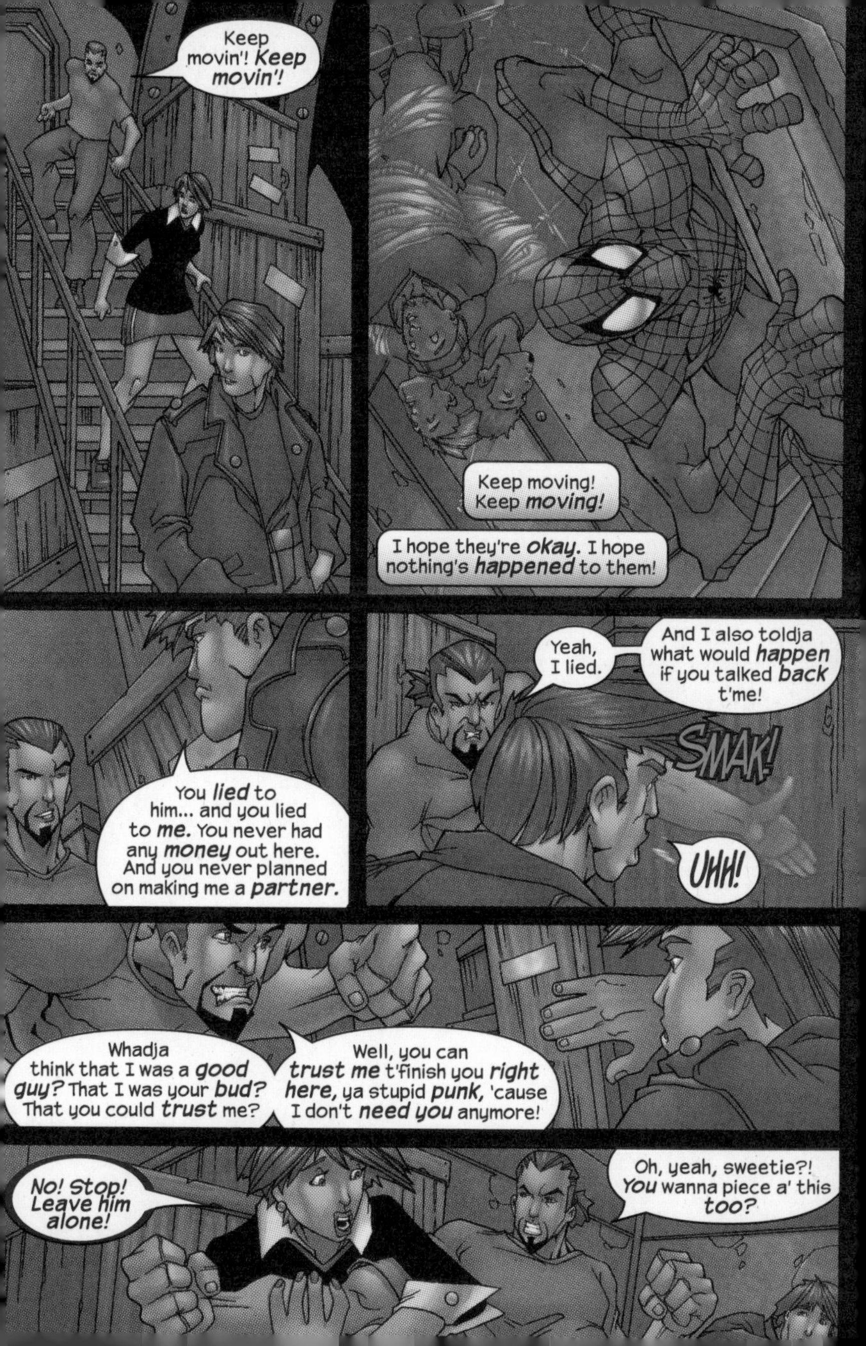
Keep movin'! Keep movin'!
Keep moving! Keep moving!
I hope they're okay. I hope nothing's happened to them!
You lied to him... and you lied to me. You never had any money out here. And you never planned on making me a partner.
Yeah, I lied.
And I also toldja what would happen if you talked back t'me!
SMAK!
UHH!
Whadja think that I was a good guy? That I was your bud? That you could trust me?
Well, you can trust me t'finish you right here, ya stupid punk, 'cause I don't need you anymore!
No! Stop! Leave him alone!
Oh, yeah, sweetie?! You wanna piece a' this too?

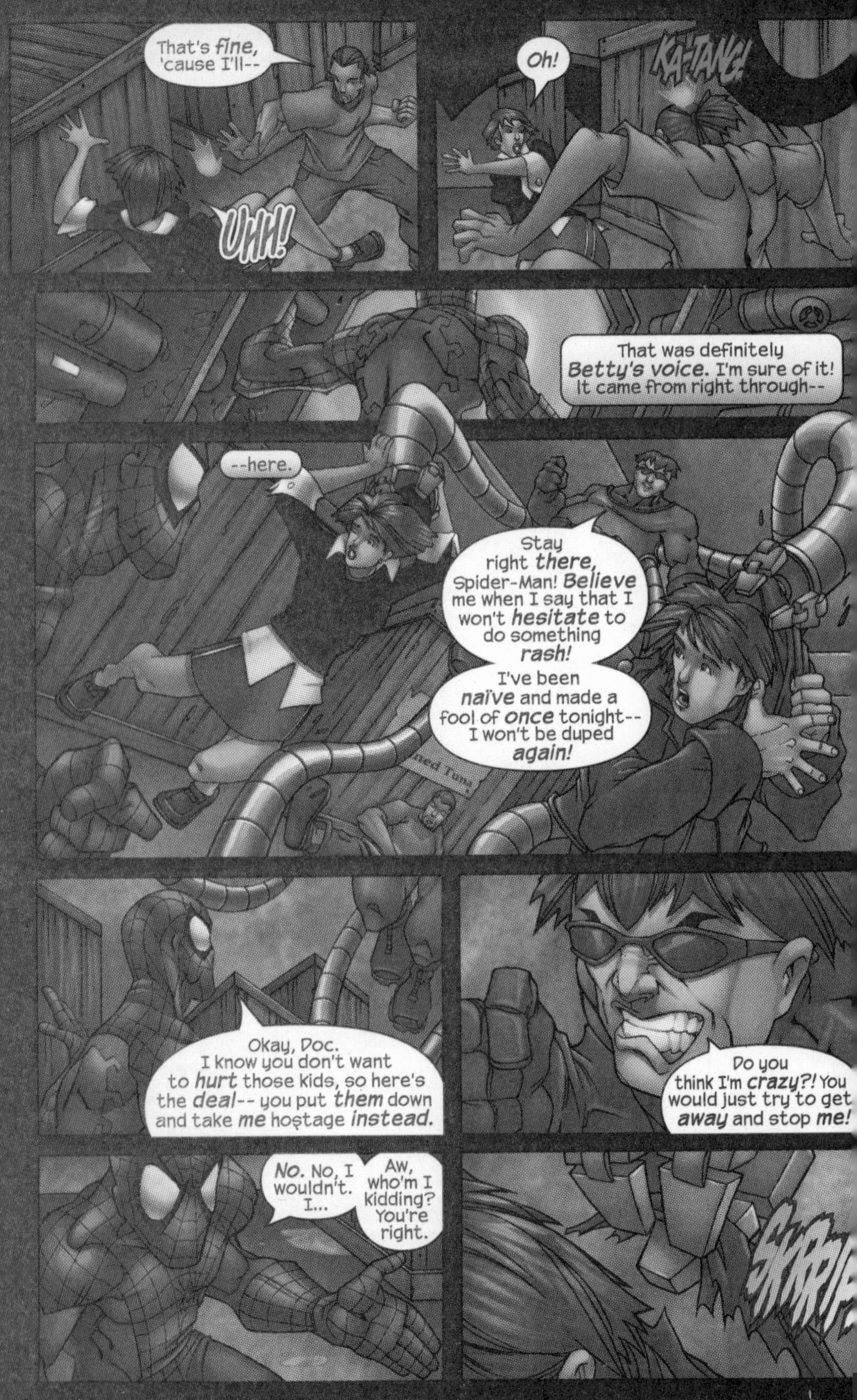

That's fine, 'cause I'll--
UHH!
Oh!
KA-TANG!
That was definitely Betty's voice. I'm sure of it! It came from right through--
--here.
Stay right there, Spider-Man! Believe me when I say that I won't hesitate to do something rash!
I've been naïve and made a fool of once tonight-- I won't be duped again!
Okay, Doc. I know you don't want to hurt those kids, so here's the deal-- you put them down and take me hostage instead.
Do you think I'm crazy?! You would just try to get away and stop me!
No. No, I wouldn't. I...
Aw, who'm I kidding? You're right.

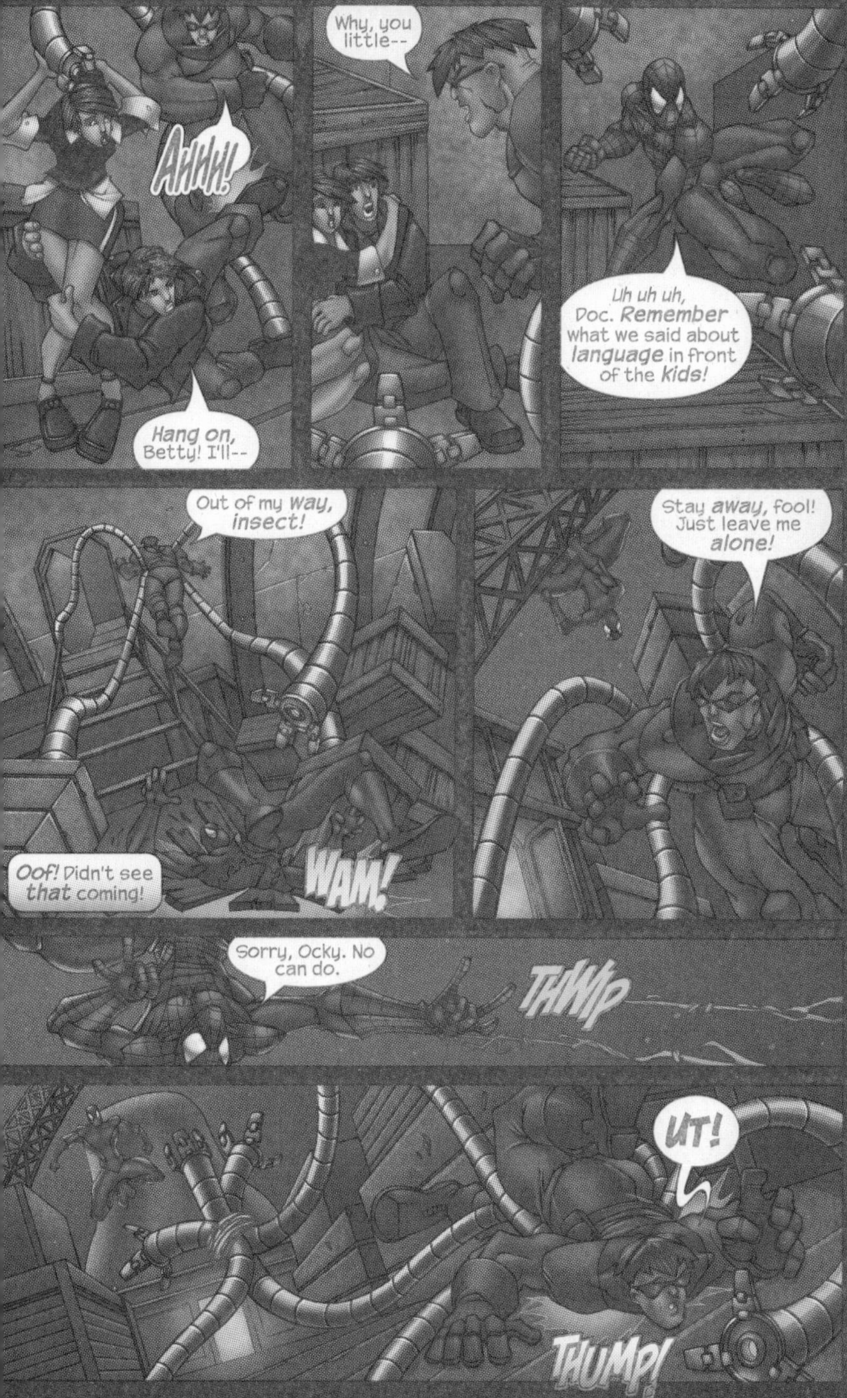
AHHH!
Hang on, Betty! I'll--
Why, you little--
Uh uh uh, Doc. Remember what we said about language in front of the kids!
Out of my way, insect!
Oof! Didn't see that coming!
WAM!
Stay away, fool! Just leave me alone!
Sorry, Ocky. No can do.
THWIP
UT!
THUMP!

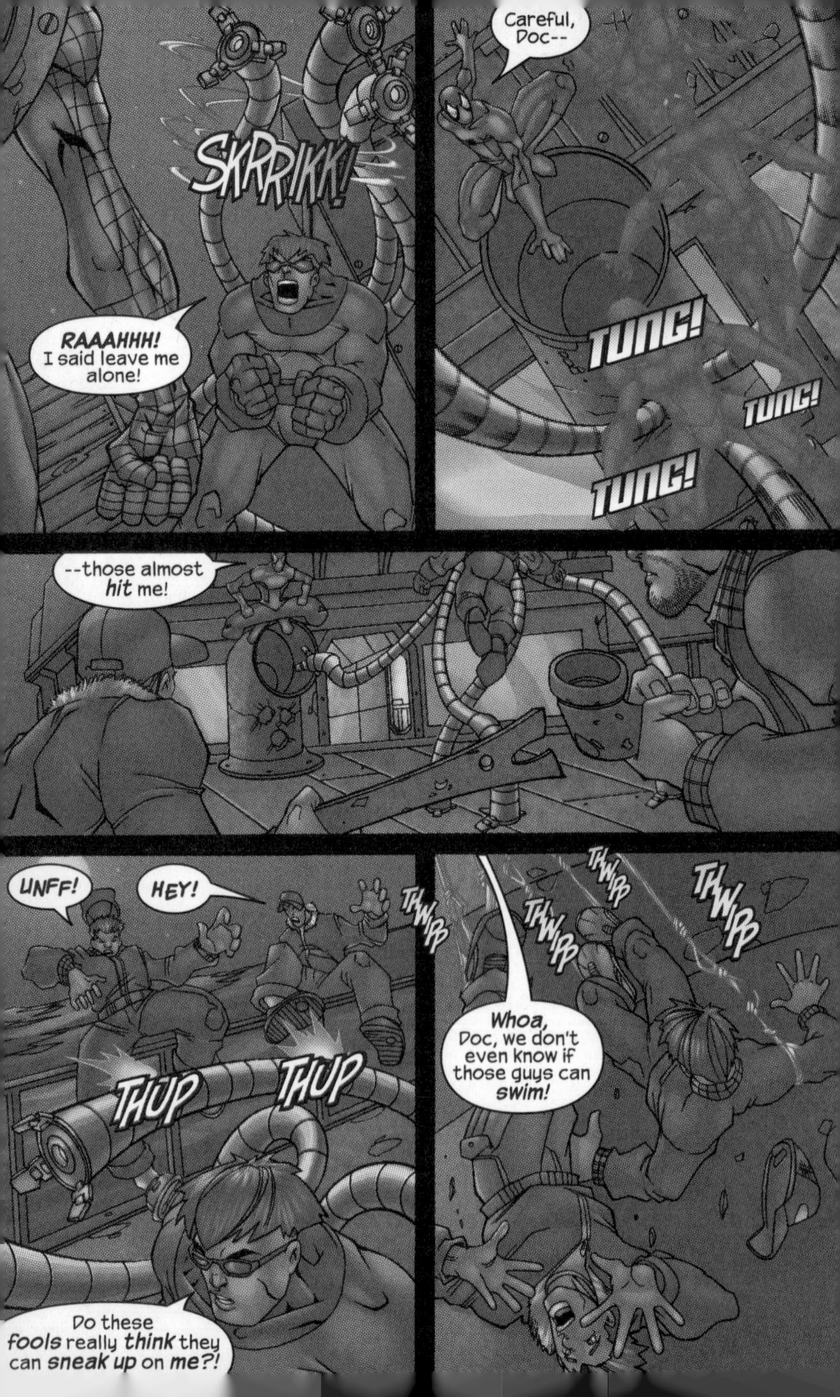
SKRRIKK!
RAAAHHH! I said leave me alone!
Careful, Doc--
TUNG!
TUNG!
TUNG!
--those almost hit me!
UNFF!
HEY!
THWIPP
THUP
THUP
Do these fools really think they can sneak up on me?!
THWIPP
THWIPP
THWIPP
Whoa, Doc, we don't even know if those guys can swim!

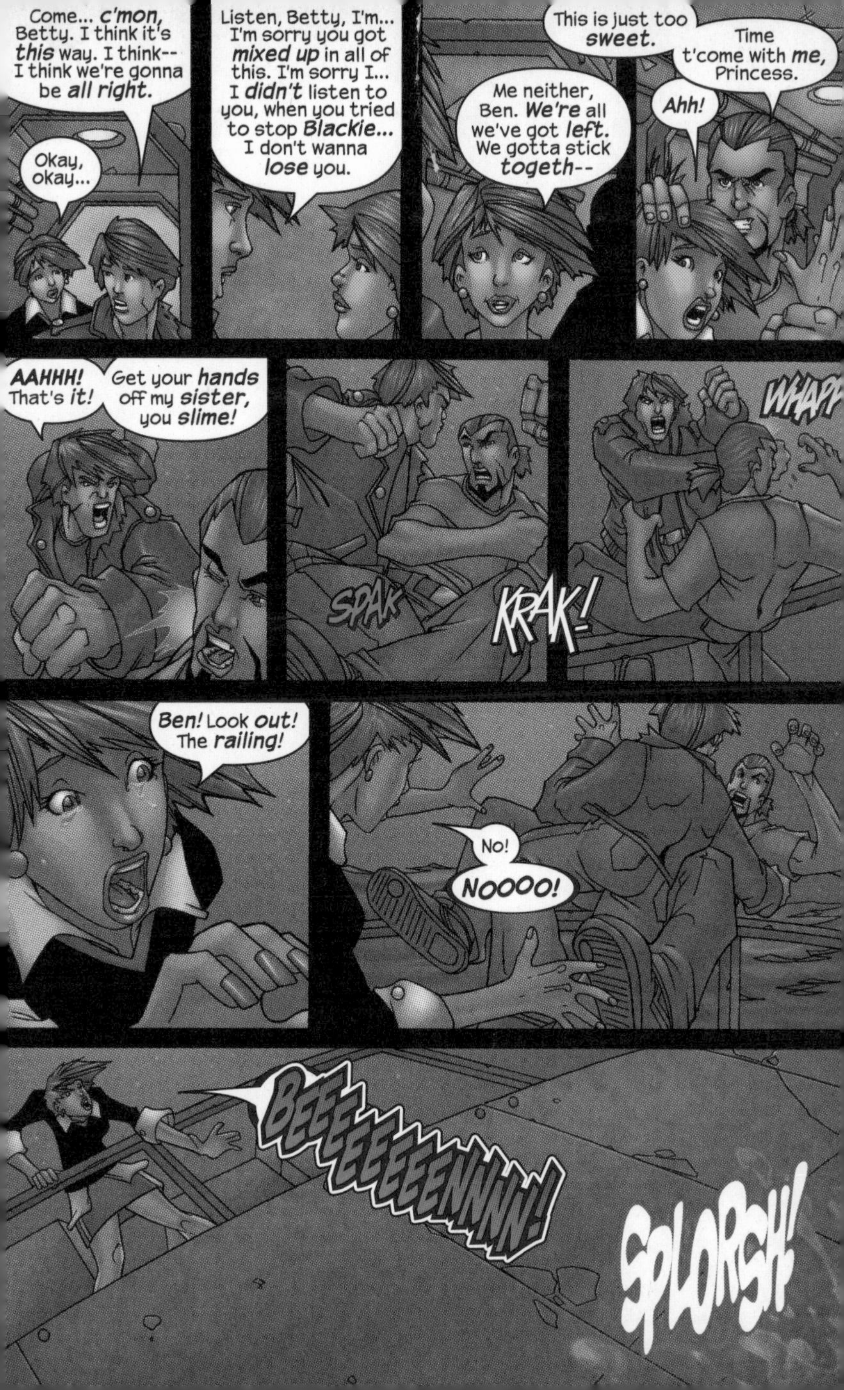
Come... c'mon, Betty. I think it's this way. I think-- I think we're gonna be all right.
Okay, okay...
Listen, Betty, I'm... I'm sorry you got mixed up in all of this. I'm sorry I... I didn't listen to you, when you tried to stop Blackie... I don't wanna lose you.
Me neither, Ben. We're all we've got left. We gotta stick togeth--
This is just too sweet.
Time t'come with me, Princess.
Ahh!
AAHHH! That's it!
Get your hands off my sister, you slime!
SPAK
KRAK!
Ben! Look out! The railing!
No!
NOOOO!
BEEEEEEEENNNN!
SPLORSH!

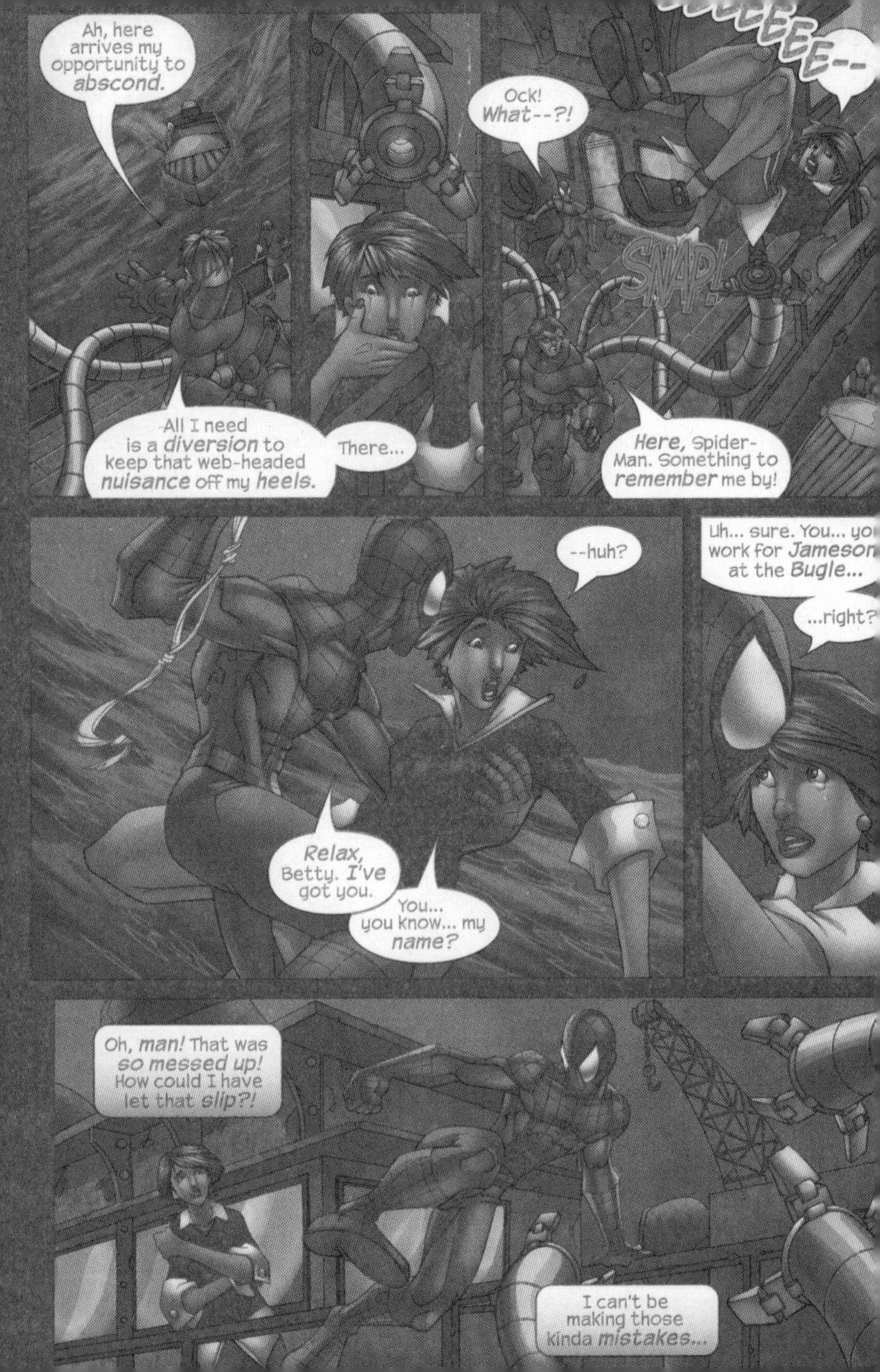
Ah, here arrives my opportunity to abscond.
All I need is a diversion to keep that web-headed nuisance off my heels.
There...
Ock! What--?!
EEEE--
SNAP!
Here, Spider-Man. Something to remember me by!
--huh?
Relax, Betty. I've got you.
You... you know... my name?
Uh... sure. You... yo work for Jameson at the Bugle...
...right?
Oh, man! That was so messed up! How could I have let that slip?!
I can't be making those kinda mistakes...

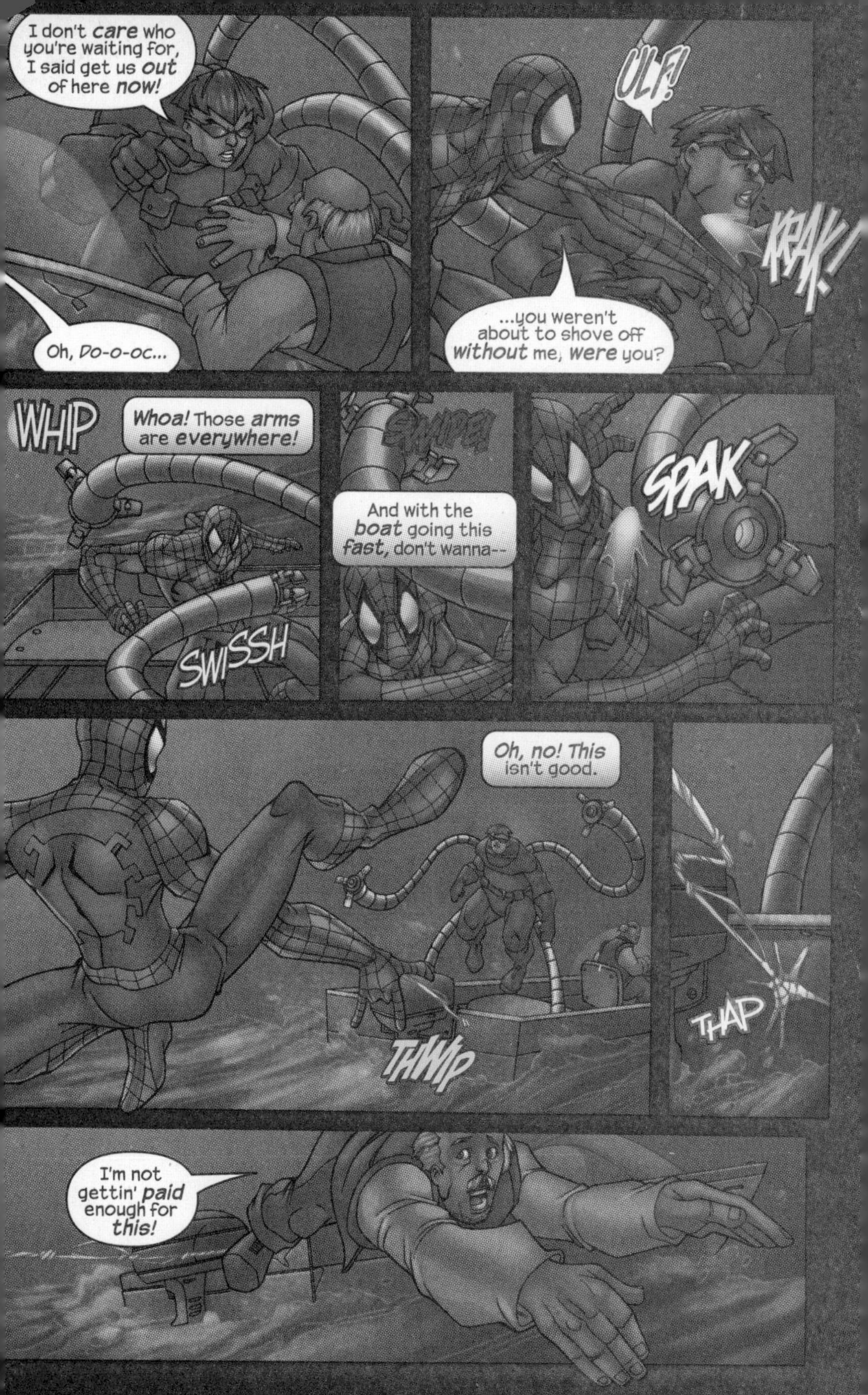
I don't care who you're waiting for, I said get us out of here now!
Oh, Do-o-oc...
ULF!
...you weren't about to shove off without me, were you?
KRAK!
WHIP
Whoa! Those arms are everywhere!
SWISSH
SWIPE!
And with the boat going this fast, don't wanna--
SPAK
Oh, no! This isn't good.
THWIP
THAP
I'm not gettin' paid enough for this!

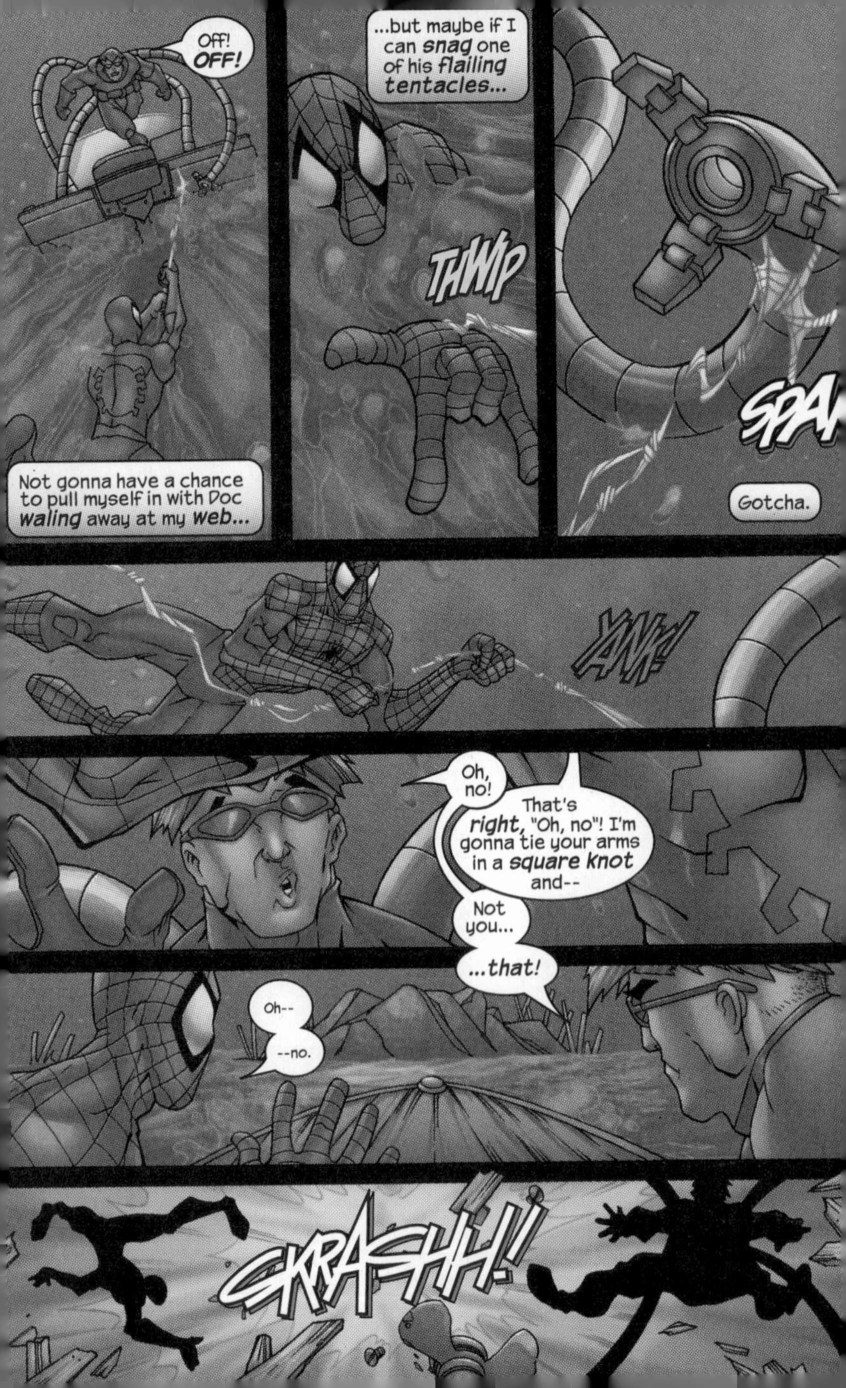
Off! OFF!
Not gonna have a chance to pull myself in with Doc waling away at my web...
...but maybe if I can snag one of his flailing tentacles...
THWIP
SPA
Gotcha.
YANK!
Oh, no!
That's right, "Oh, no"! I'm gonna tie your arms in a square knot and--
Not you...
...that!
Oh--
--no.
GKRASHH!

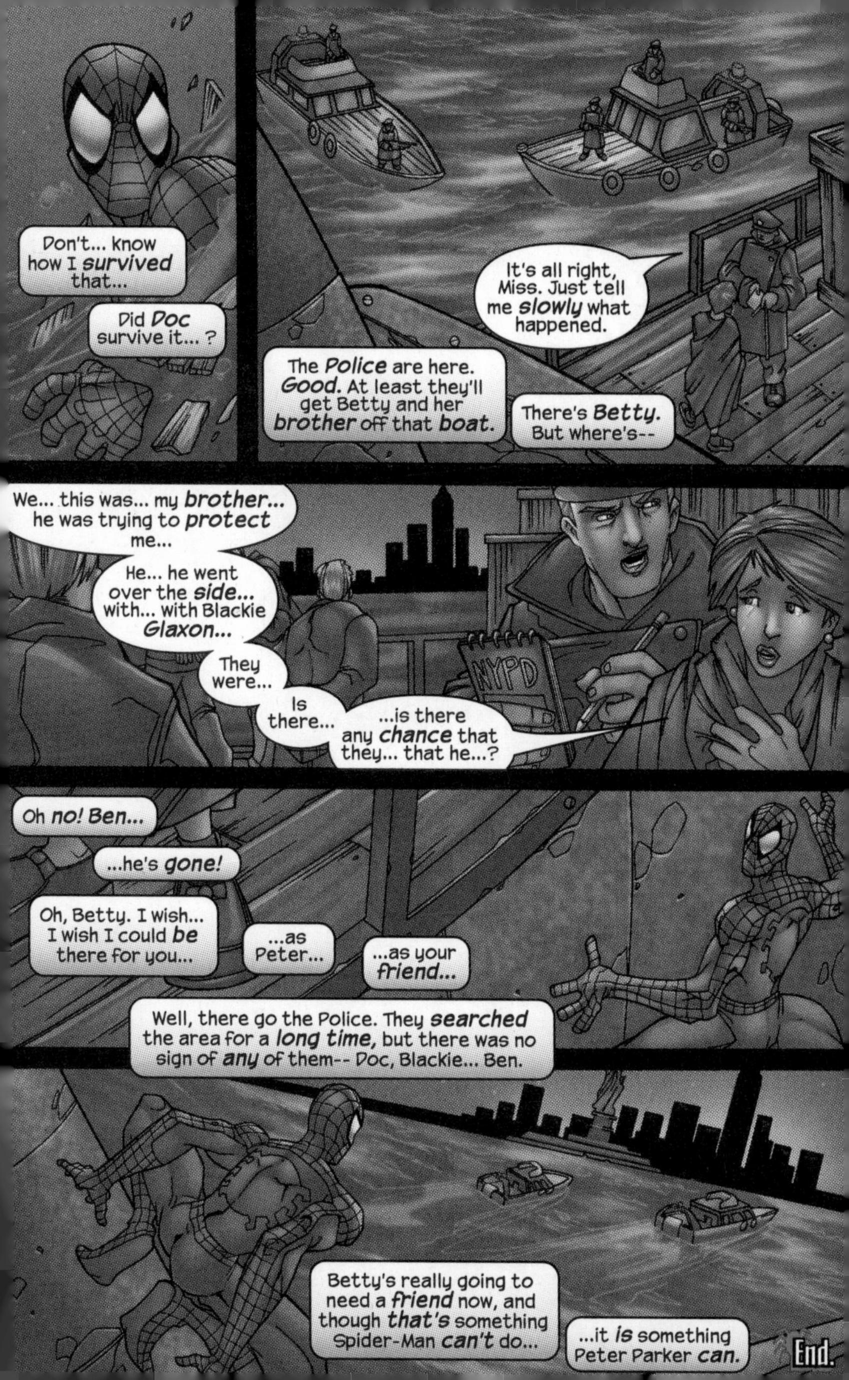

Don't... know how I survived that...
Did Doc survive it... ?
The Police are here. Good. At least they'll get Betty and her brother off that boat.
It's all right, Miss. Just tell me slowly what happened.
There's Betty. But where's--
We... this was... my brother... he was trying to protect me...
He... he went over the side... with... with Blackie Glaxon...
They were...
Is there...
...is there any chance that they... that he...?
NYPD
Oh no! Ben...
...he's gone!
Oh, Betty. I wish... I wish I could be there for you...
...as Peter...
...as your friend...
Well, there go the Police. They searched the area for a long time, but there was no sign of any of them-- Doc, Blackie... Ben.
Betty's really going to need a friend now, and though that's something Spider-Man can't do...
...it is something Peter Parker can.
End.

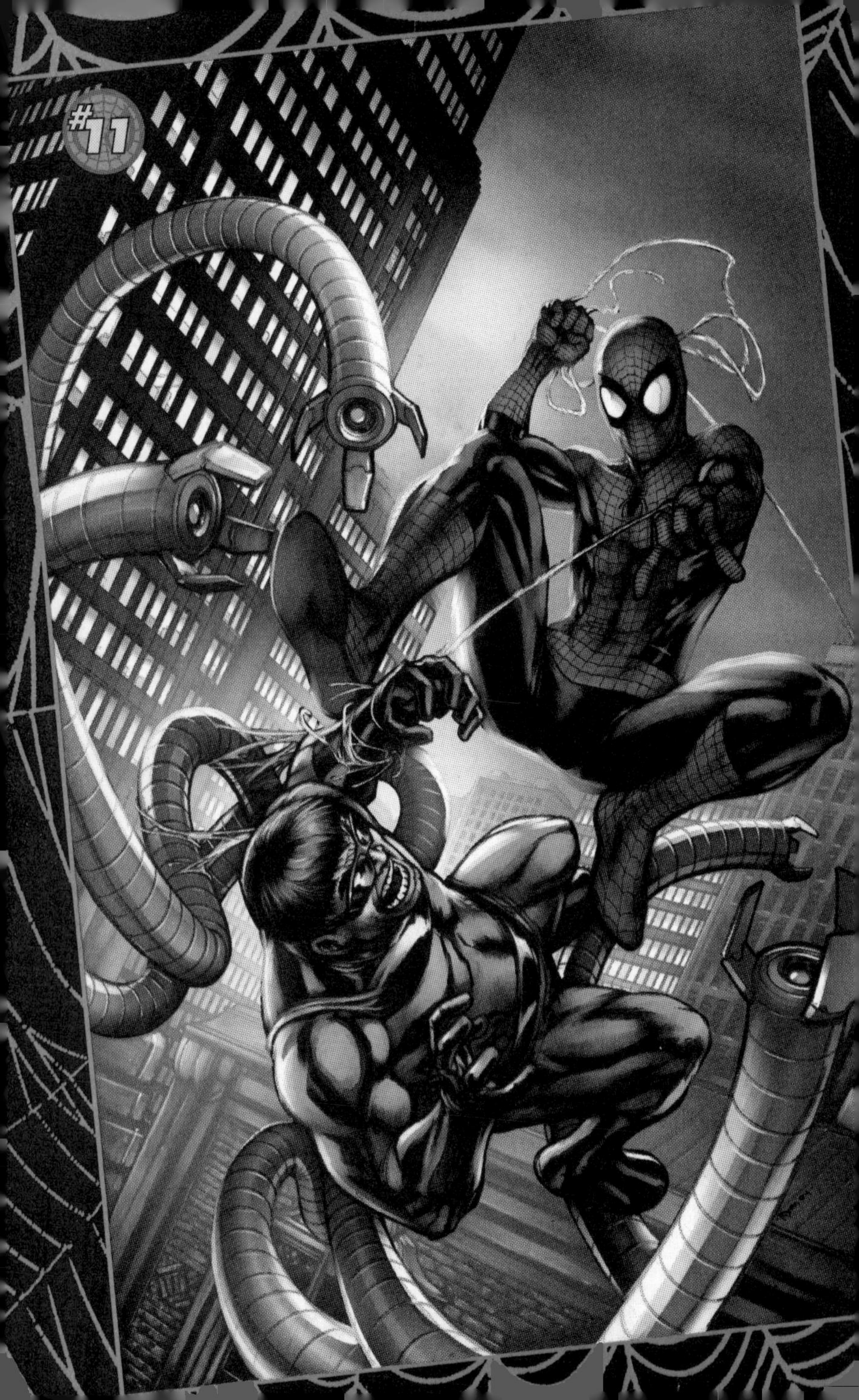
#11

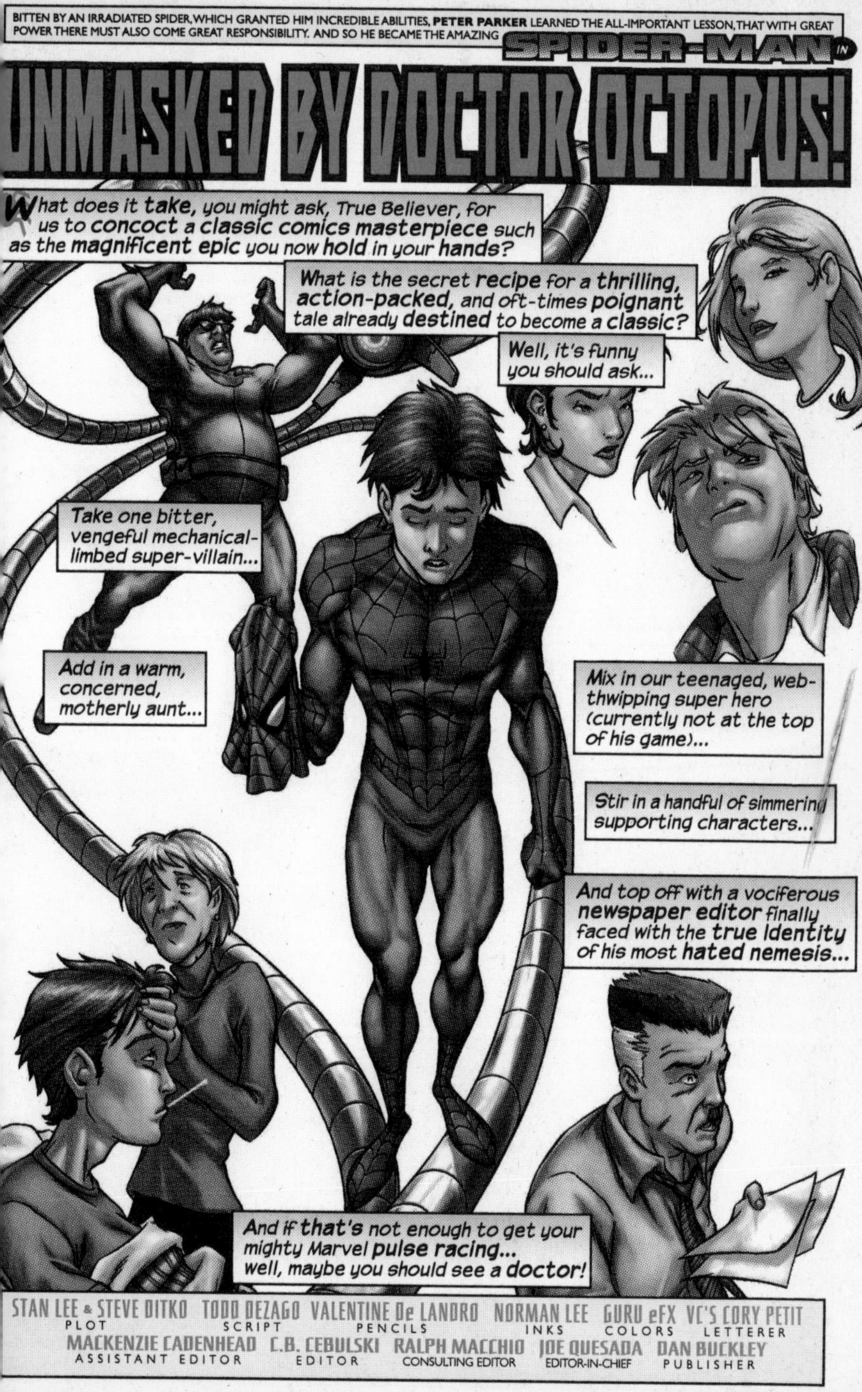
BITTEN BY AN IRRADIATED SPIDER, WHICH GRANTED HIM INCREDIBLE ABILITIES, PETER PARKER LEARNED THE ALL-IMPORTANT LESSON, THAT WITH GREAT POWER THERE MUST ALSO COME GREAT RESPONSIBILITY. AND SO HE BECAME THE AMAZING SPIDER-MAN IN
UNMASKED BY DOCTOR OCTOPUS!
What does it take, you might ask, True Believer, for us to concoct a classic comics masterpiece such as the magnificent epic you now hold in your hands?
What is the secret recipe for a thrilling, action-packed, and oft-times poignant tale already destined to become a classic?
Well, it's funny you should ask...
Take one bitter, vengeful mechanical-limbed super-villain...
Add in a warm, concerned, motherly aunt...
Mix in our teenaged, web-thwipping super hero (currently not at the top of his game)...
Stir in a handful of simmering supporting characters...
And top off with a vociferous newspaper editor finally faced with the true identity of his most hated nemesis...
And if that's not enough to get your mighty Marvel pulse racing... well, maybe you should see a doctor!
STAN LEE & STEVE DITKO PLOT
TODD DEZAGO SCRIPT
VALENTINE De LANDRO PENCILS
NORMAN LEE INKS
GURU eFX COLORS
VC'S CORY PETIT LETTERER
MACKENZIE CADENHEAD ASSISTANT EDITOR
C.B. CEBULSKI EDITOR
RALPH MACCHIO CONSULTING EDITOR
JOE QUESADA EDITOR-IN-CHIEF
DAN BUCKLEY PUBLISHER

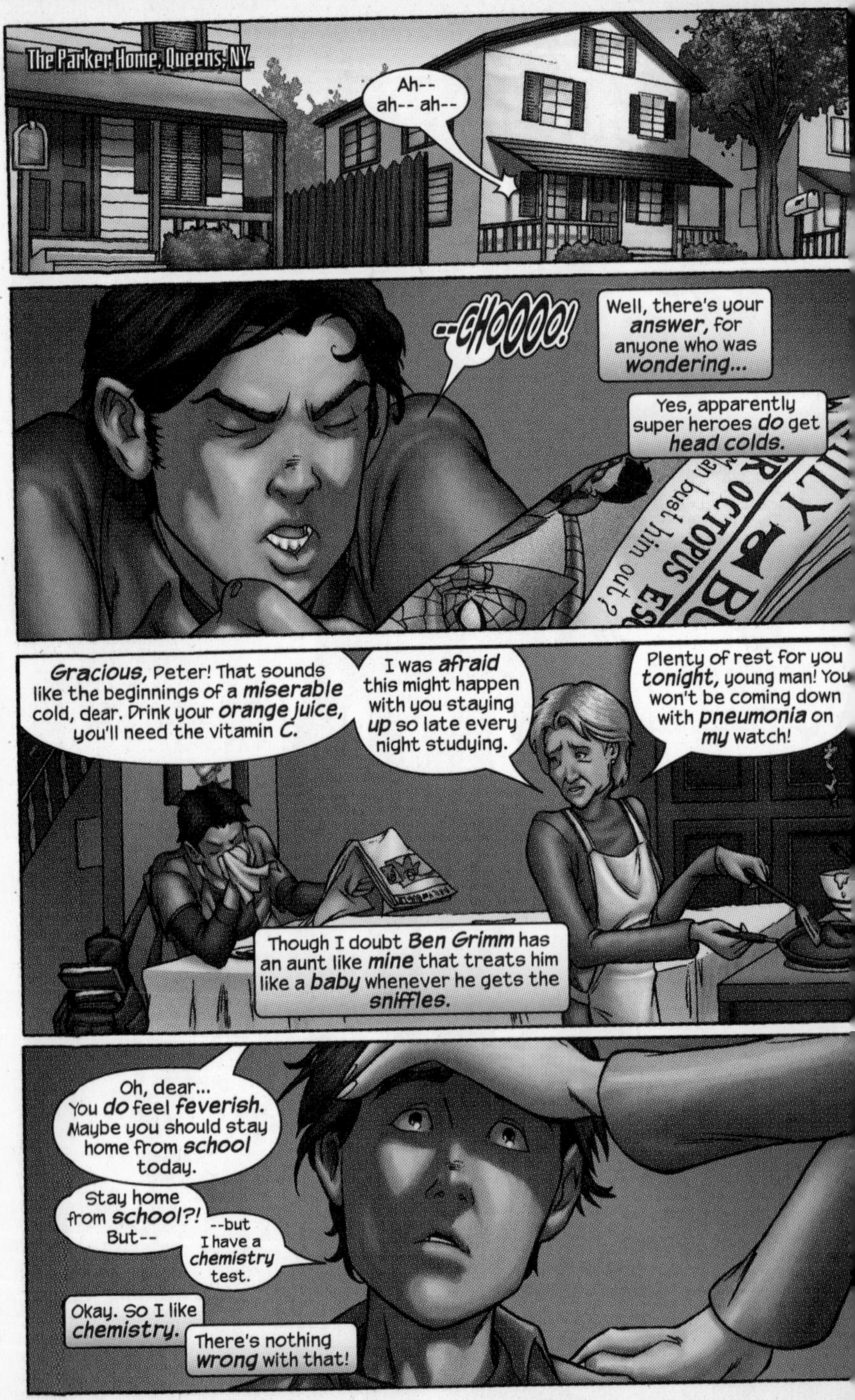

The Parker Home, Queens, NY.
Ah-- ah-- ah--
--CHOOOO!
Well, there's your answer, for anyone who was wondering...
Yes, apparently super heroes do get head colds.
Gracious, Peter! That sounds like the beginnings of a miserable cold, dear. Drink your orange juice, you'll need the vitamin C.
I was afraid this might happen with you staying up so late every night studying.
Plenty of rest for you tonight, young man! You won't be coming down with pneumonia on my watch!
Though I doubt Ben Grimm has an aunt like mine that treats him like a baby whenever he gets the sniffles.
Oh, dear... You do feel feverish. Maybe you should stay home from school today.
Stay home from school?! But--
--but I have a chemistry test.
Okay. So I like chemistry.
There's nothing wrong with that!

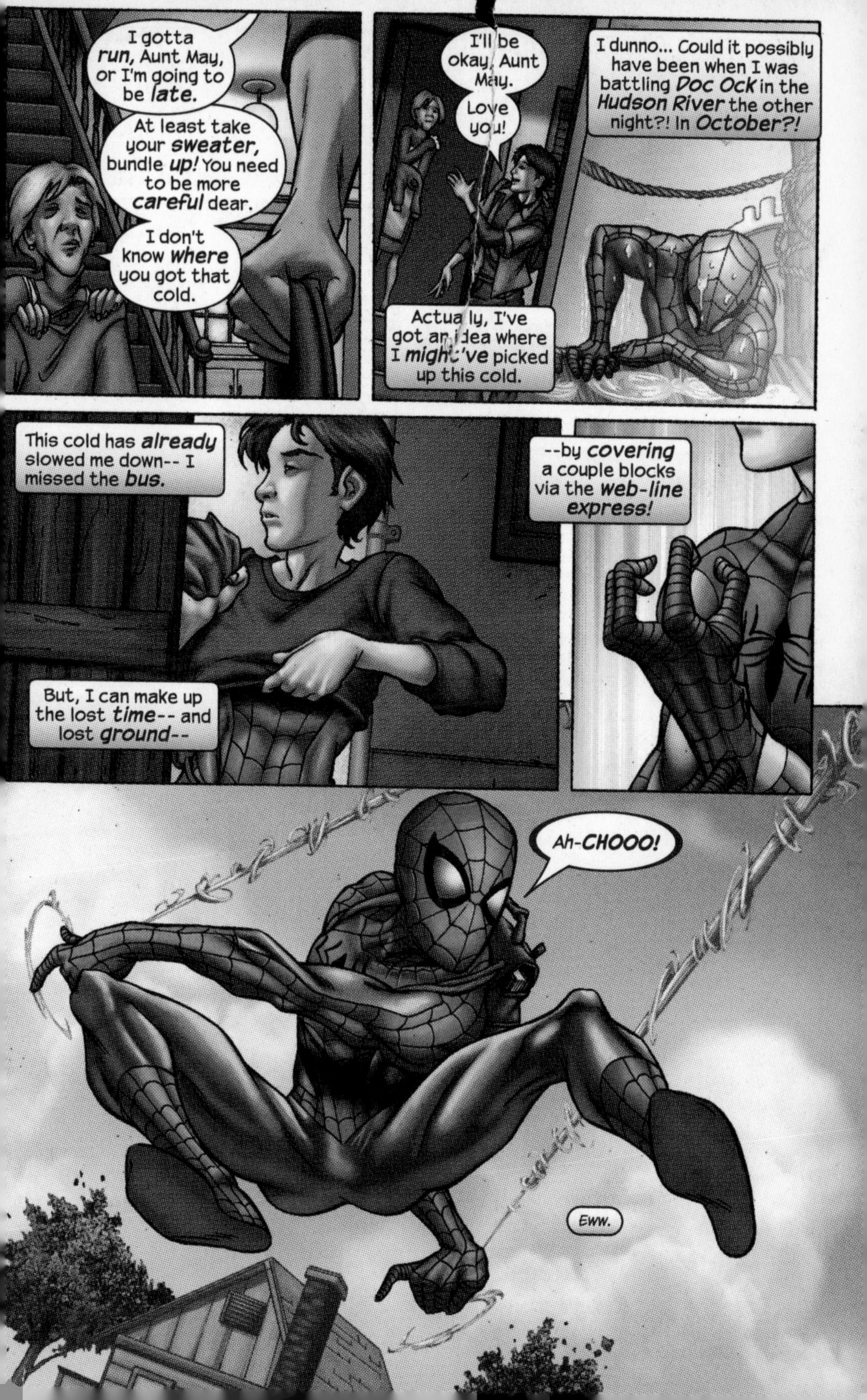
I gotta run, Aunt May, or I'm going to be late.
At least take your sweater, bundle up! You need to be more careful dear.
I don't know where you got that cold.
I'll be okay, Aunt May.
Love you!
Actually, I've got an idea where I might've picked up this cold.
I dunno... Could it possibly have been when I was battling Doc Ock in the Hudson River the other night?! In October?!
This cold has already slowed me down-- I missed the bus.
But, I can make up the lost time-- and lost ground--
--by covering a couple blocks via the web-line express!
Ah-CHOOO!
Eww.

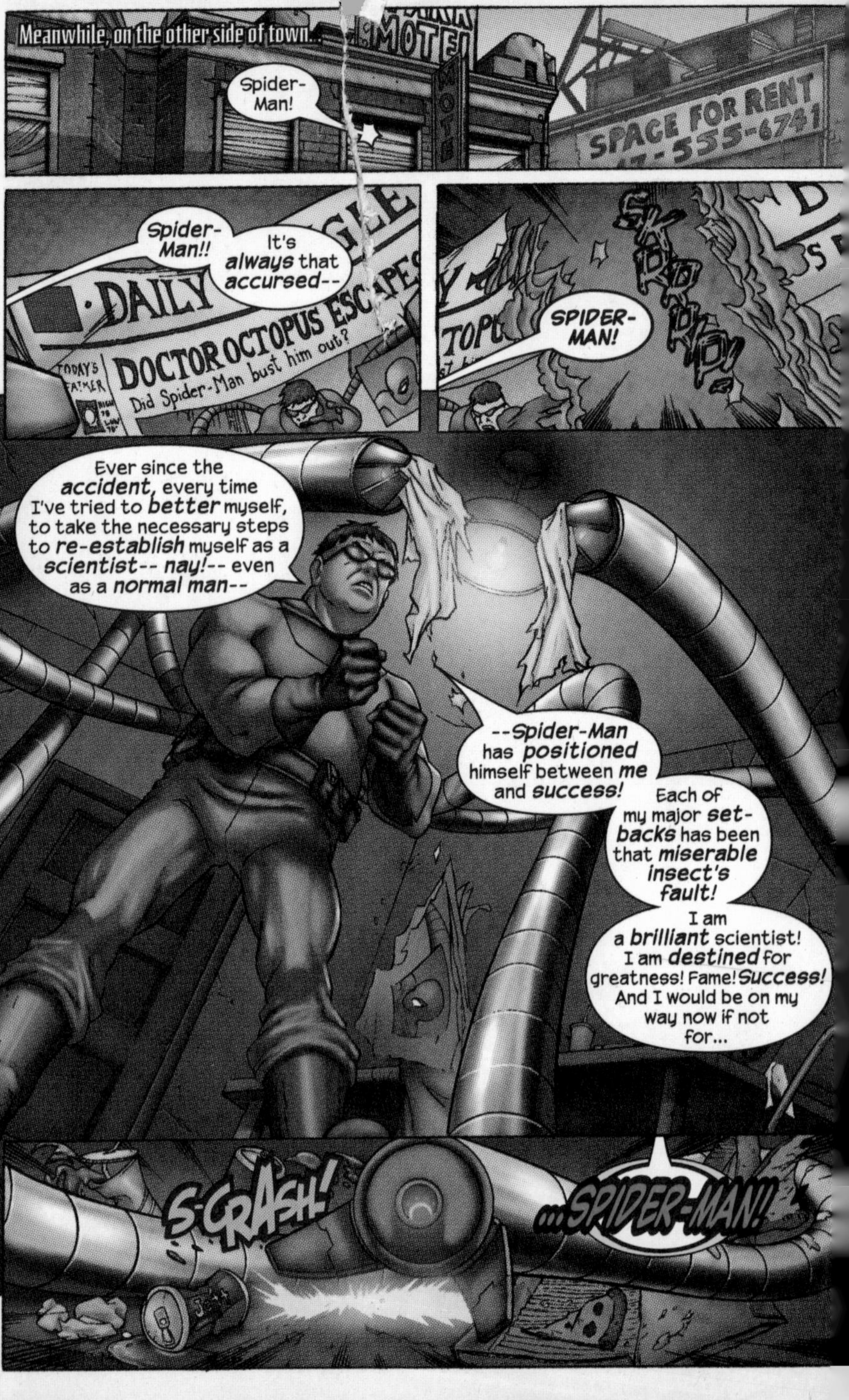

Meanwhile, on the other side of town...
MOTEL
Spider-Man!
SPACE FOR RENT
555-6741
Spider-Man!!
It's always that accursed--
DAILY
DOCTOR OCTOPUS ESCAPES
Did Spider-Man bust him out?
TODAY'S FARMER
SKRRRUNCH
SPIDER-MAN!
Ever since the accident, every time I've tried to better myself, to take the necessary steps to re-establish myself as a scientist-- nay!-- even as a normal man--
--Spider-Man has positioned himself between me and success!
Each of my major set-backs has been that miserable insect's fault!
I am a brilliant scientist! I am destined for greatness! Fame! Success! And I would be on my way now if not for...
S-CRASH!
...SPIDER-MAN!

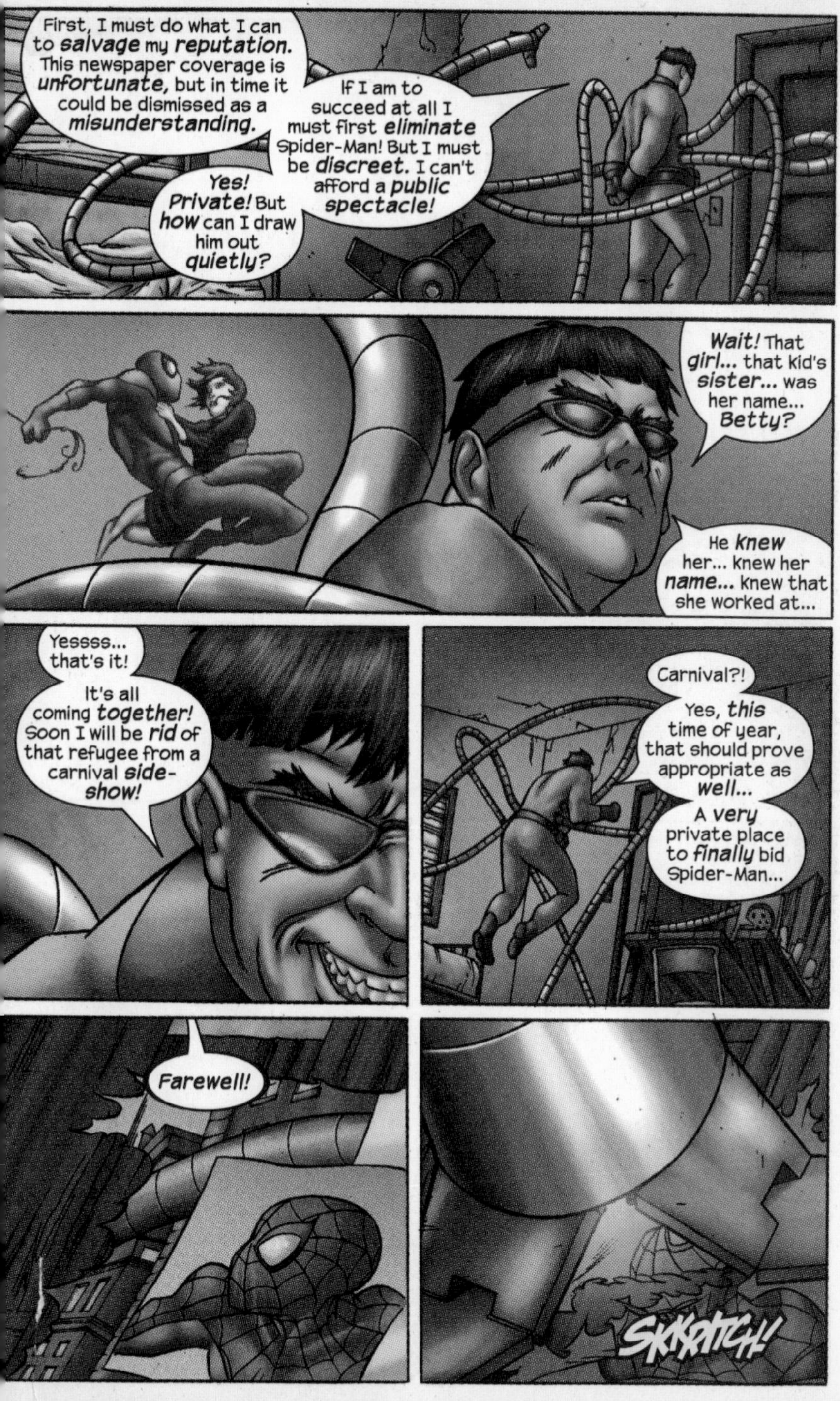
First, I must do what I can to salvage my reputation. This newspaper coverage is unfortunate, but in time it could be dismissed as a misunderstanding.
If I am to succeed at all I must first eliminate Spider-Man! But I must be discreet. I can't afford a public spectacle!
Yes! Private! But how can I draw him out quietly?
Wait! That girl... that kid's sister... was her name... Betty?
He knew her... knew her name... knew that she worked at...
Yessss... that's it!
It's all coming together! Soon I will be rid of that refugee from a carnival side-show!
Carnival?!
Yes, this time of year, that should prove appropriate as well...
A very private place to finally bid Spider-Man...
Farewell!
SKKRITCH!

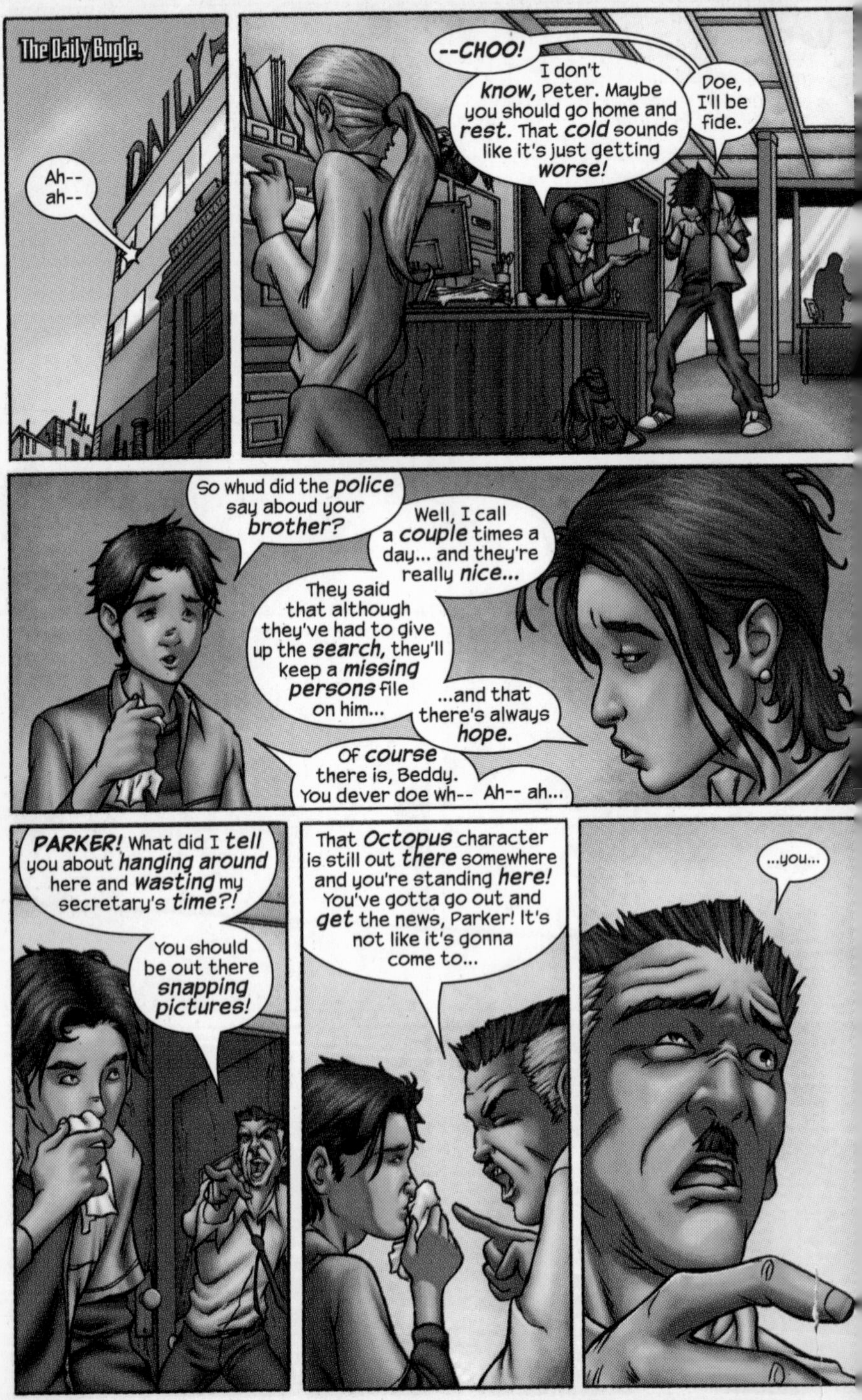
The Daily Bugle.
Ah-- ah--
--CHOO!
I don't know, Peter. Maybe you should go home and rest. That cold sounds like it's just getting worse!
Doe, I'll be fide.
So whud did the police say aboud your brother?
Well, I call a couple times a day... and they're really nice...
They said that although they've had to give up the search, they'll keep a missing persons file on him...
...and that there's always hope.
Of course there is, Beddy. You dever doe wh-- Ah-- ah...
PARKER! What did I tell you about hanging around here and wasting my secretary's time?!
You should be out there snapping pictures!
That Octopus character is still out there somewhere and you're standing here! You've gotta go out and get the news, Parker! It's not like it's gonna come to...
...you...

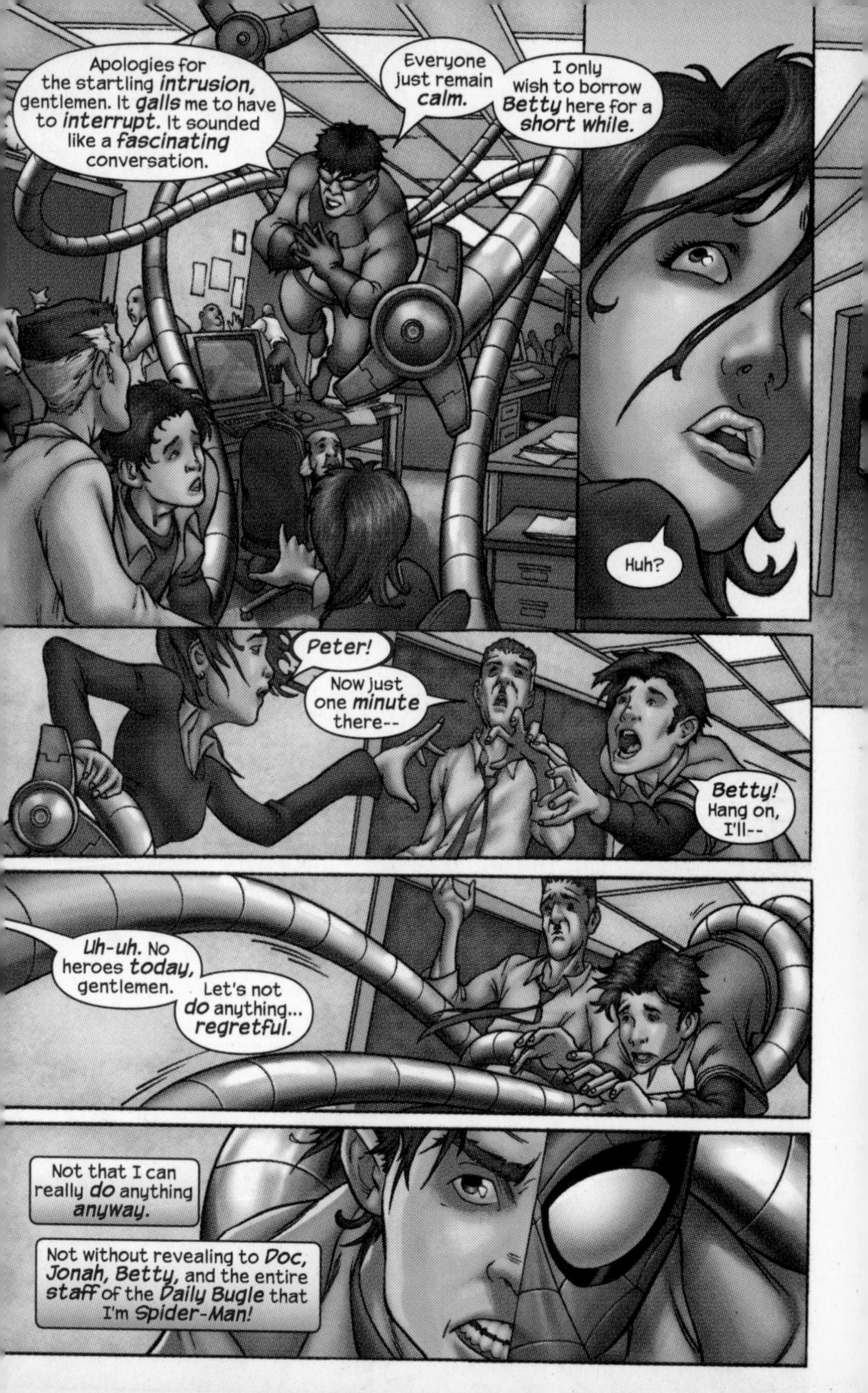
Apologies for the startling *intrusion,* gentlemen. It *galls* me to have to *interrupt.* It sounded like a *fascinating* conversation.
Everyone just remain *calm.*
I only wish to borrow *Betty* here for a *short while.*
Huh?
Peter!
Now just one *minute* there--
Betty! Hang on, I'll--
Uh-uh. No heroes *today,* gentlemen.
Let's not *do* anything... *regretful.*
Not that I can really *do* anything *anyway.*
Not without revealing to *Doc, Jonah, Betty,* and the entire *staff* of the *Daily Bugle* that I'm *Spider-Man!*

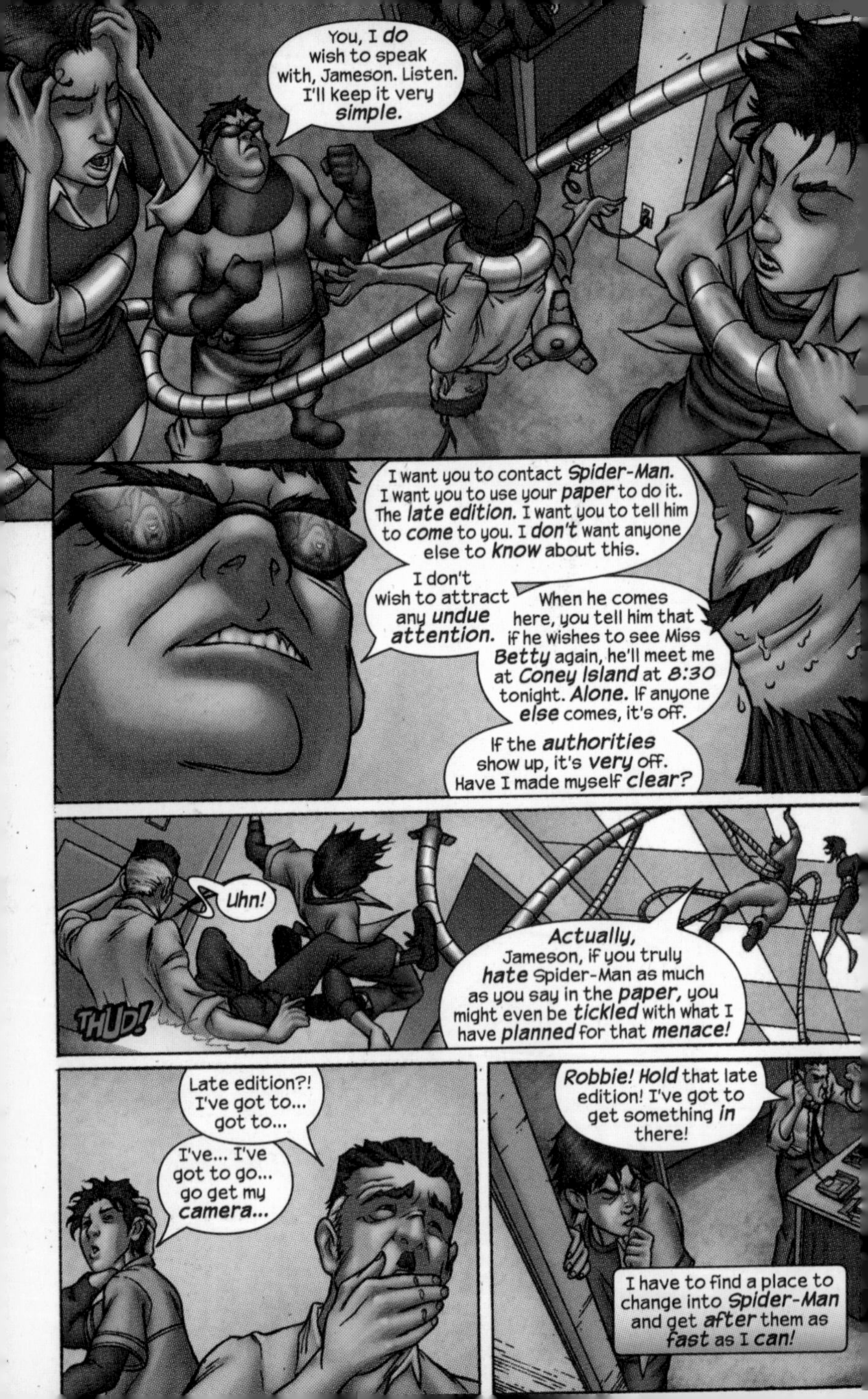
You, I do wish to speak with, Jameson. Listen. I'll keep it very simple.
I want you to contact Spider-Man. I want you to use your paper to do it. The late edition. I want you to tell him to come to you. I don't want anyone else to know about this.
I don't wish to attract any undue attention.
When he comes here, you tell him that if he wishes to see Miss Betty again, he'll meet me at Coney Island at 8:30 tonight. Alone. If anyone else comes, it's off.
If the authorities show up, it's very off. Have I made myself clear?
Uhn!
THUD!
Actually, Jameson, if you truly hate Spider-Man as much as you say in the paper, you might even be tickled with what I have planned for that menace!
Late edition?! I've got to... got to...
I've... I've got to go... go get my camera...
Robbie! Hold that late edition! I've got to get something in there!
I have to find a place to change into Spider-Man and get after them as fast as I can!

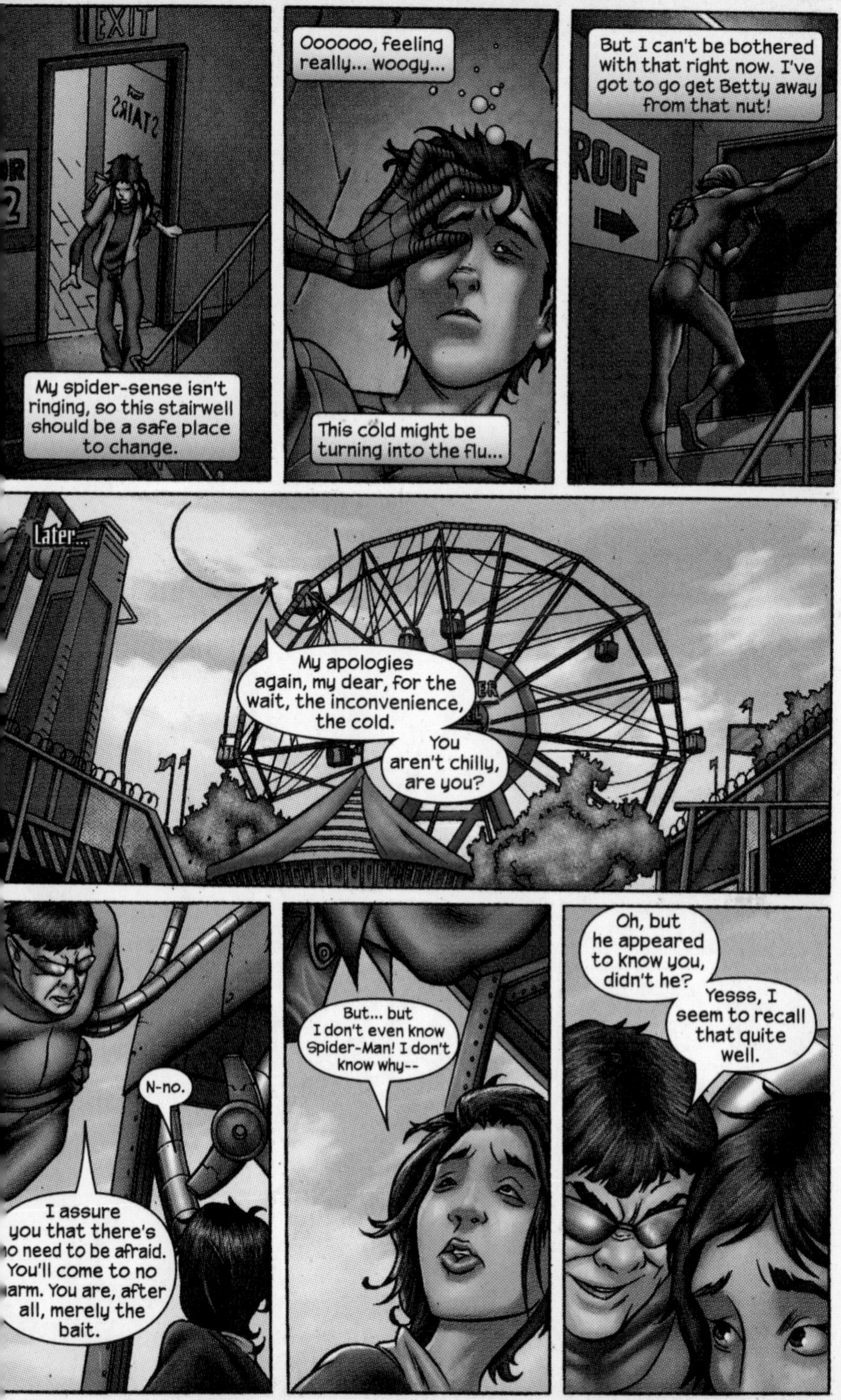
EXIT
STAIRS
My spider-sense isn't ringing, so this stairwell should be a safe place to change.
Oooooo, feeling really... woogy...
This cold might be turning into the flu...
But I can't be bothered with that right now. I've got to go get Betty away from that nut!
ROOF
Later...
My apologies again, my dear, for the wait, the inconvenience, the cold.
You aren't chilly, are you?
N-no.
I assure you that there's no need to be afraid. You'll come to no harm. You are, after all, merely the bait.
But... but I don't even know Spider-Man! I don't know why--
Oh, but he appeared to know you, didn't he?
Yesss, I seem to recall that quite well.

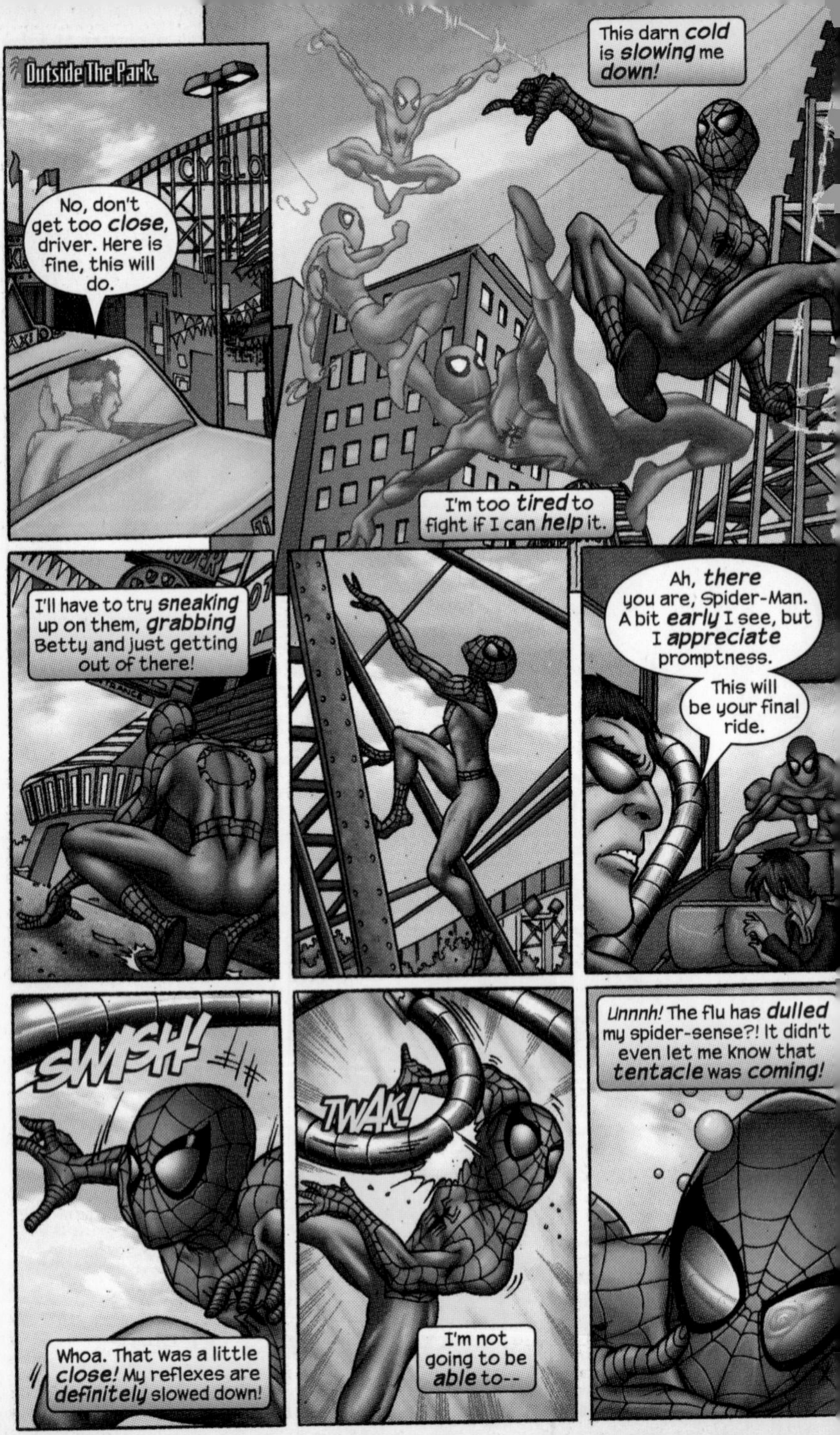
Outside The Park.
No, don't get too close, driver. Here is fine, this will do.
This darn cold is slowing me down!
I'm too tired to fight if I can help it.
I'll have to try sneaking up on them, grabbing Betty and just getting out of there!
Ah, there you are, Spider-Man. A bit early I see, but I appreciate promptness.
This will be your final ride.
SWISH!
Whoa. That was a little close! My reflexes are definitely slowed down!
TWAK!
I'm not going to be able to--
Unnnh! The flu has dulled my spider-sense?! It didn't even let me know that tentacle was coming!

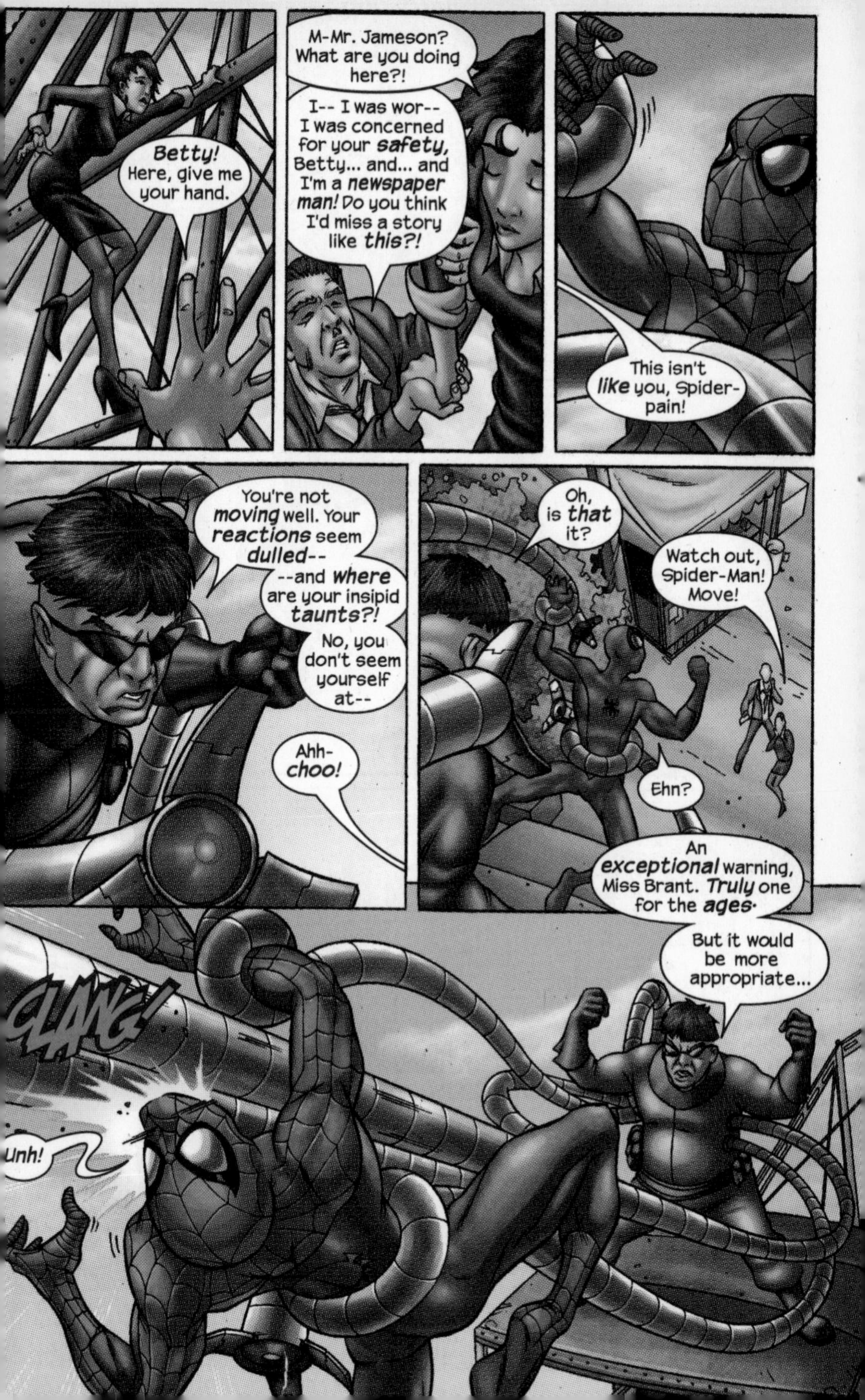
Betty! Here, give me your hand.
M-Mr. Jameson? What are you doing here?!
I-- I was wor-- I was concerned for your safety, Betty... and... and I'm a newspaper man! Do you think I'd miss a story like this?!
This isn't like you, Spider-pain!
You're not moving well. Your reactions seem dulled--
--and where are your insipid taunts?!
No, you don't seem yourself at--
Ahh-choo!
Oh, is that it?
Watch out, Spider-Man! Move!
Ehn?
An exceptional warning, Miss Brant. Truly one for the ages.
But it would be more appropriate...
CLANG!
Unh!

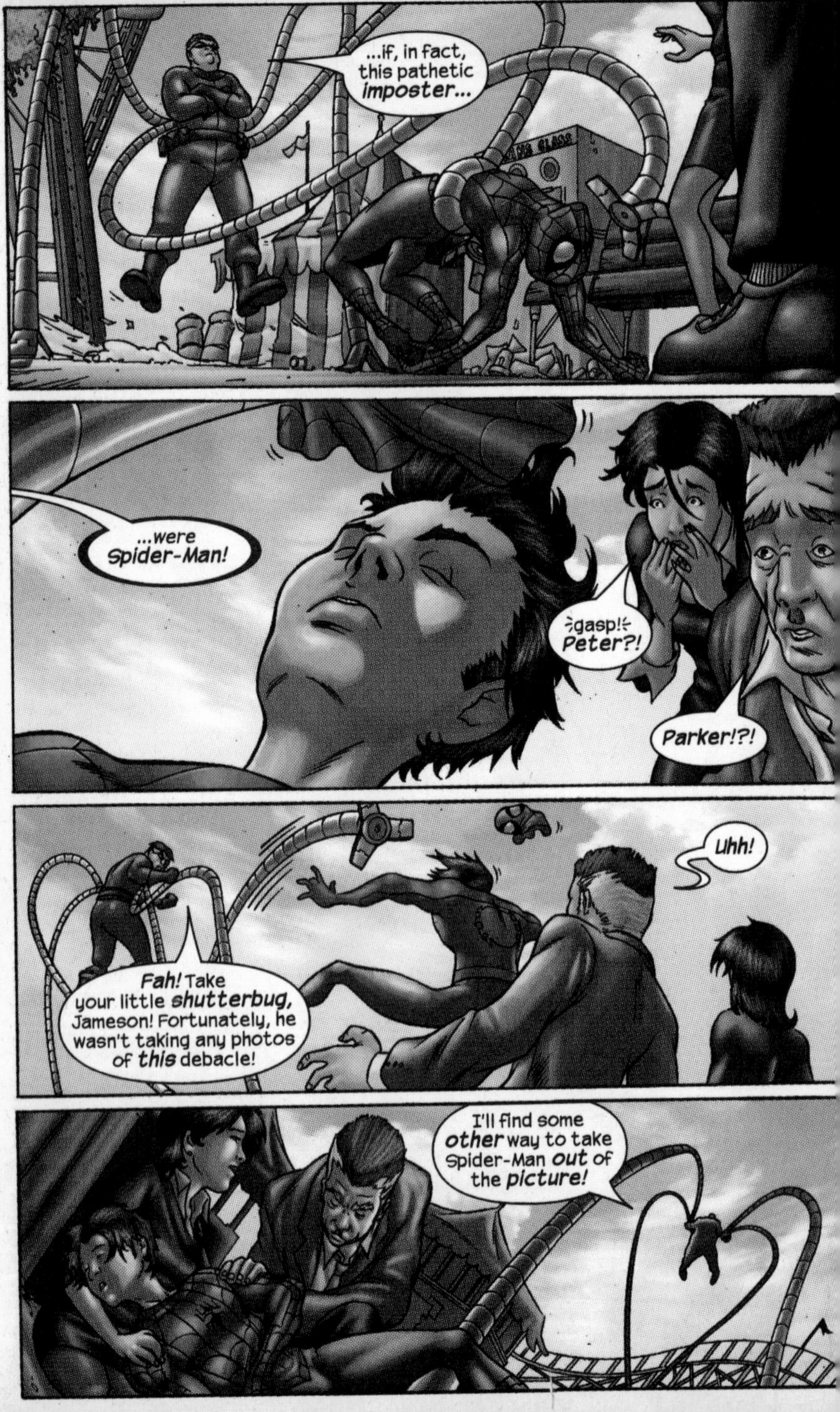
...if, in fact, this pathetic imposter...
...were Spider-Man!
¦gasp!¦ Peter?!
Parker!?!
Uhh!
Fah! Take your little shutterbug, Jameson! Fortunately, he wasn't taking any photos of this debacle!
I'll find some other way to take Spider-Man out of the picture!

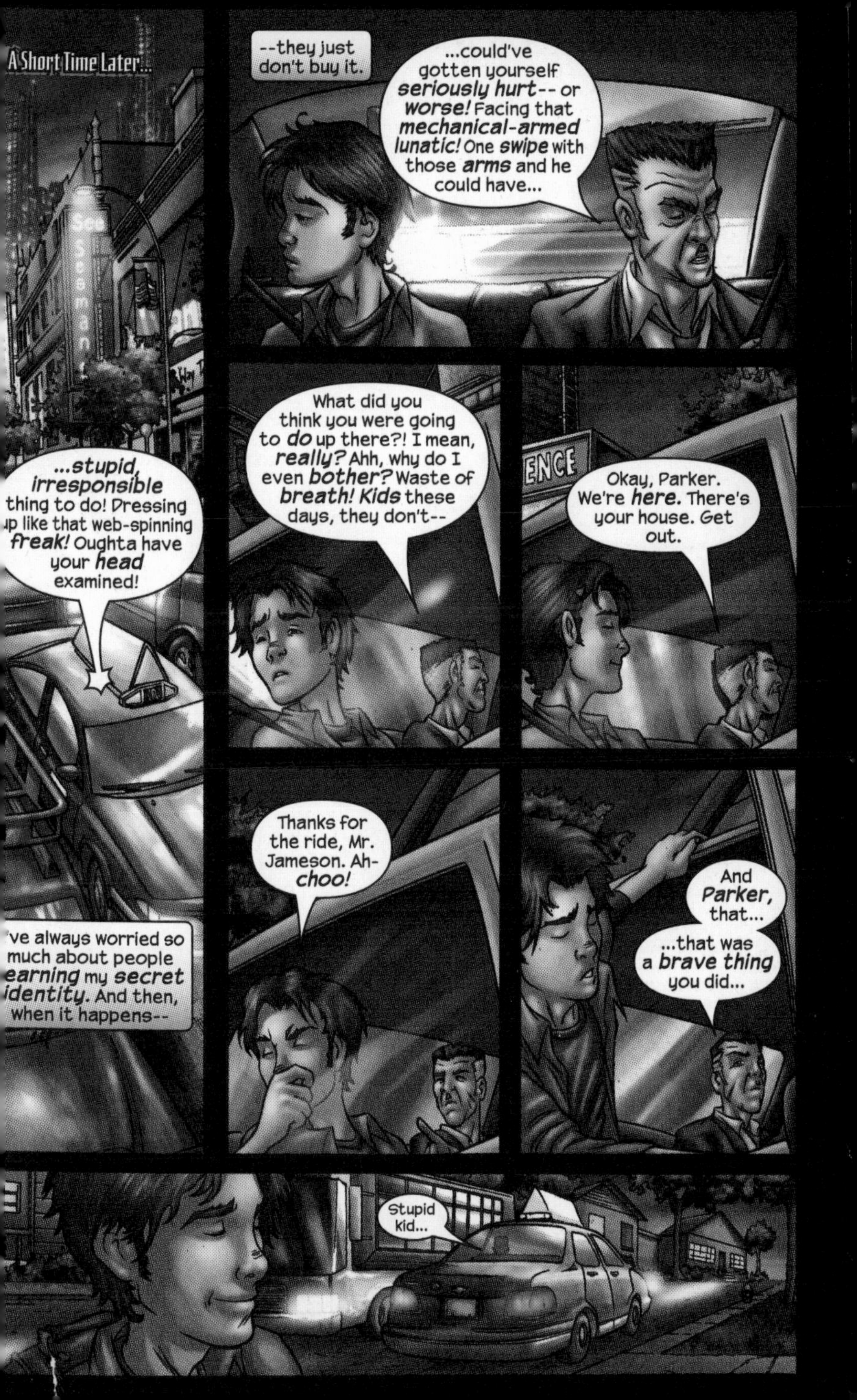
A Short Time Later...
--they just don't buy it.
...could've gotten yourself seriously hurt-- or worse! Facing that mechanical-armed lunatic! One swipe with those arms and he could have...
...stupid, irresponsible thing to do! Dressing up like that web-spinning freak! Oughta have your head examined!
What did you think you were going to do up there?! I mean, really? Ahh, why do I even bother? Waste of breath! Kids these days, they don't--
Okay, Parker. We're here. There's your house. Get out.
've always worried so much about people earning my secret identity. And then, when it happens--
Thanks for the ride, Mr. Jameson. Ah-choo!
And Parker, that...
...that was a brave thing you did...
Stupid kid...

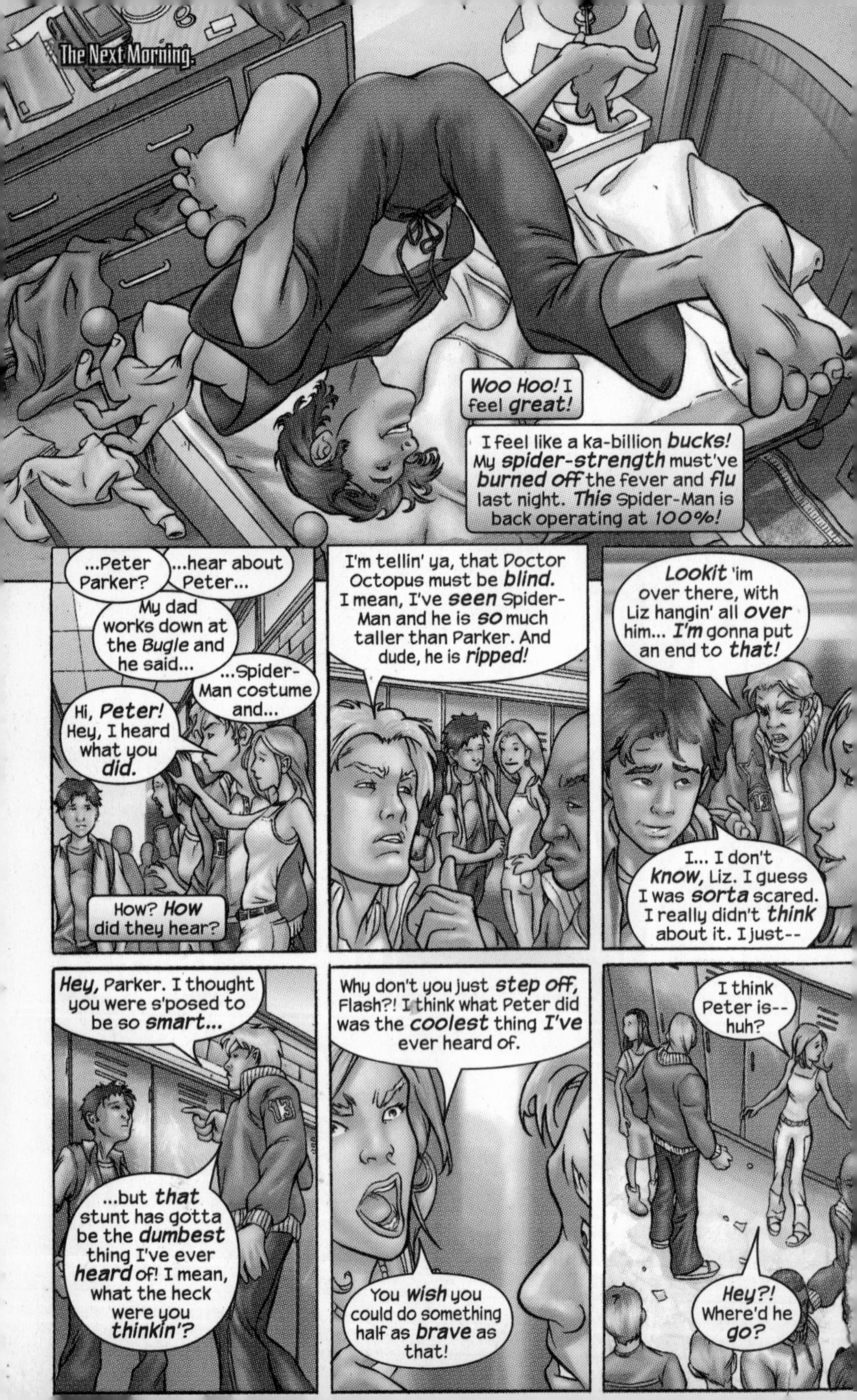
The Next Morning.
Woo Hoo! I feel great!
I feel like a ka-billion bucks! My spider-strength must've burned off the fever and flu last night. This Spider-Man is back operating at 100%!
...Peter Parker?
...hear about Peter...
My dad works down at the Bugle and he said...
...Spider-Man costume and...
Hi, Peter! Hey, I heard what you did.
How? How did they hear?
I'm tellin' ya, that Doctor Octopus must be blind. I mean, I've seen Spider-Man and he is so much taller than Parker. And dude, he is ripped!
Lookit 'im over there, with Liz hangin' all over him... I'm gonna put an end to that!
I... I don't know, Liz. I guess I was sorta scared. I really didn't think about it. I just--
Hey, Parker. I thought you were s'posed to be so smart...
...but that stunt has gotta be the dumbest thing I've ever heard of! I mean, what the heck were you thinkin'?
Why don't you just step off, Flash?! I think what Peter did was the coolest thing I've ever heard of.
You wish you could do something half as brave as that!
I think Peter is--huh?
Hey?! Where'd he go?

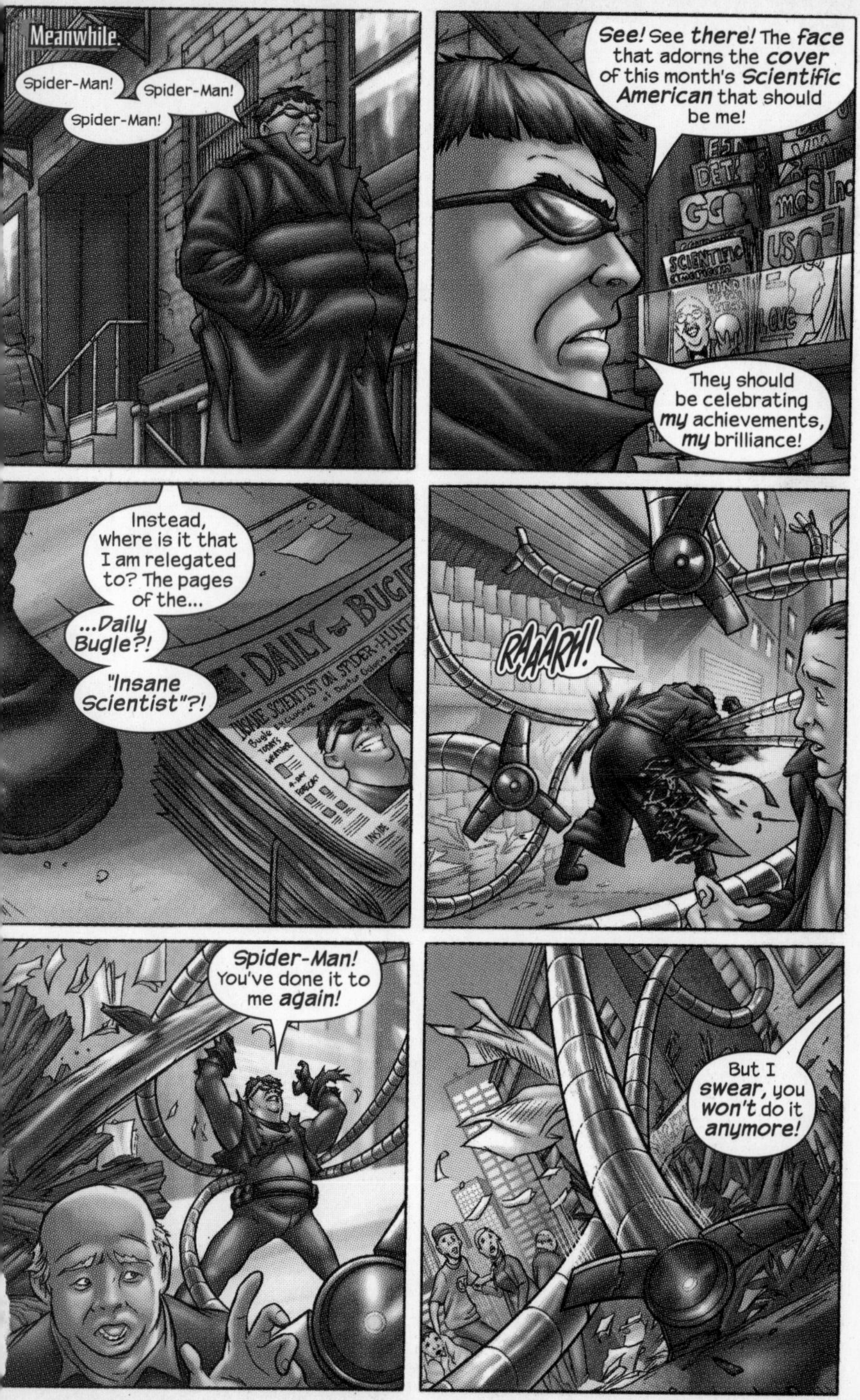
Meanwhile.
Spider-Man!
Spider-Man!
Spider-Man!
See! See there! The face that adorns the cover of this month's Scientific American that should be me!
They should be celebrating my achievements, my brilliance!
Instead, where is it that I am relegated to? The pages of the...
...Daily Bugle?!
"Insane Scientist"?!
DAILY BUGLE
RAAARH!
Spider-Man! You've done it to me again!
But I swear, you won't do it anymore!

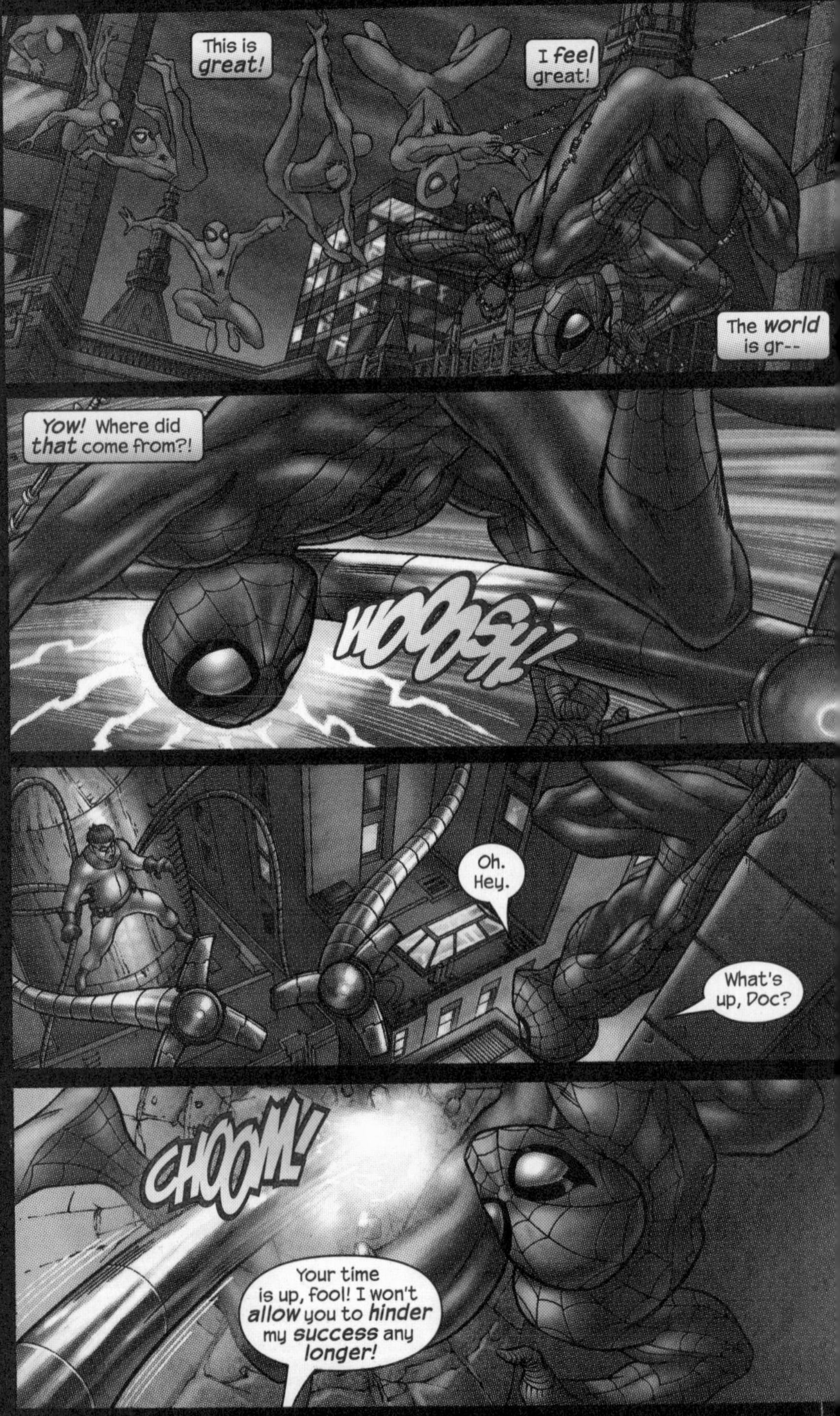
This is great!
I feel great!
The world is gr--
Yow! Where did that come from?!
WOOSH!
Oh. Hey.
What's up, Doc?
CHOOM!
Your time is up, fool! I won't allow you to hinder my success any longer!

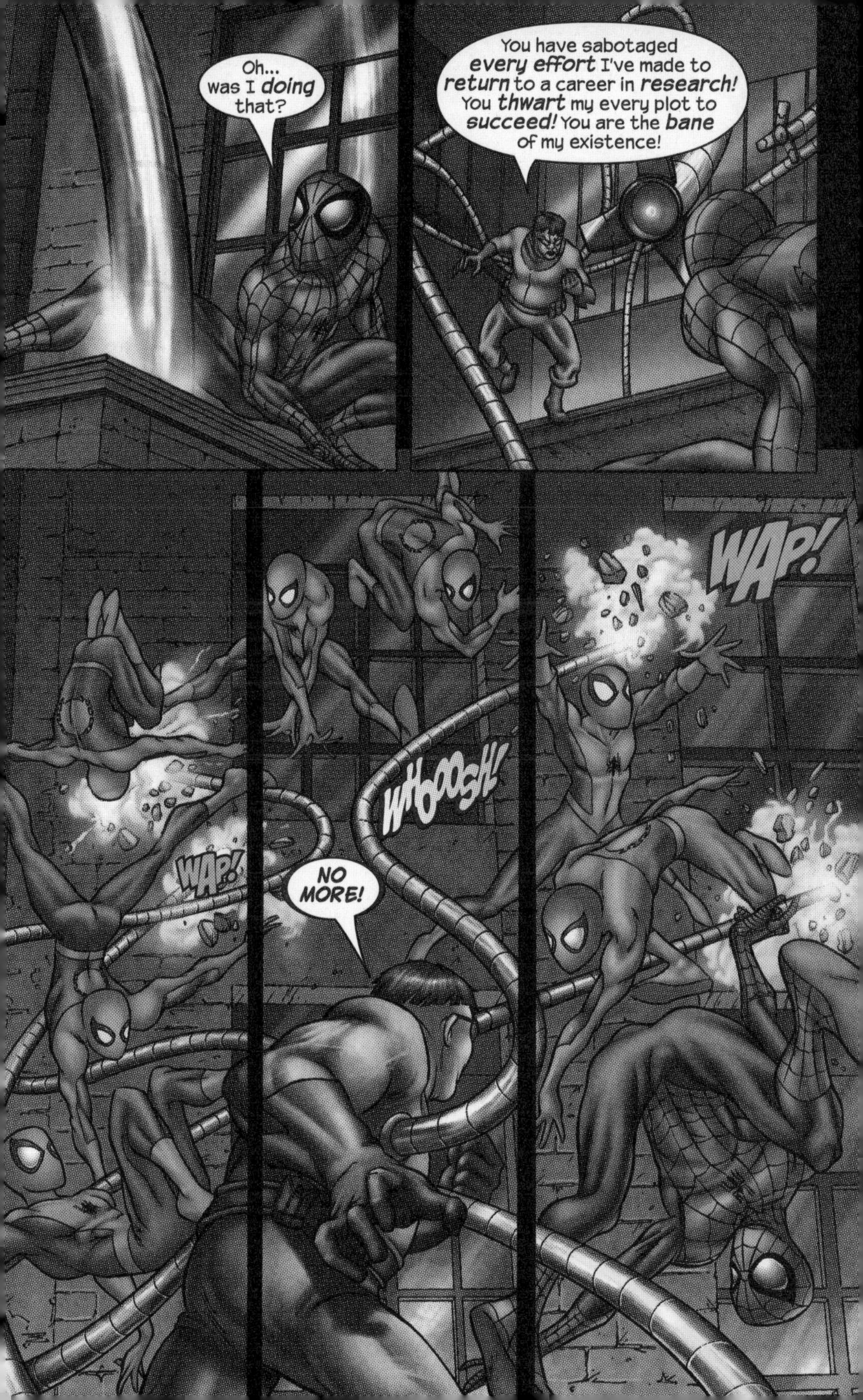

Oh... was I doing that?
You have sabotaged every effort I've made to return to a career in research! You thwart my every plot to succeed! You are the bane of my existence!
WAP!
WHOOOSH!
NO MORE!
WAP!

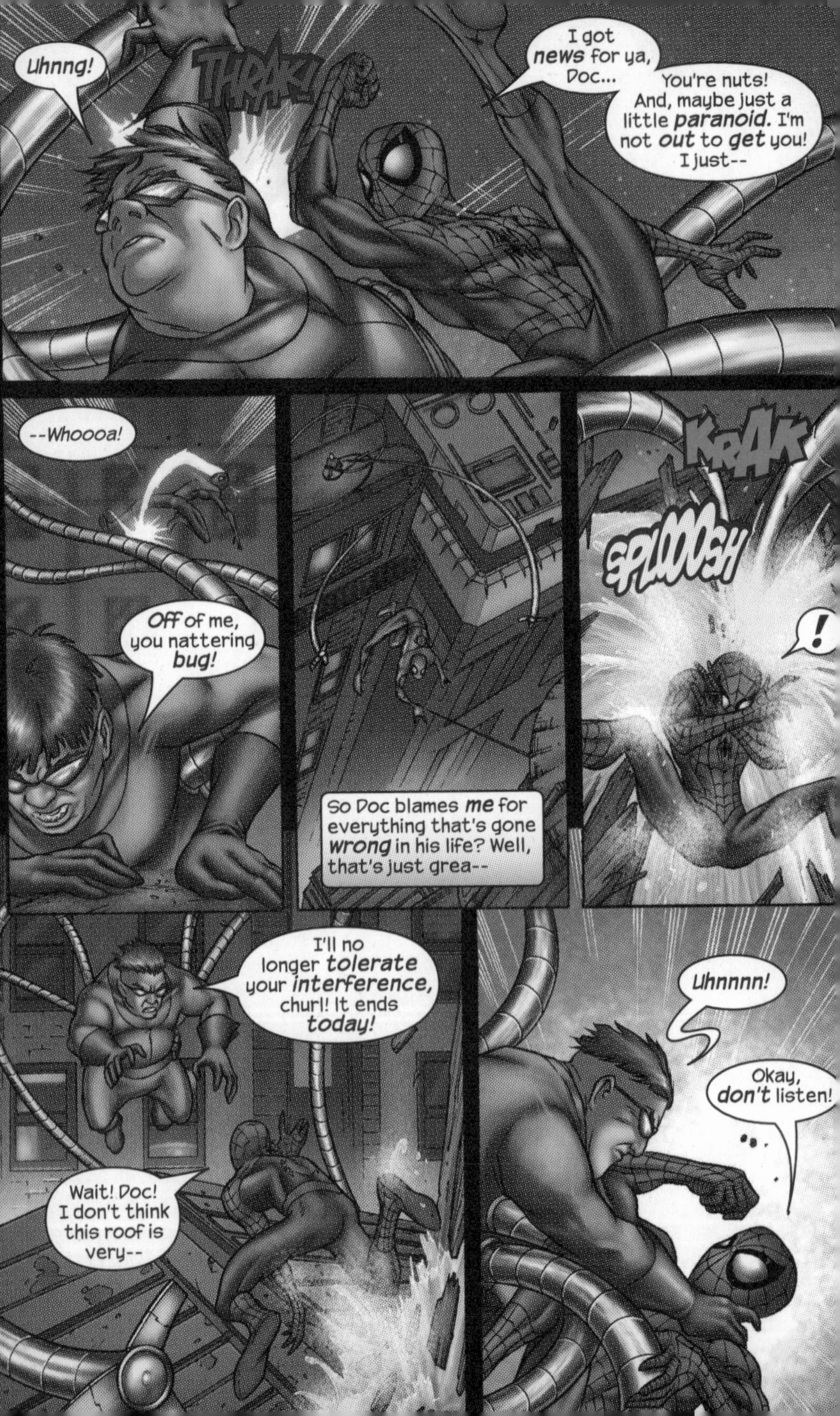
Uhnng!
THRAK!
I got news for ya, Doc...
You're nuts! And, maybe just a little paranoid. I'm not out to get you! I just--
--Whoooa!
Off of me, you nattering bug!
So Doc blames me for everything that's gone wrong in his life? Well, that's just grea--
KRAK
SPLOOOSH
!
I'll no longer tolerate your interference, churl! It ends today!
Wait! Doc! I don't think this roof is very--
Uhnnnn!
Okay, don't listen!

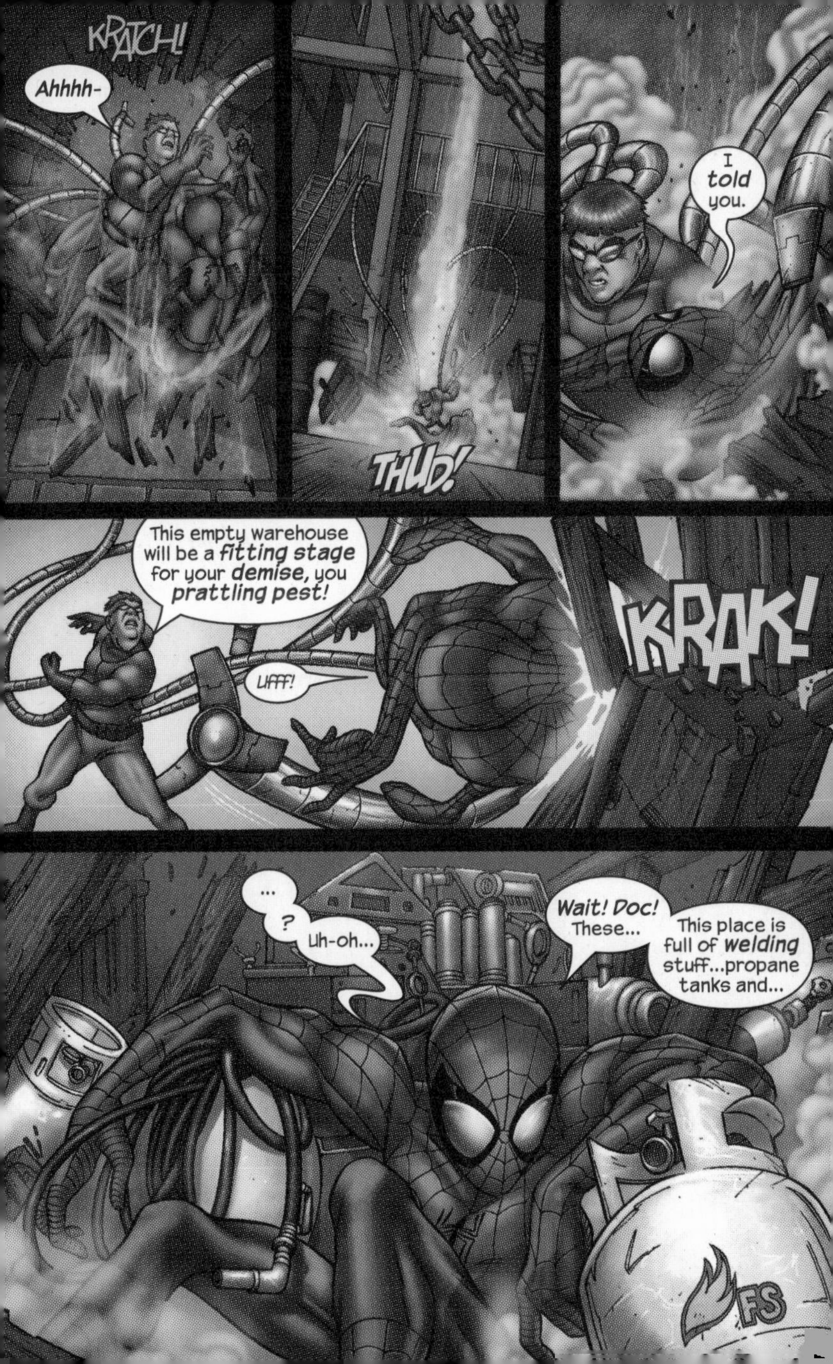
KRATCH!
Ahhhh-
THUD!
I told you.
This empty warehouse will be a fitting stage for your demise, you prattling pest!
UFFF!
KRAK!
...
?
Uh-oh...
Wait! Doc! These...
This place is full of welding stuff...propane tanks and...
FS

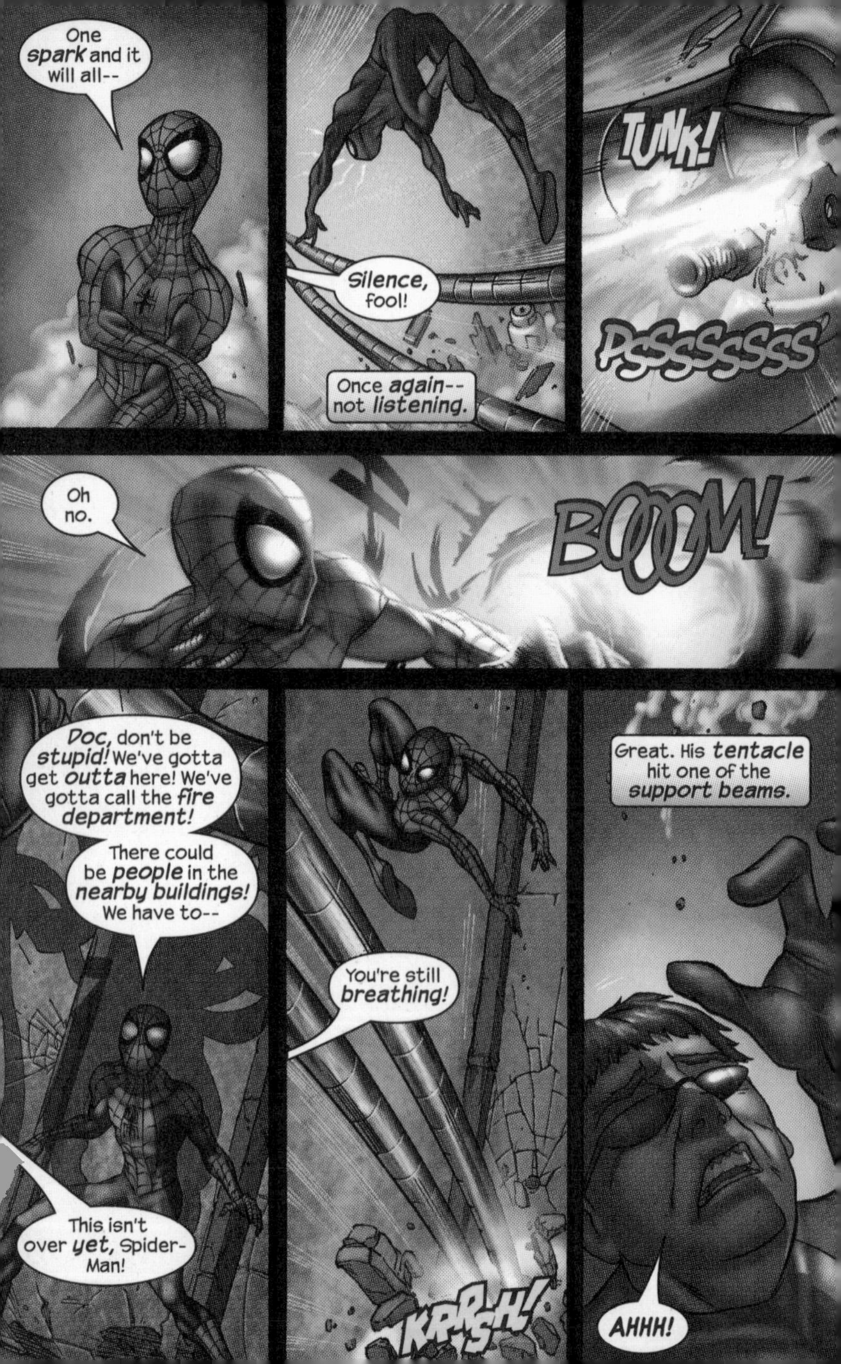
One spark and it will all--
Silence, fool!
Once again-- not listening.
TUNK!
PSSSSSSS
Oh no.
BOOOM!
Doc, don't be stupid! We've gotta get outta here! We've gotta call the fire department!
There could be people in the nearby buildings! We have to--
This isn't over yet, Spider-Man!
You're still breathing!
KRRSH!
Great. His tentacle hit one of the support beams.
AHHH!

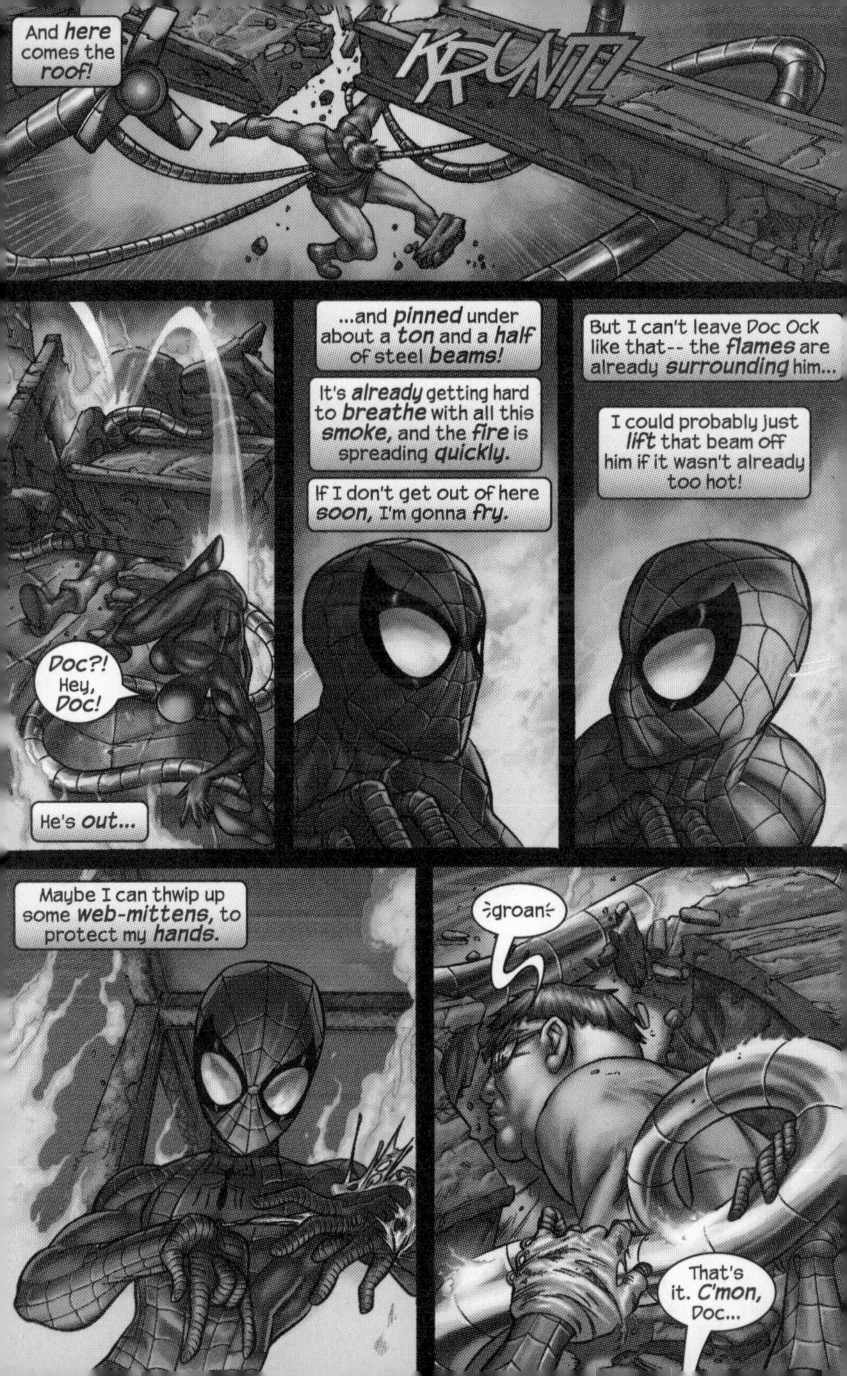
And here comes the roof!
KRUNTZ
Doc?! Hey, Doc!
He's out...
...and pinned under about a ton and a half of steel beams!
It's already getting hard to breathe with all this smoke, and the fire is spreading quickly.
If I don't get out of here soon, I'm gonna fry.
But I can't leave Doc Ock like that-- the flames are already surrounding him...
I could probably just lift that beam off him if it wasn't already too hot!
Maybe I can thwip up some web-mittens, to protect my hands.
groan
That's it. C'mon, Doc...

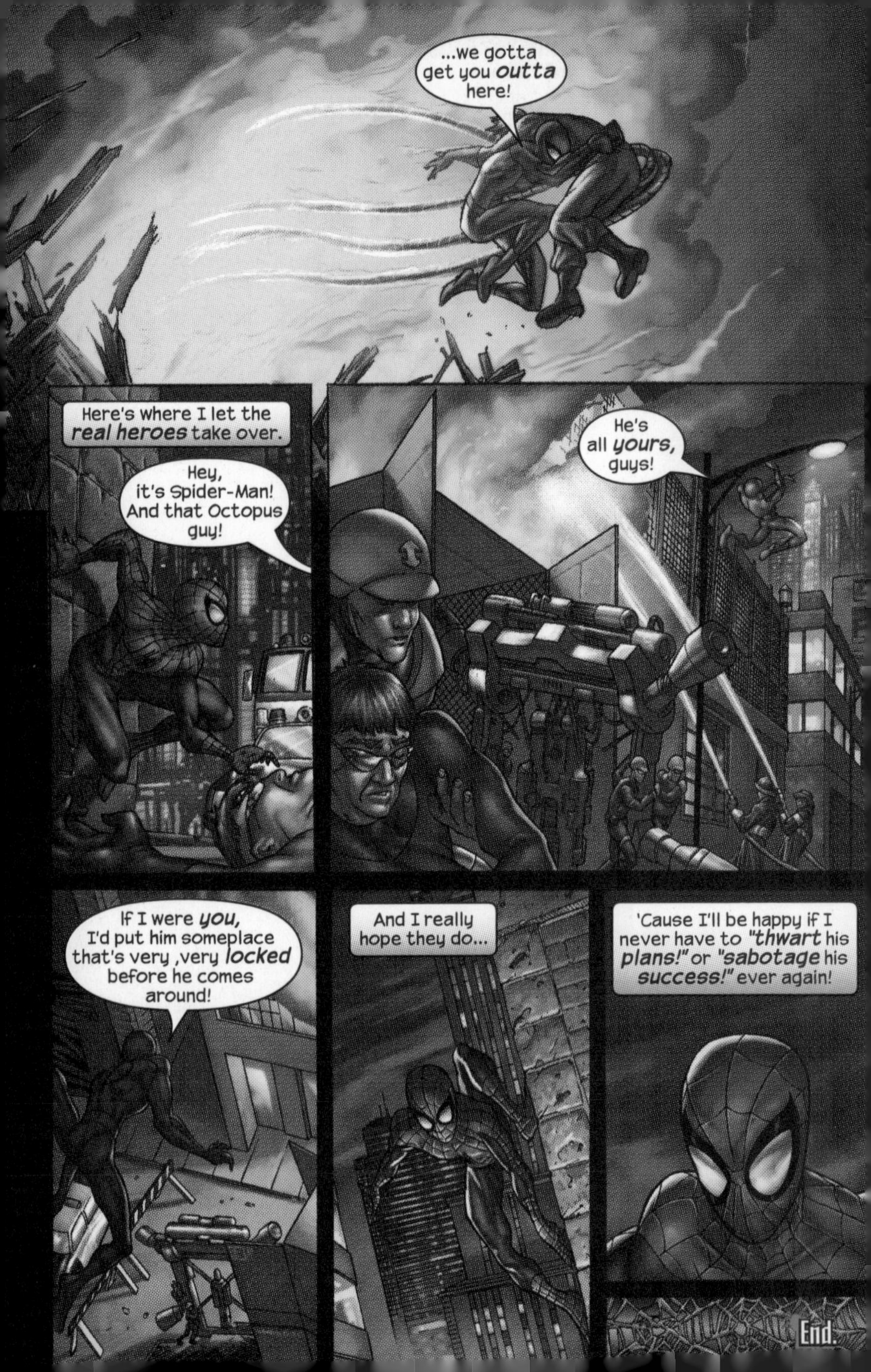
...we gotta get you outta here!
Here's where I let the real heroes take over.
Hey, it's Spider-Man! And that Octopus guy!
He's all yours, guys!
If I were you, I'd put him someplace that's very ,very locked before he comes around!
And I really hope they do...
'Cause I'll be happy if I never have to "thwart his plans!" or "sabotage his success!" ever again!
End.

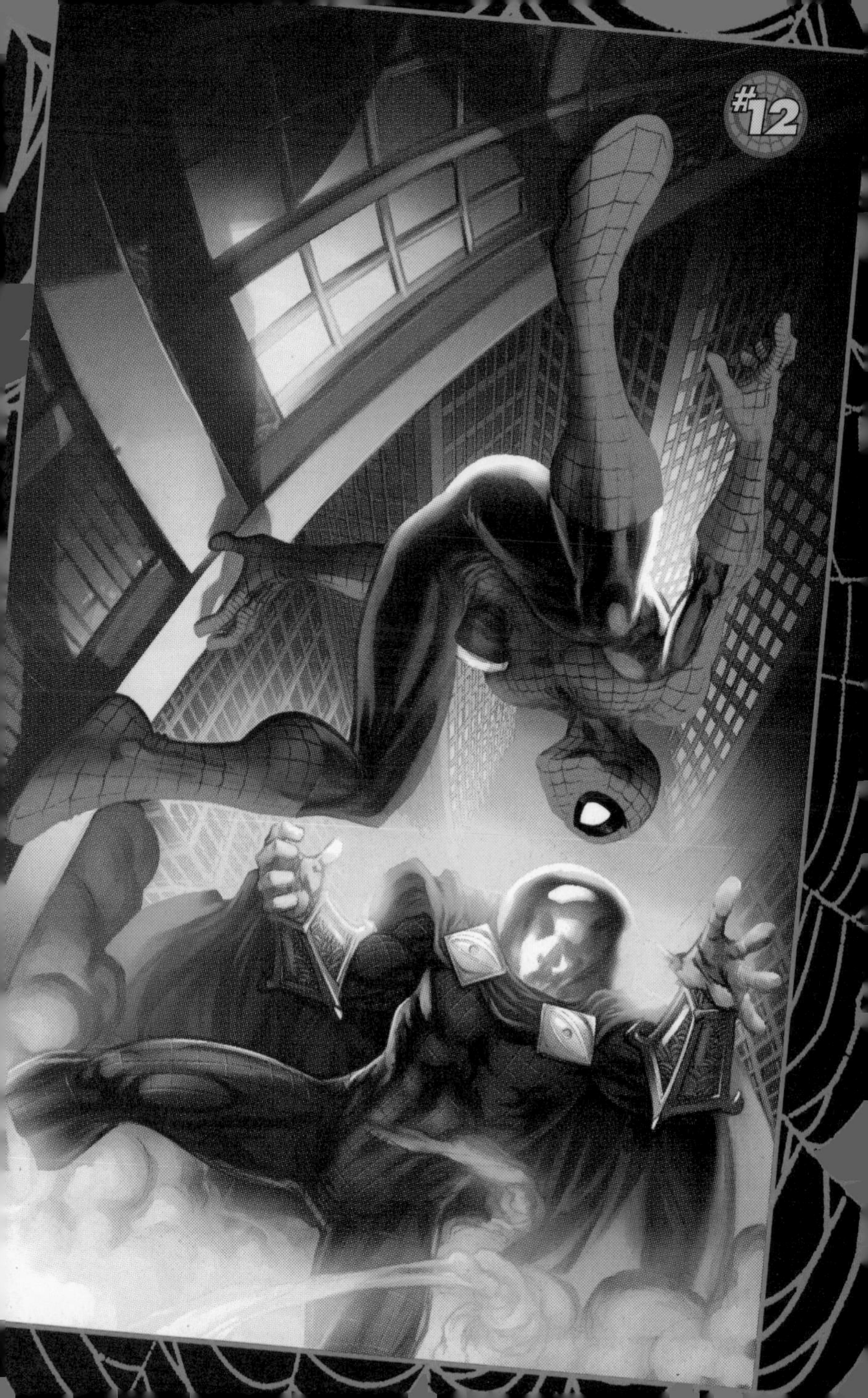
#12

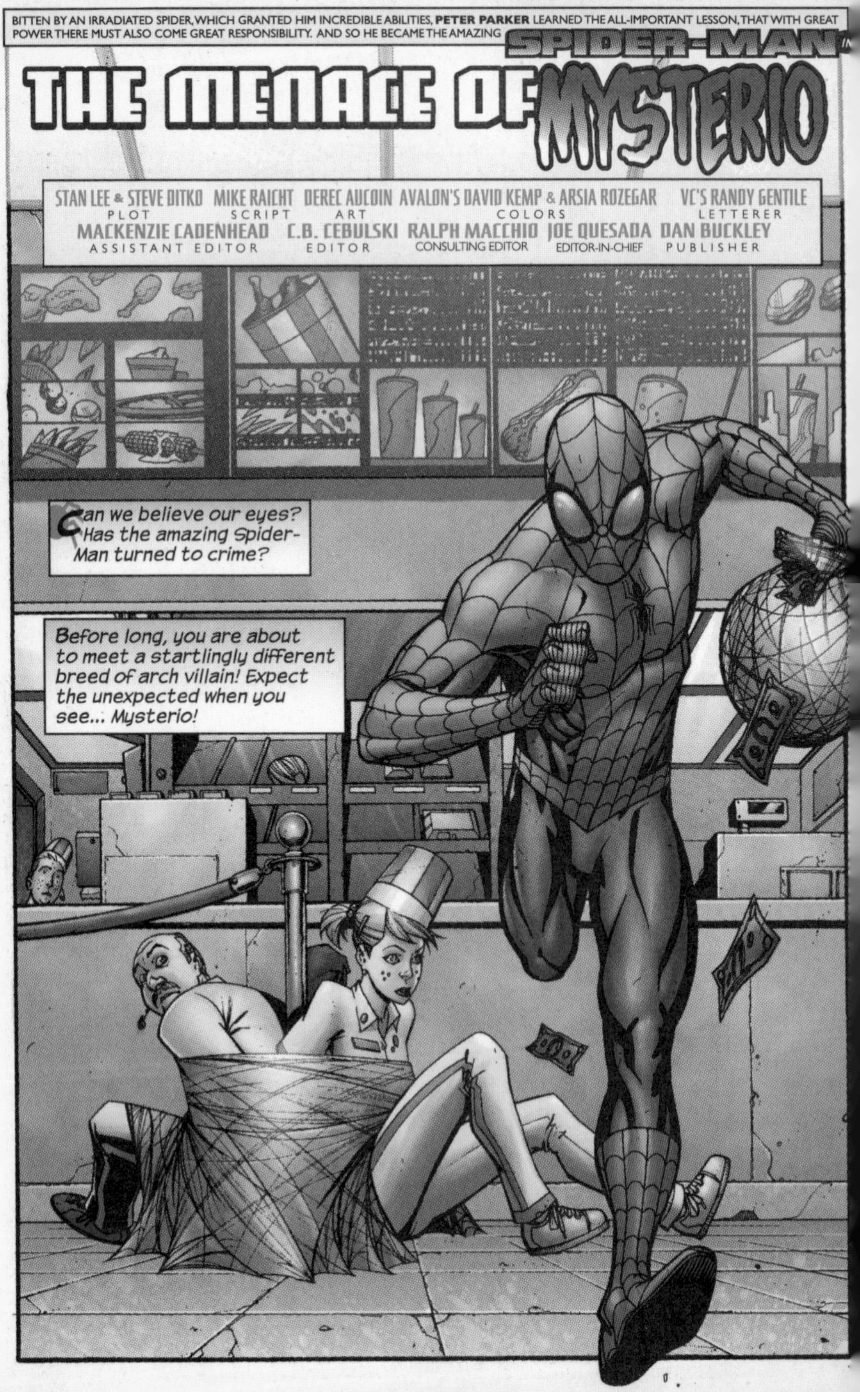
BITTEN BY AN IRRADIATED SPIDER, WHICH GRANTED HIM INCREDIBLE ABILITIES, PETER PARKER LEARNED THE ALL-IMPORTANT LESSON, THAT WITH GREAT POWER THERE MUST ALSO COME GREAT RESPONSIBILITY. AND SO HE BECAME THE AMAZING SPIDER-MAN
THE MENACE OF MYSTERIO
STAN LEE & STEVE DITKO PLOT MIKE RAICHT SCRIPT DEREC AUCOIN ART AVALON'S DAVID KEMP & ARSIA ROZEGAR COLORS VC'S RANDY GENTILE LETTERER
MACKENZIE CADENHEAD ASSISTANT EDITOR C.B. CEBULSKI EDITOR RALPH MACCHIO CONSULTING EDITOR JOE QUESADA EDITOR-IN-CHIEF DAN BUCKLEY PUBLISHER
Can we believe our eyes? Has the amazing Spider-Man turned to crime?
Before long, you are about to meet a startlingly different breed of arch villain! Expect the unexpected when you see... Mysterio!

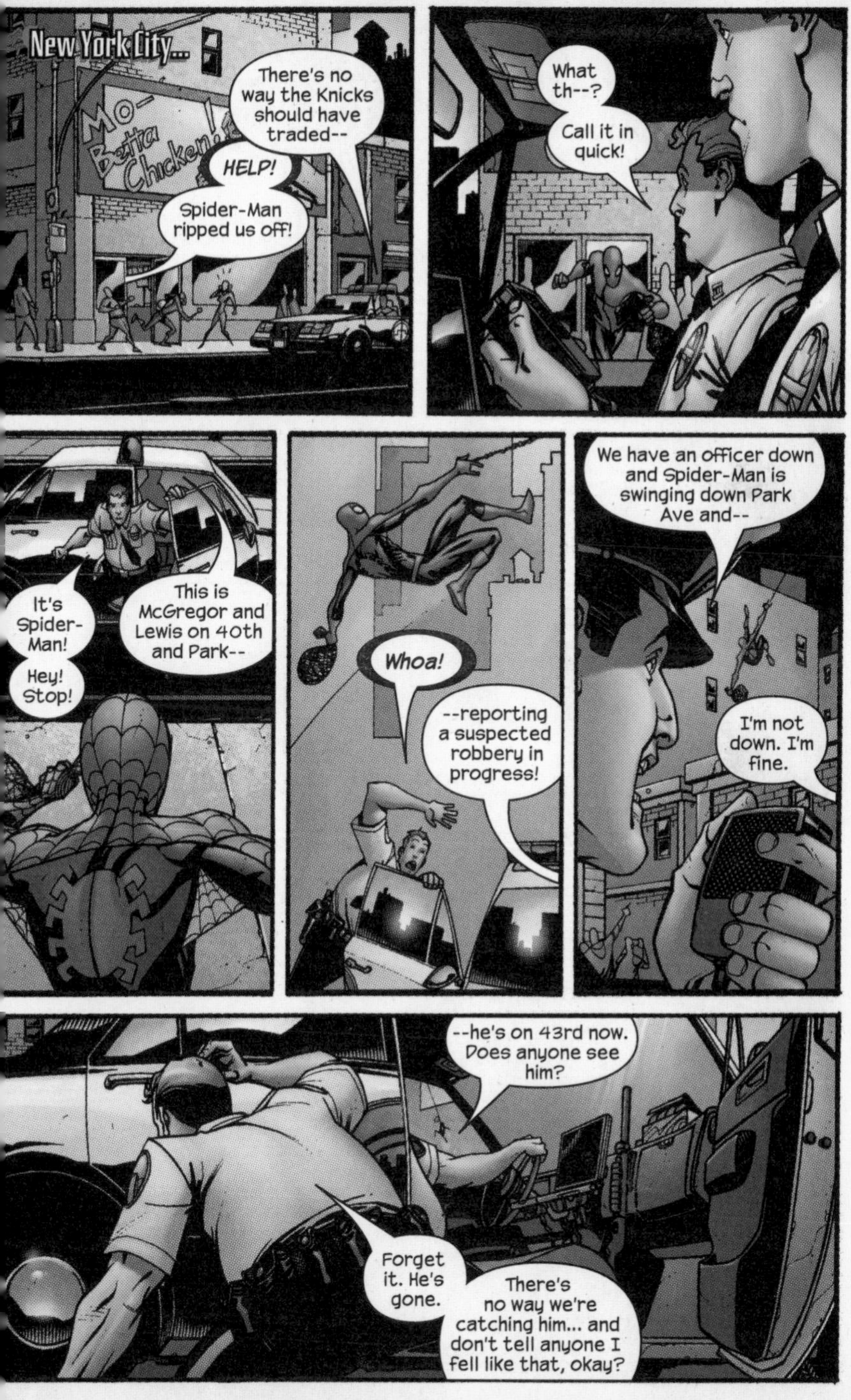
New York City...
There's no way the Knicks should have traded--
HELP!
Spider-Man ripped us off!
What th--?
Call it in quick!
It's Spider-Man!
Hey! Stop!
This is McGregor and Lewis on 40th and Park--
Whoa!
--reporting a suspected robbery in progress!
We have an officer down and Spider-Man is swinging down Park Ave and--
I'm not down. I'm fine.
--he's on 43rd now. Does anyone see him?
Forget it. He's gone.
There's no way we're catching him... and don't tell anyone I fell like that, okay?

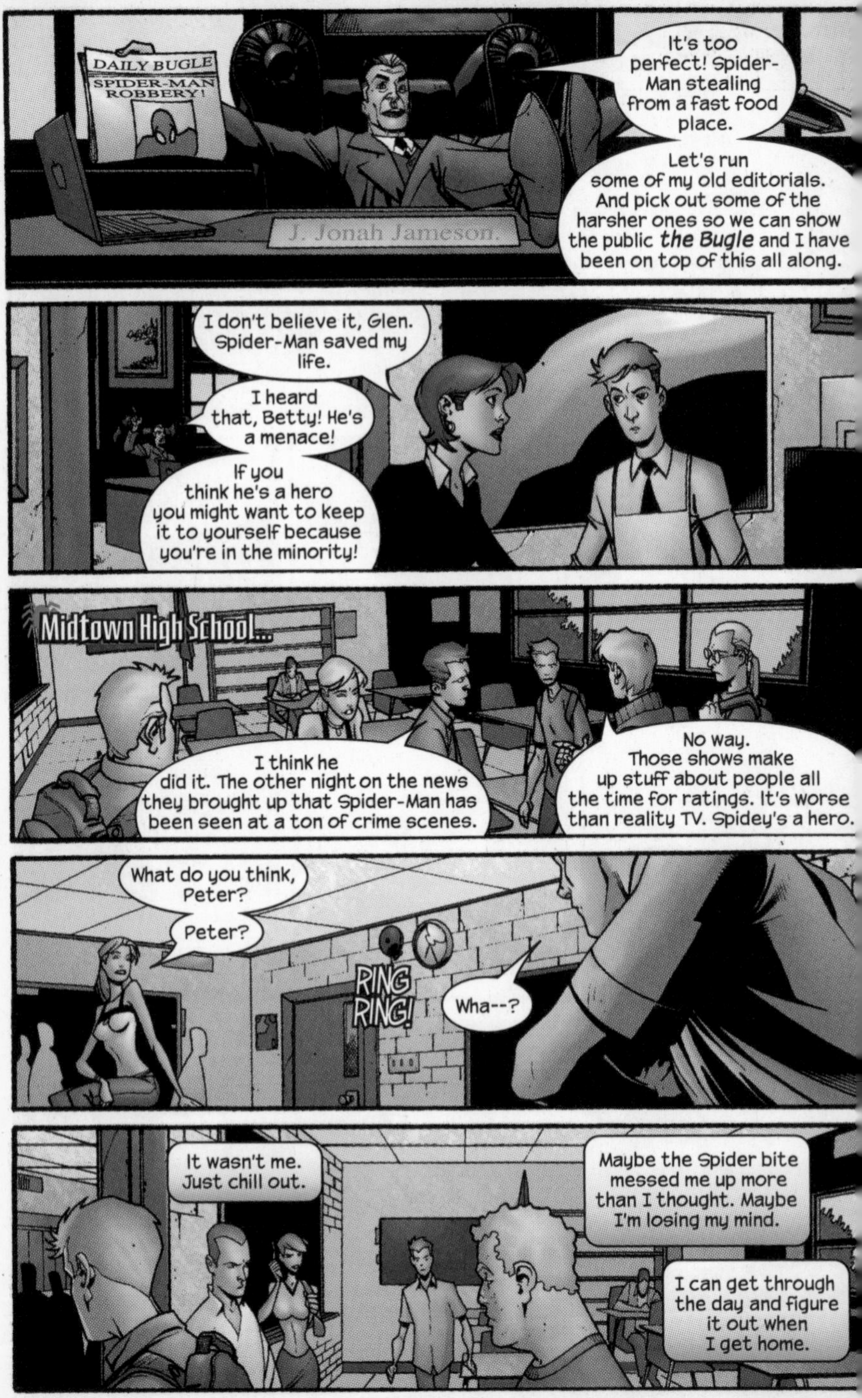
DAILY BUGLE
SPIDER-MAN ROBBERY!
J. Jonah Jameson.
It's too perfect! Spider-Man stealing from a fast food place.
Let's run some of my old editorials. And pick out some of the harsher ones so we can show the public *the Bugle* and I have been on top of this all along.
I don't believe it, Glen. Spider-Man saved my life.
I heard that, Betty! He's a menace!
If you think he's a hero you might want to keep it to yourself because you're in the minority!
Midtown High School...
I think he did it. The other night on the news they brought up that Spider-Man has been seen at a ton of crime scenes.
No way. Those shows make up stuff about people all the time for ratings. It's worse than reality TV. Spidey's a hero.
What do you think, Peter?
Peter?
RING RING!
Wha--?
It wasn't me. Just chill out.
Maybe the Spider bite messed me up more than I thought. Maybe I'm losing my mind.
I can get through the day and figure it out when I get home.

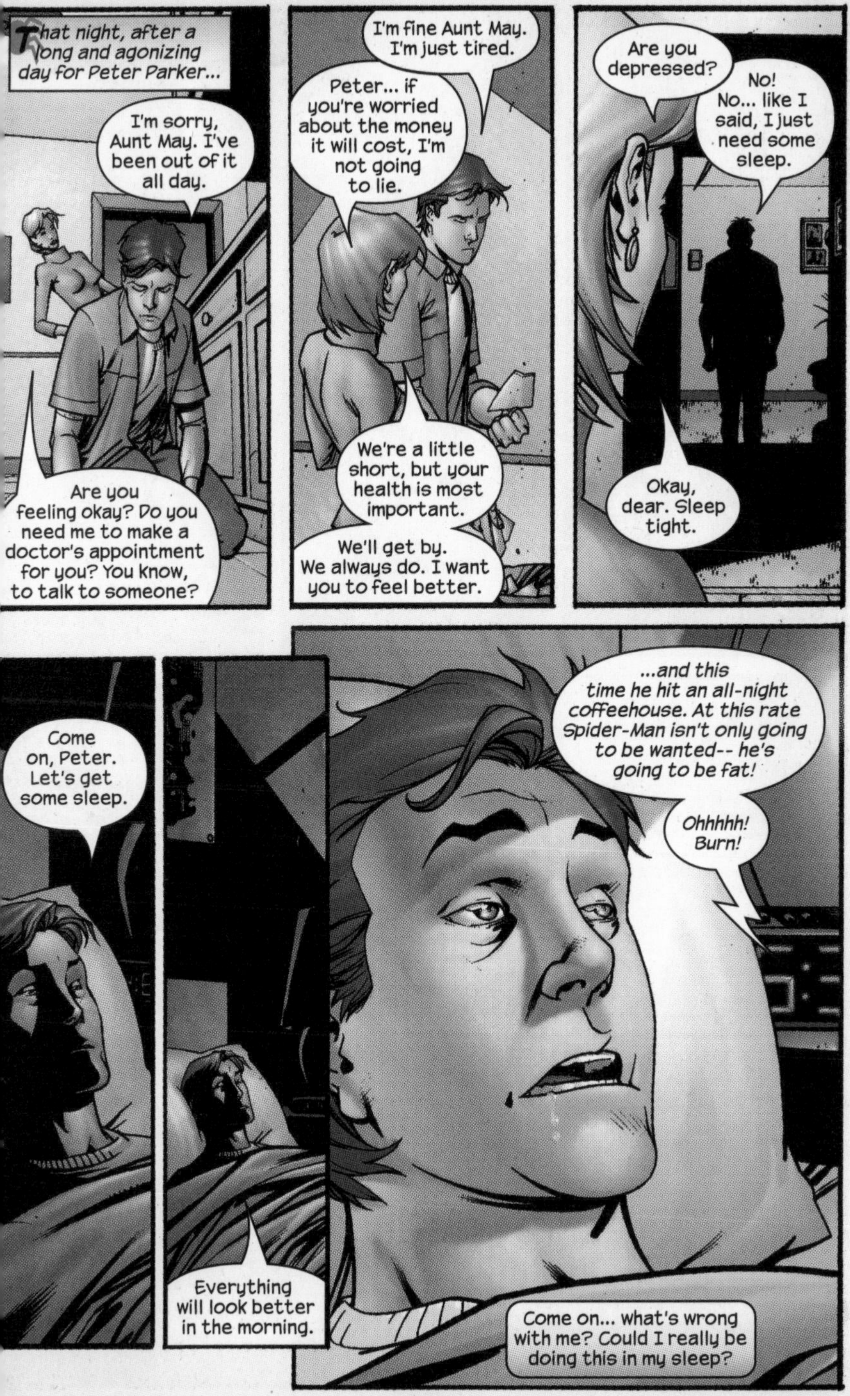

That night, after a long and agonizing day for Peter Parker...
I'm sorry, Aunt May. I've been out of it all day.
Are you feeling okay? Do you need me to make a doctor's appointment for you? You know, to talk to someone?
I'm fine Aunt May. I'm just tired.
Peter... if you're worried about the money it will cost, I'm not going to lie.
We're a little short, but your health is most important.
We'll get by. We always do. I want you to feel better.
Are you depressed?
No! No... like I said, I just need some sleep.
Okay, dear. Sleep tight.
Come on, Peter. Let's get some sleep.
Everything will look better in the morning.
...and this time he hit an all-night coffeehouse. At this rate Spider-Man isn't only going to be wanted-- he's going to be fat!
Ohhhhh! Burn!
Come on... what's wrong with me? Could I really be doing this in my sleep?

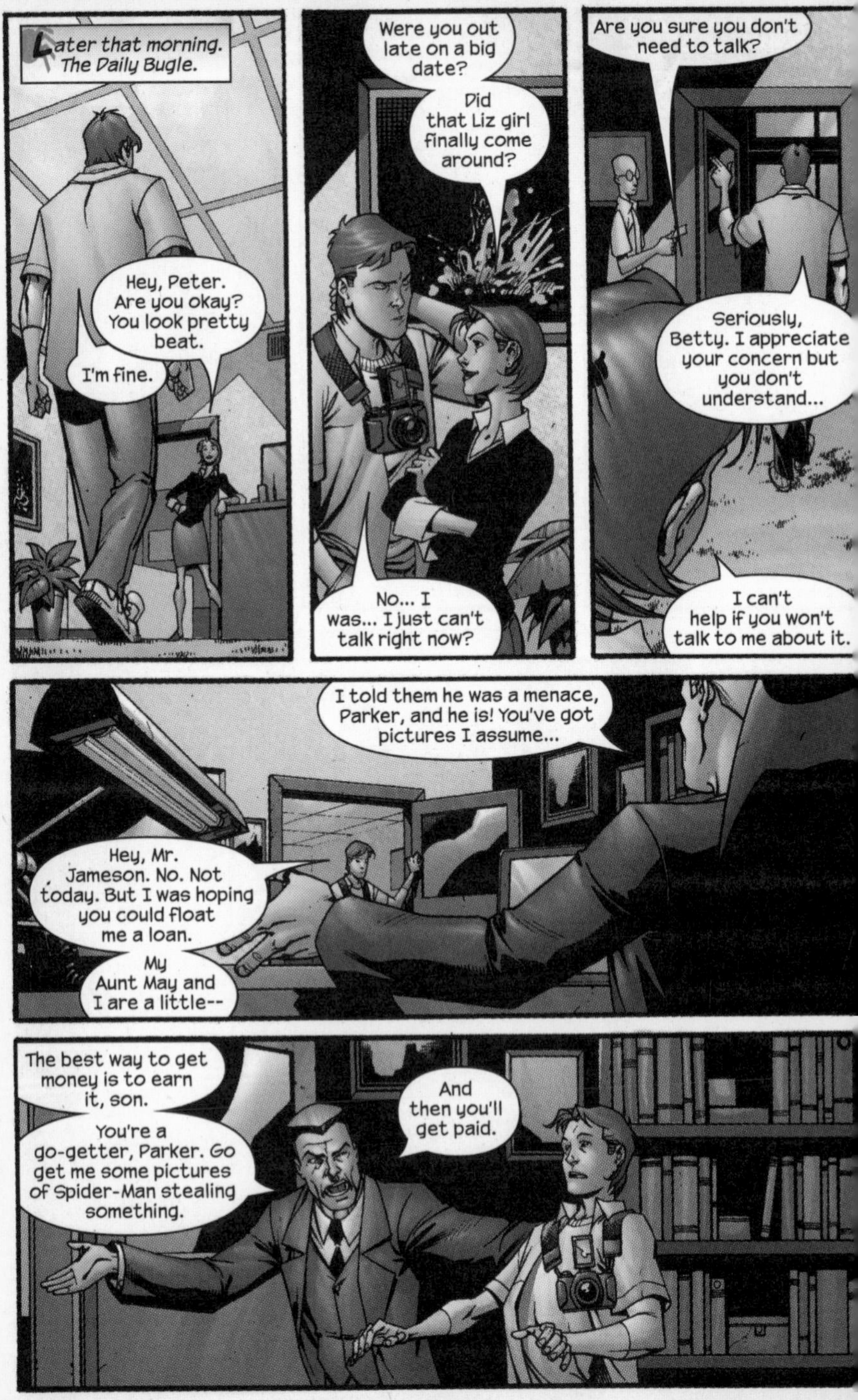
Later that morning. The Daily Bugle.
Hey, Peter. Are you okay? You look pretty beat.
I'm fine.
Were you out late on a big date?
Did that Liz girl finally come around?
No... I was... I just can't talk right now?
Are you sure you don't need to talk?
Seriously, Betty. I appreciate your concern but you don't understand...
I can't help if you won't talk to me about it.
I told them he was a menace, Parker, and he is! You've got pictures I assume...
Hey, Mr. Jameson. No. Not today. But I was hoping you could float me a loan.
My Aunt May and I are a little--
The best way to get money is to earn it, son.
You're a go-getter, Parker. Go get me some pictures of Spider-Man stealing something.
And then you'll get paid.

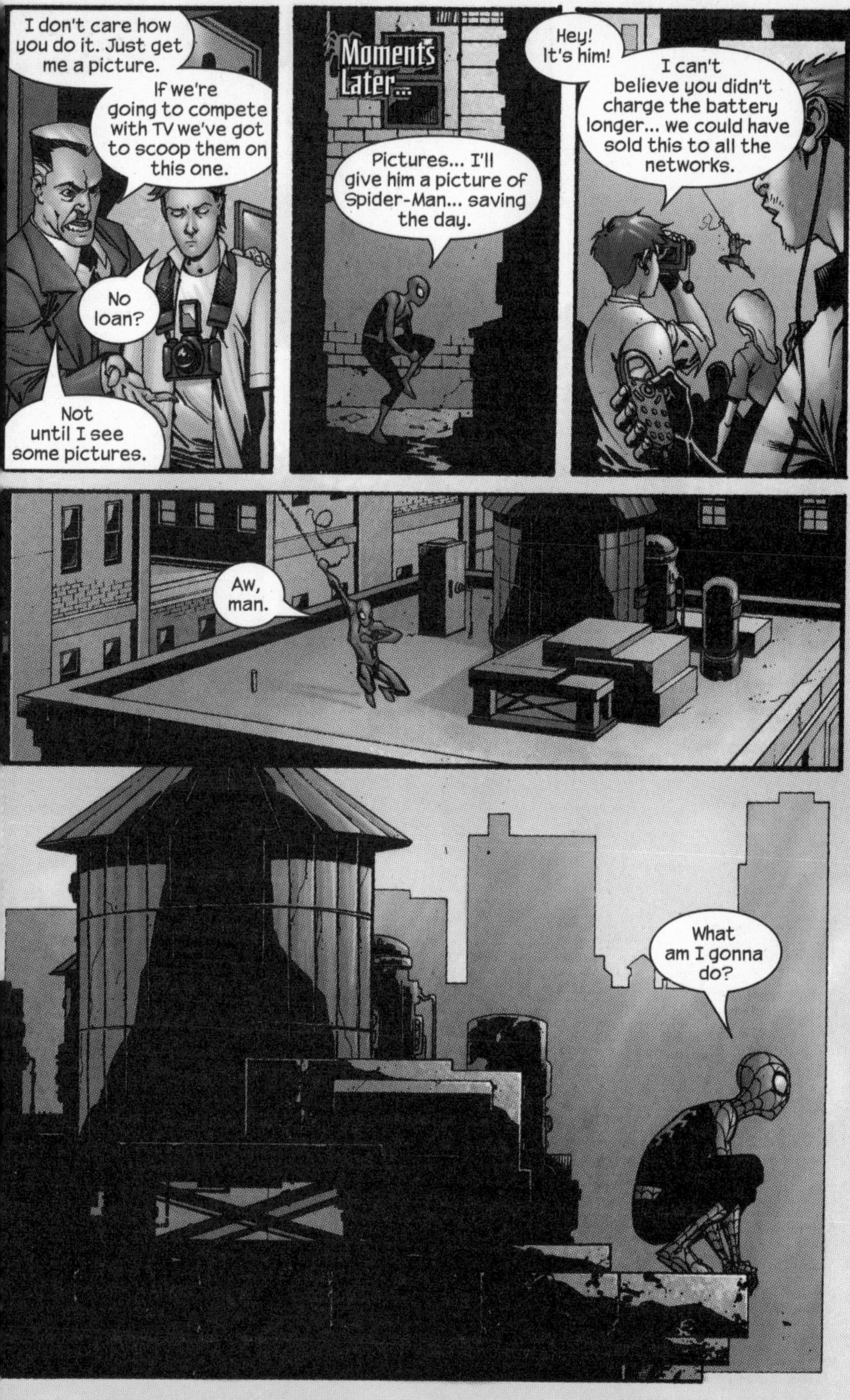
I don't care how you do it. Just get me a picture.
If we're going to compete with TV we've got to scoop them on this one.
No loan?
Not until I see some pictures.
Moments Later...
Pictures... I'll give him a picture of Spider-Man... saving the day.
Hey! It's him!
I can't believe you didn't charge the battery longer... we could have sold this to all the networks.
Aw, man.
What am I gonna do?

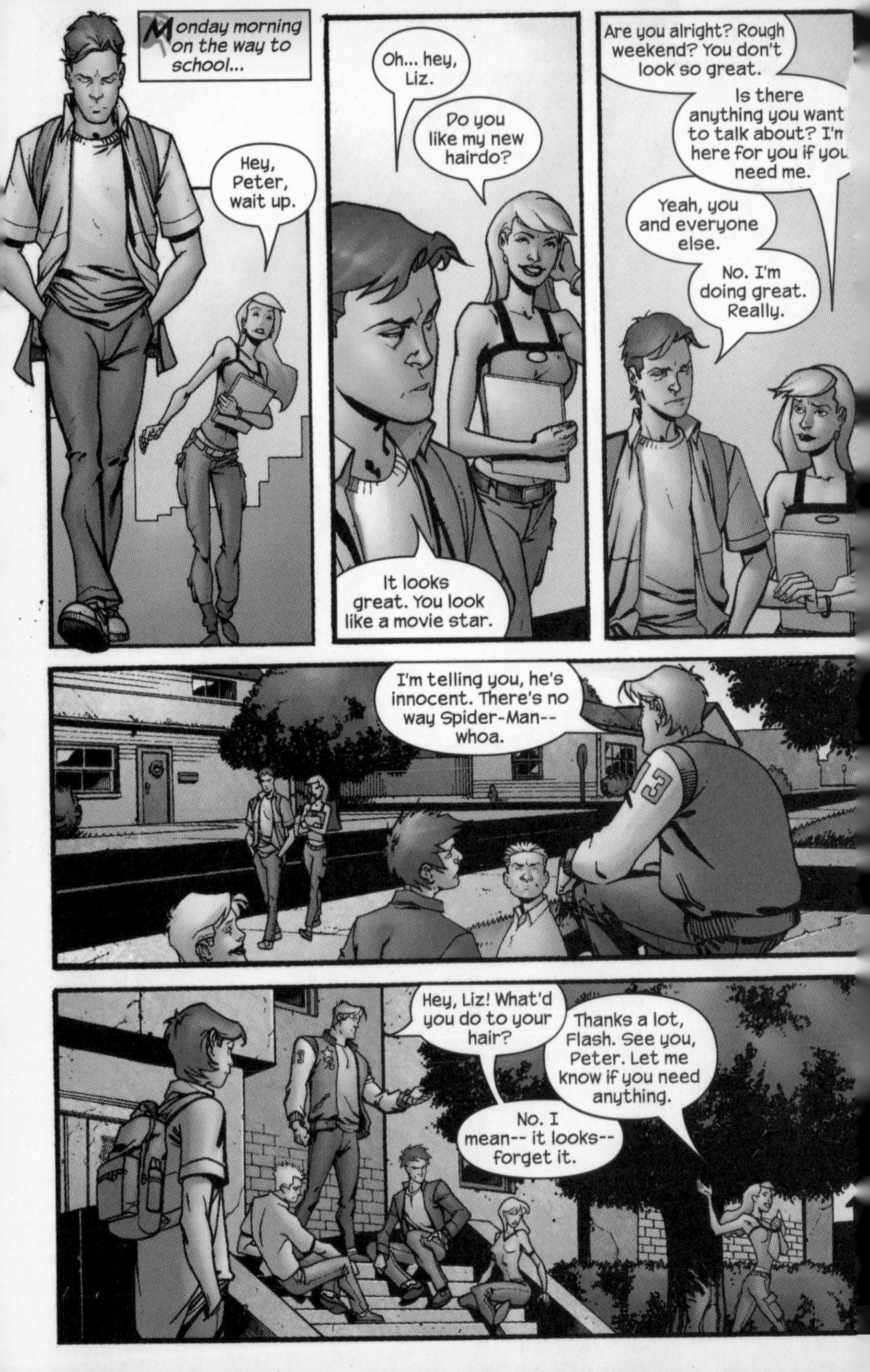
Monday morning on the way to school...
Hey, Peter, wait up.
Oh... hey, Liz.
Do you like my new hairdo?
It looks great. You look like a movie star.
Are you alright? Rough weekend? You don't look so great.
Is there anything you want to talk about? I'm here for you if you need me.
Yeah, you and everyone else.
No. I'm doing great. Really.
I'm telling you, he's innocent. There's no way Spider-Man-- whoa.
Hey, Liz! What'd you do to your hair?
Thanks a lot, Flash. See you, Peter. Let me know if you need anything.
No. I mean-- it looks-- forget it.

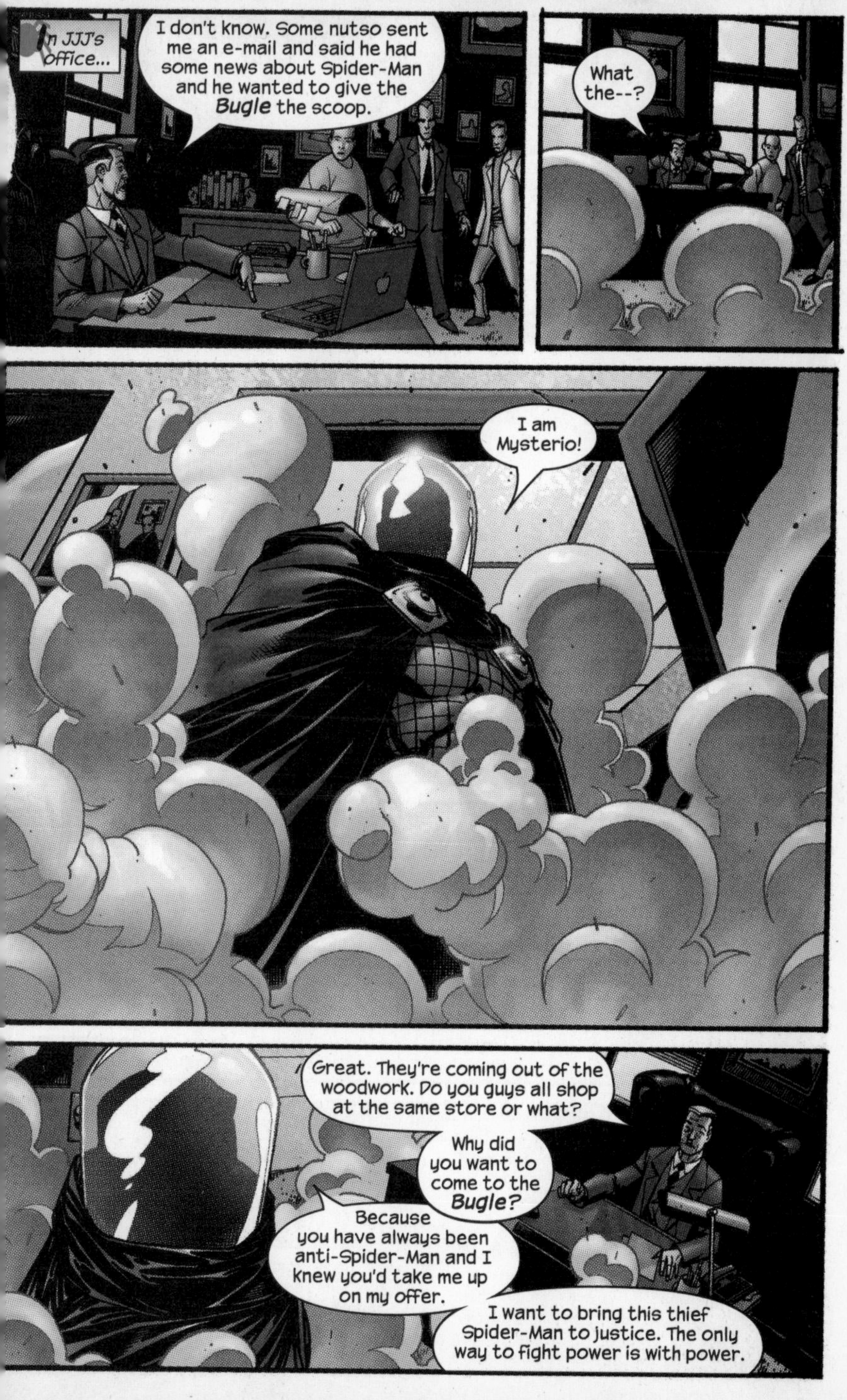
In JJJ's office...
I don't know. Some nutso sent me an e-mail and said he had some news about Spider-Man and he wanted to give the *Bugle* the scoop.
What the--?
I am Mysterio!
Great. They're coming out of the woodwork. Do you guys all shop at the same store or what?
Why did you want to come to the *Bugle?*
Because you have always been anti-Spider-Man and I knew you'd take me up on my offer.
I want to bring this thief Spider-Man to justice. The only way to fight power is with power.

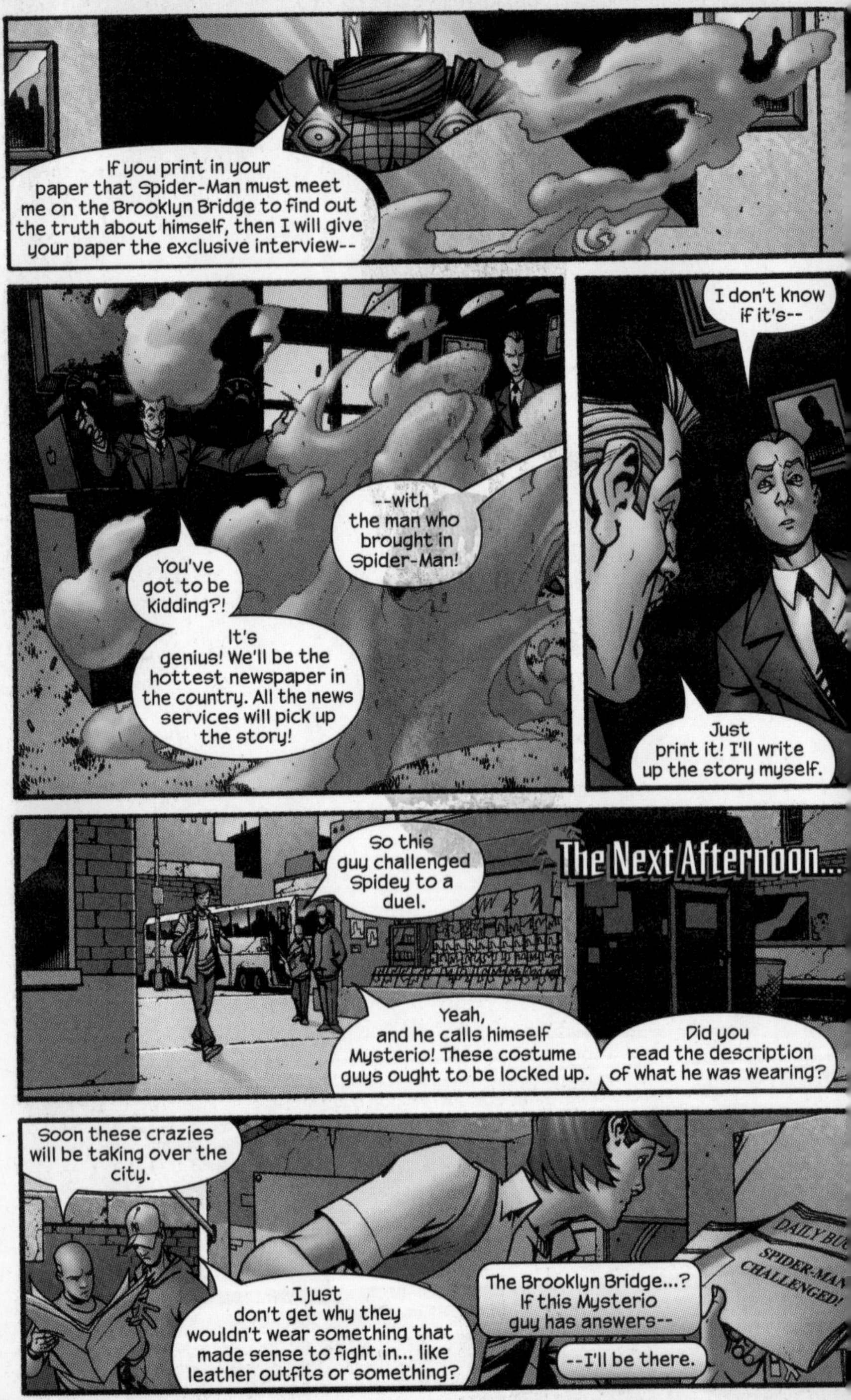
If you print in your paper that Spider-Man must meet me on the Brooklyn Bridge to find out the truth about himself, then I will give your paper the exclusive interview--
--with the man who brought in Spider-Man!
You've got to be kidding?!
It's genius! We'll be the hottest newspaper in the country. All the news services will pick up the story!
I don't know if it's--
Just print it! I'll write up the story myself.
The Next Afternoon...
So this guy challenged Spidey to a duel.
Yeah, and he calls himself Mysterio! These costume guys ought to be locked up.
Did you read the description of what he was wearing?
Soon these crazies will be taking over the city.
I just don't get why they wouldn't wear something that made sense to fight in... like leather outfits or something?
DAILY BU
SPIDER-MAN CHALLENGED!
The Brooklyn Bridge...? If this Mysterio guy has answers--
--I'll be there.

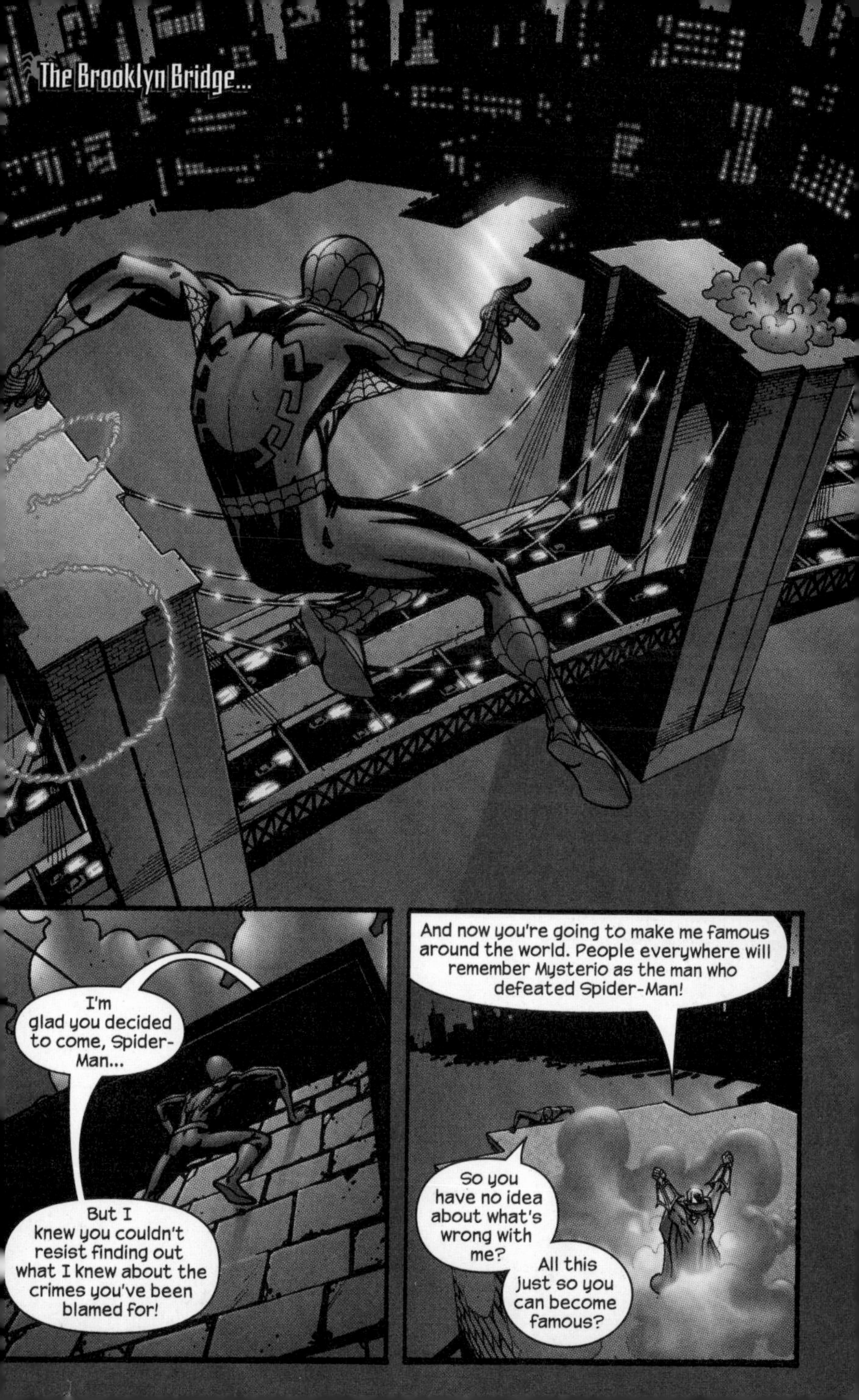
The Brooklyn Bridge...
I'm glad you decided to come, Spider-Man...
But I knew you couldn't resist finding out what I knew about the crimes you've been blamed for!
And now you're going to make me famous around the world. People everywhere will remember Mysterio as the man who defeated Spider-Man!
So you have no idea about what's wrong with me?
All this just so you can become famous?

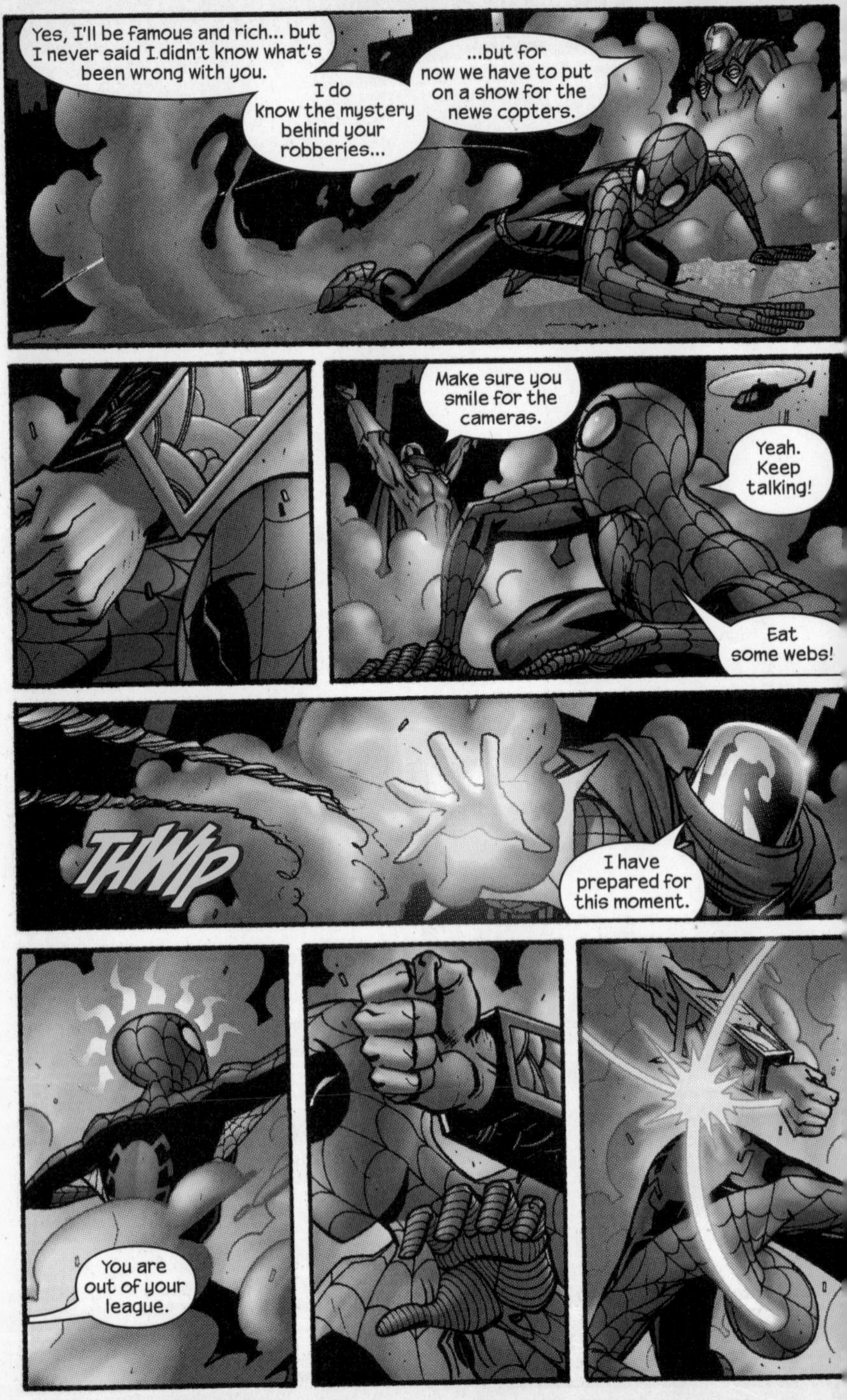

Yes, I'll be famous and rich... but I never said I didn't know what's been wrong with you.
I do know the mystery behind your robberies...
...but for now we have to put on a show for the news copters.
Make sure you smile for the cameras.
Yeah. Keep talking!
Eat some webs!
THWIP
I have prepared for this moment.
You are out of your league.

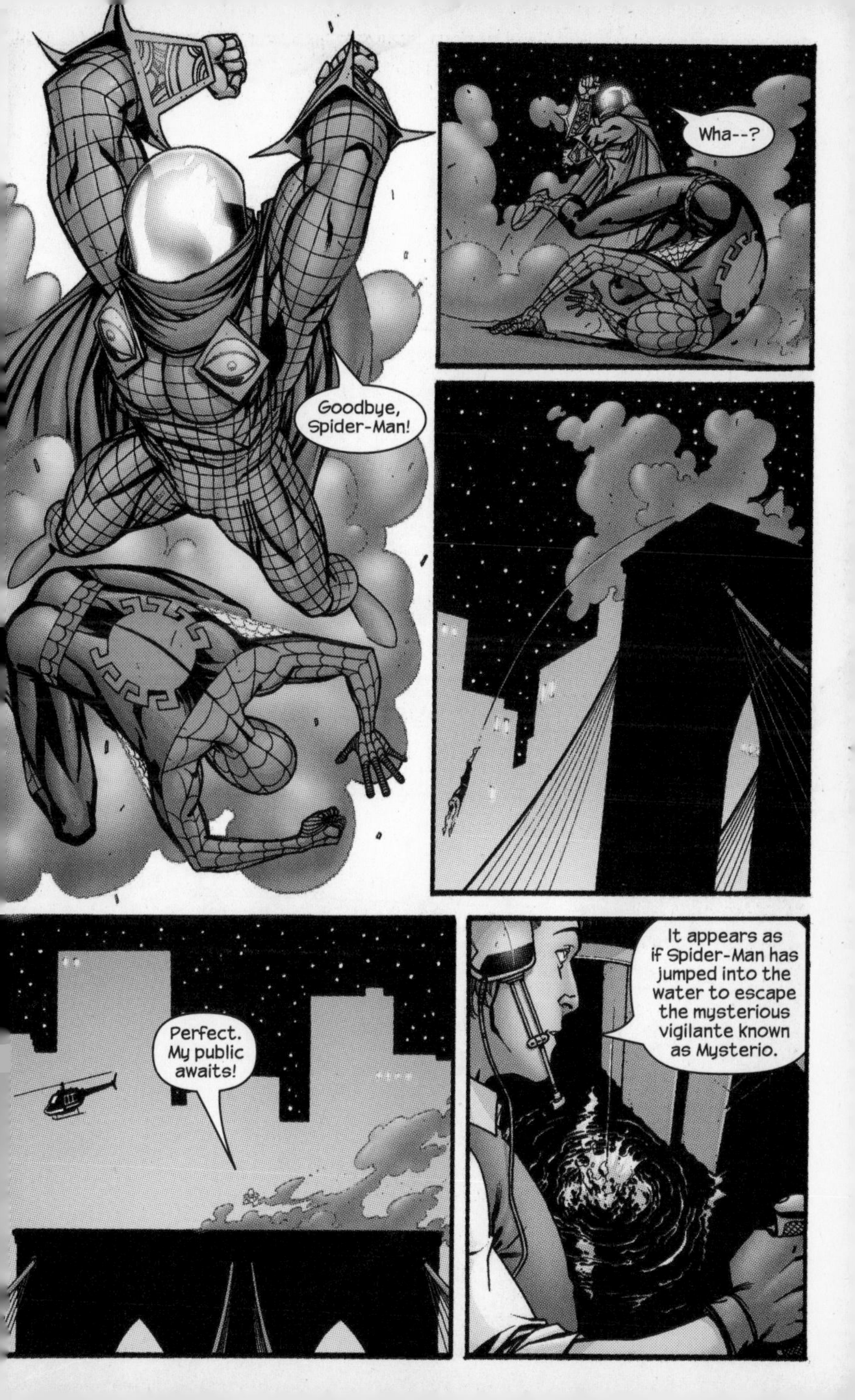
Goodbye, Spider-Man!
Wha--?
Perfect. My public awaits!
It appears as if Spider-Man has jumped into the water to escape the mysterious vigilante known as Mysterio.

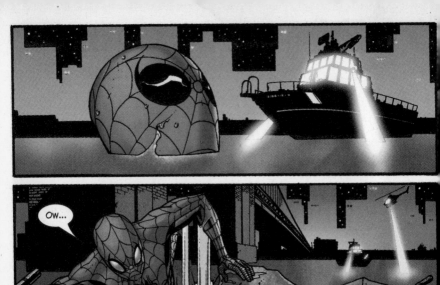

OW...

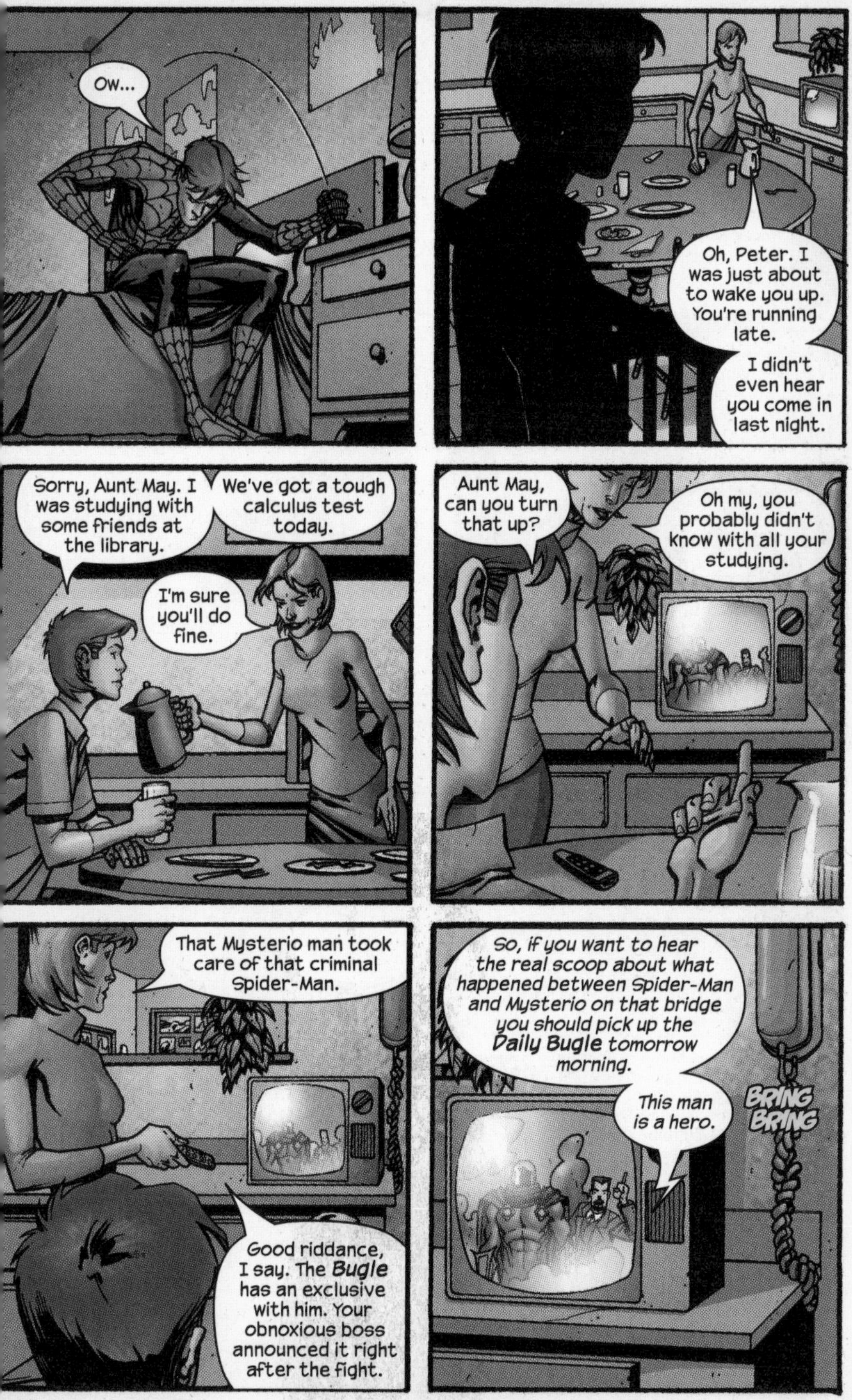
OW...
Oh, Peter. I was just about to wake you up. You're running late.
I didn't even hear you come in last night.
Sorry, Aunt May. I was studying with some friends at the library.
We've got a tough calculus test today.
I'm sure you'll do fine.
Aunt May, can you turn that up?
Oh my, you probably didn't know with all your studying.
That Mysterio man took care of that criminal Spider-Man.
Good riddance, I say. The *Bugle* has an exclusive with him. Your obnoxious boss announced it right after the fight.
So, if you want to hear the real scoop about what happened between Spider-Man and Mysterio on that bridge you should pick up the *Daily Bugle* tomorrow morning.
This man is a hero.
BRING BRING

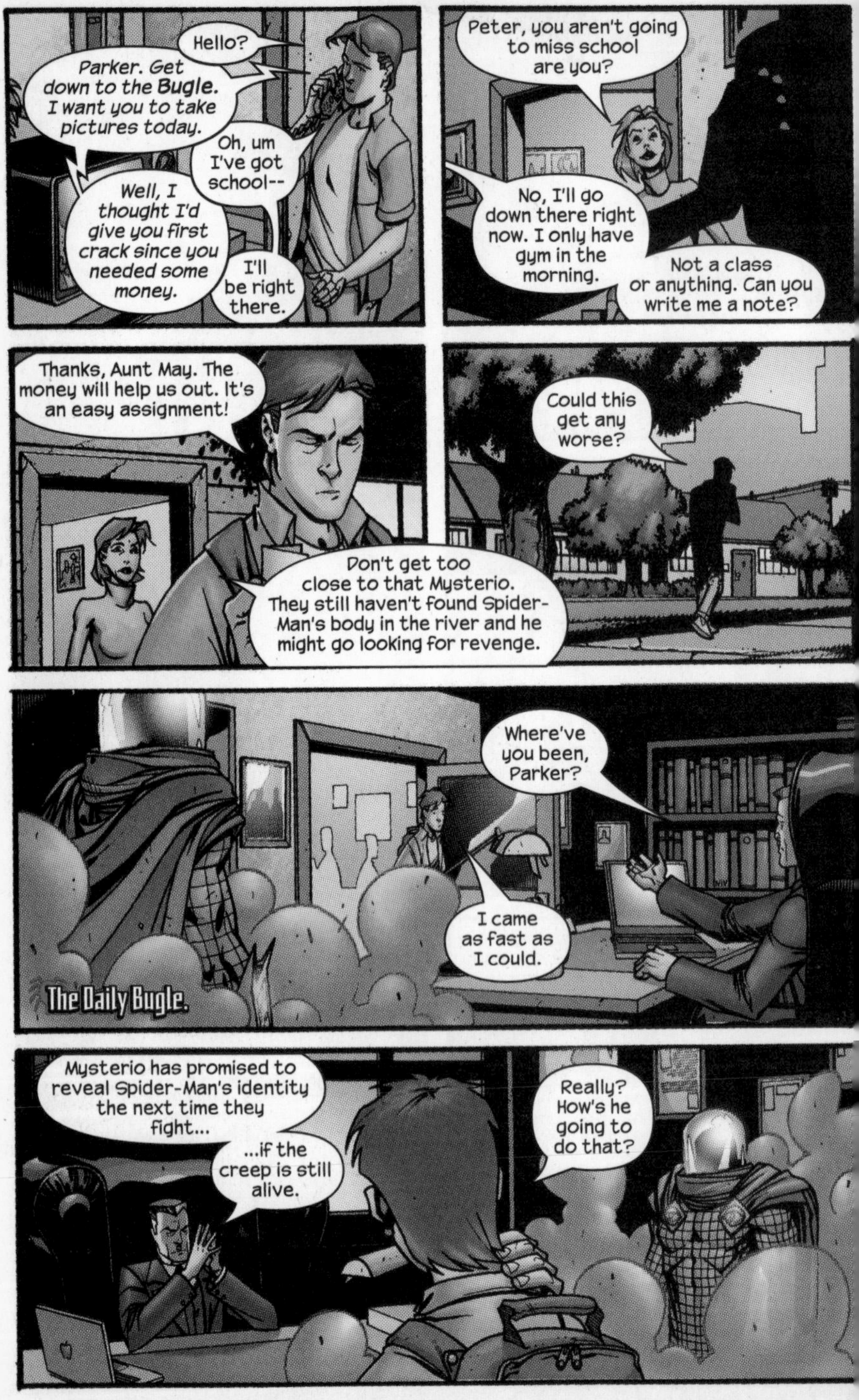
Hello?
Parker. Get down to the Bugle. I want you to take pictures today.
Oh, um I've got school--
Well, I thought I'd give you first crack since you needed some money.
I'll be right there.
Peter, you aren't going to miss school are you?
No, I'll go down there right now. I only have gym in the morning.
Not a class or anything. Can you write me a note?
Thanks, Aunt May. The money will help us out. It's an easy assignment!
Don't get too close to that Mysterio. They still haven't found Spider-Man's body in the river and he might go looking for revenge.
Could this get any worse?
The Daily Bugle.
Where've you been, Parker?
I came as fast as I could.
Mysterio has promised to reveal Spider-Man's identity the next time they fight...
...if the creep is still alive.
Really? How's he going to do that?

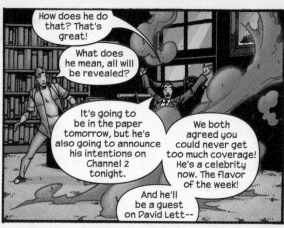

How does he do that? That's great!

What does he mean, all will be revealed?

It's going to be in the paper tomorrow, but he's also going to announce his intentions on Channel 2 tonight.

We both agreed you could never get too much coverage! He's a celebrity now. The flavor of the week!

And he'll be a guest on David Lett--

All will be revealed shortly.

Thanks for the job, Mr. Jameson. I've got to head to school!

Make sure you get that picture! I want a close-up of Spider-Man's face when Mysterio pulls his mask off. A close-up!

Later that night...

Oh, you've got to be kidding me. He's giving autographs?!?

Well, let's hope this works.

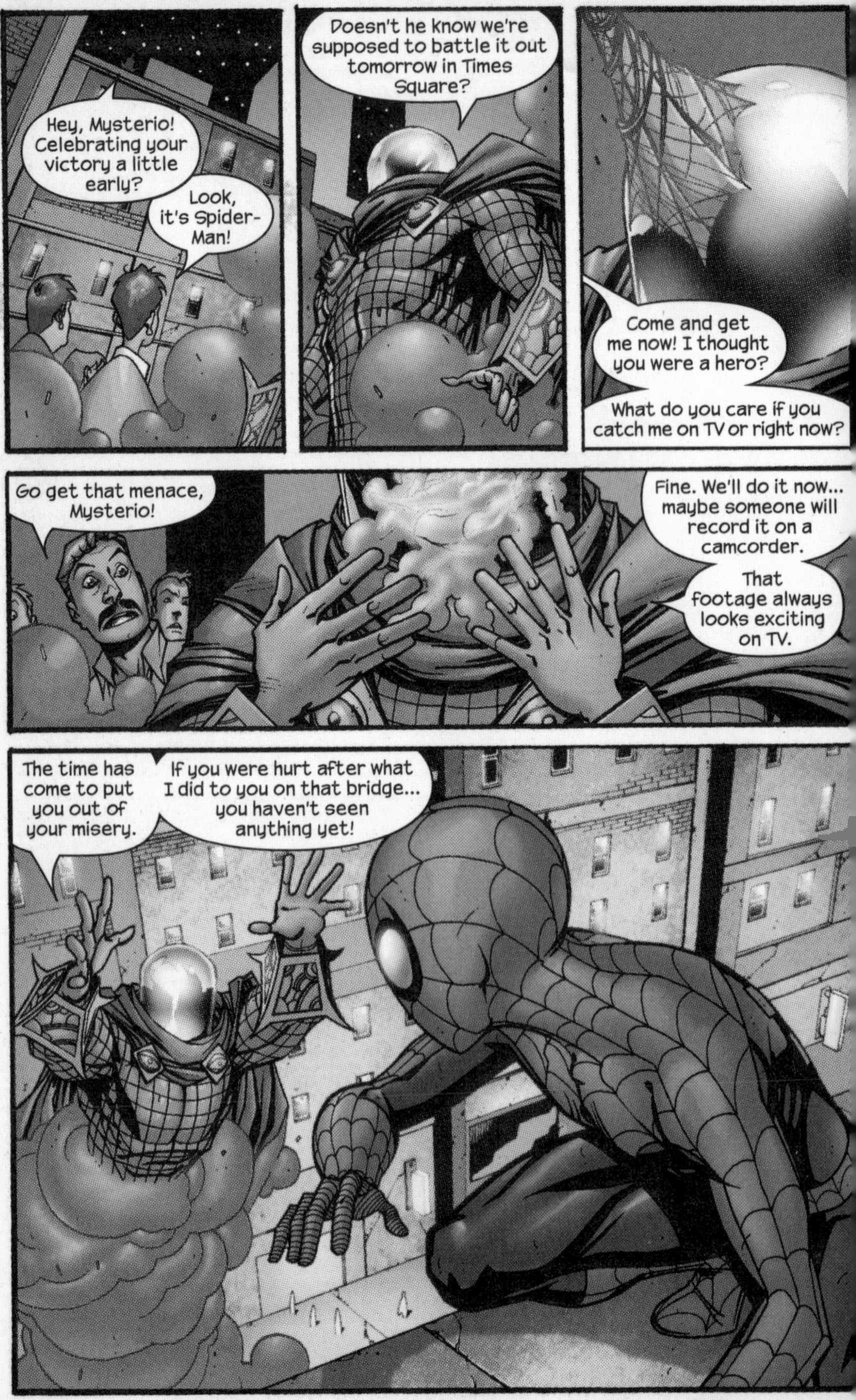
Hey, Mysterio! Celebrating your victory a little early?
Look, it's Spider-Man!
Doesn't he know we're supposed to battle it out tomorrow in Times Square?
Come and get me now! I thought you were a hero?
What do you care if you catch me on TV or right now?
Go get that menace, Mysterio!
Fine. We'll do it now... maybe someone will record it on a camcorder.
That footage always looks exciting on TV.
The time has come to put you out of your misery.
If you were hurt after what I did to you on that bridge... you haven't seen anything yet!

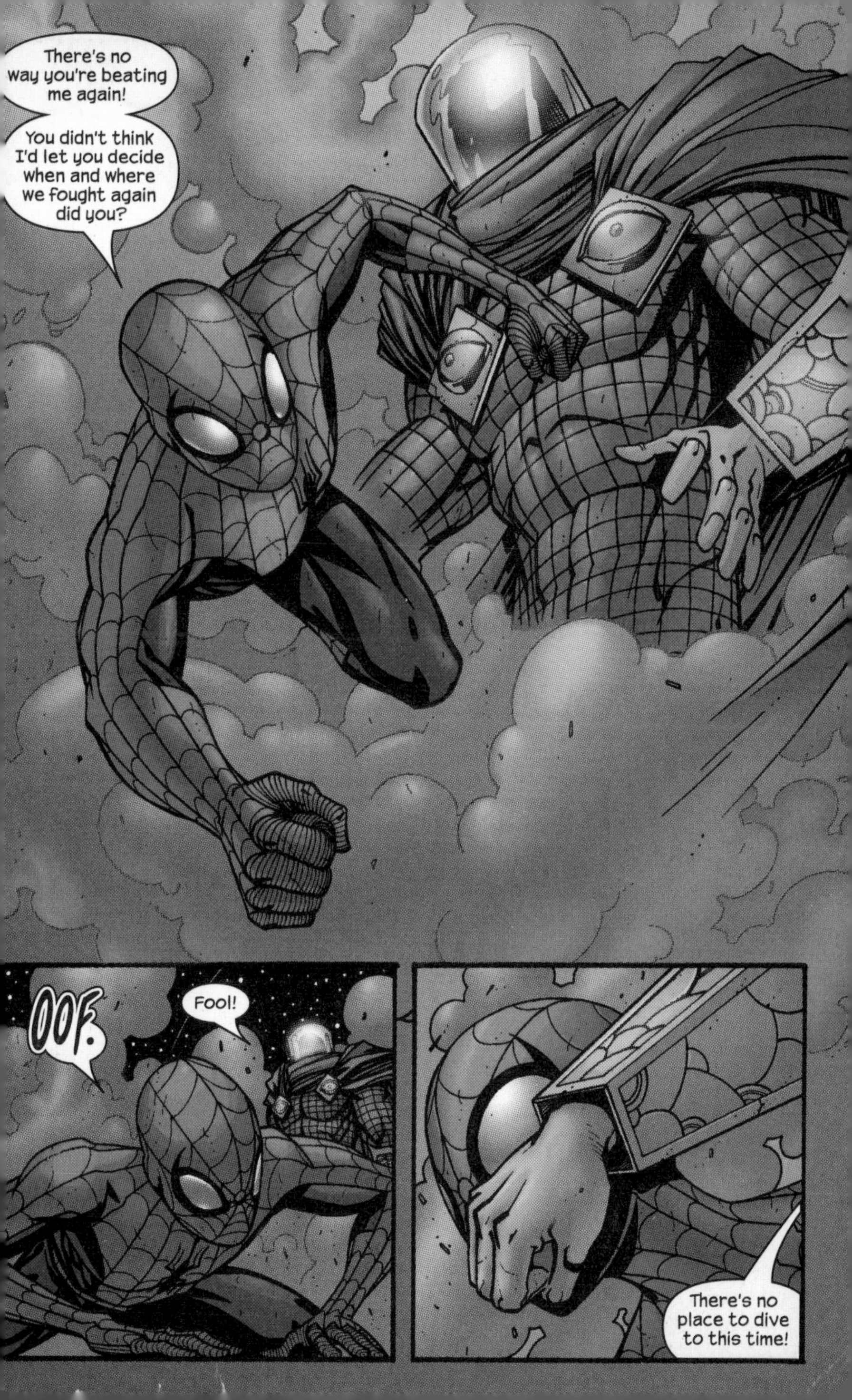
There's no way you're beating me again!
You didn't think I'd let you decide when and where we fought again did you?
OOF.
Fool!
There's no place to dive to this time!

I've worked too hard to have you defeat me now!

Worked too hard at what? What does all of this have to do with my robbery spree?

You actually believed you were behind those robberies?

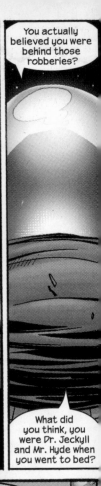

What did you think, you were Dr. Jeckyll and Mr. Hyde when you went to bed?

I was a special effects maker in Hollywood...

...I watched you on TV and wondered if I could do those things. Create props to help me perform those amazing stunts.

And I could.

So, you robbed all those places as me? But why become Mysterio?

Because after I used you to make the money I decided I wanted to be the hero, too.

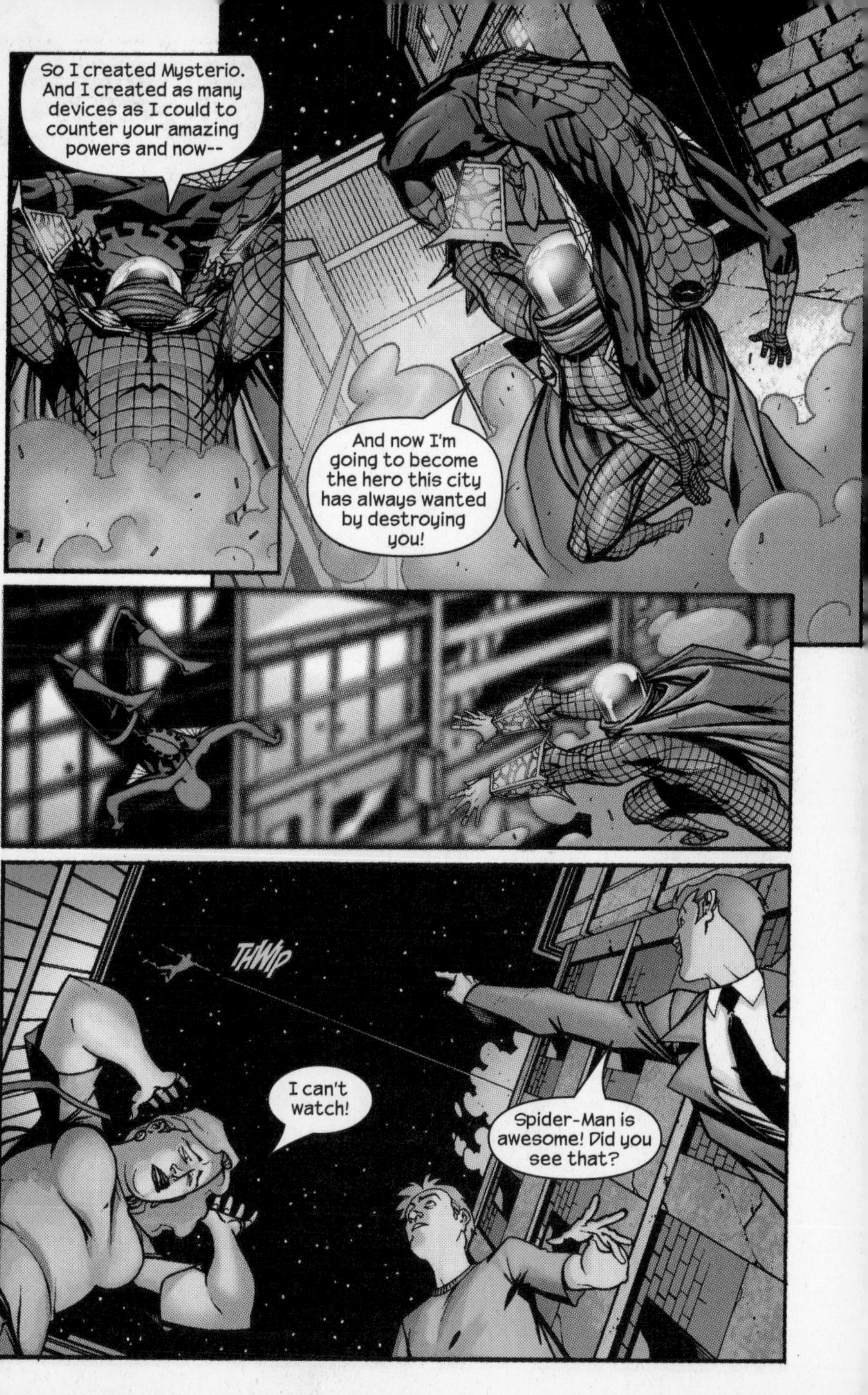
So I created Mysterio. And I created as many devices as I could to counter your amazing powers and now--
And now I'm going to become the hero this city has always wanted by destroying you!
THWIP
I can't watch!
Spider-Man is awesome! Did you see that?

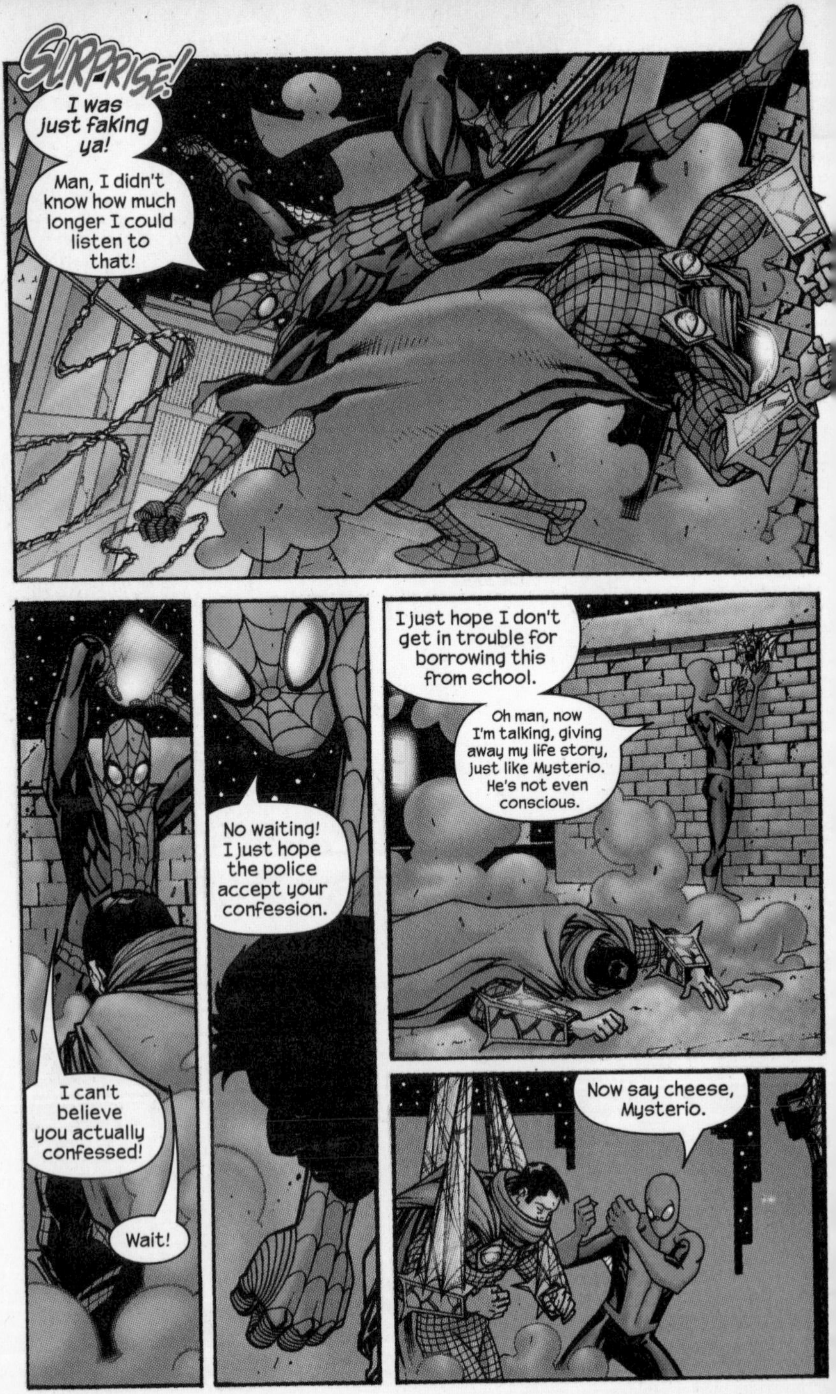
SURPRISE!
I was just faking ya!
Man, I didn't know how much longer I could listen to that!
I can't believe you actually confessed!
Wait!
No waiting! I just hope the police accept your confession.
I just hope I don't get in trouble for borrowing this from school.
Oh man, now I'm talking, giving away my life story, just like Mysterio. He's not even conscious.
Now say cheese, Mysterio.

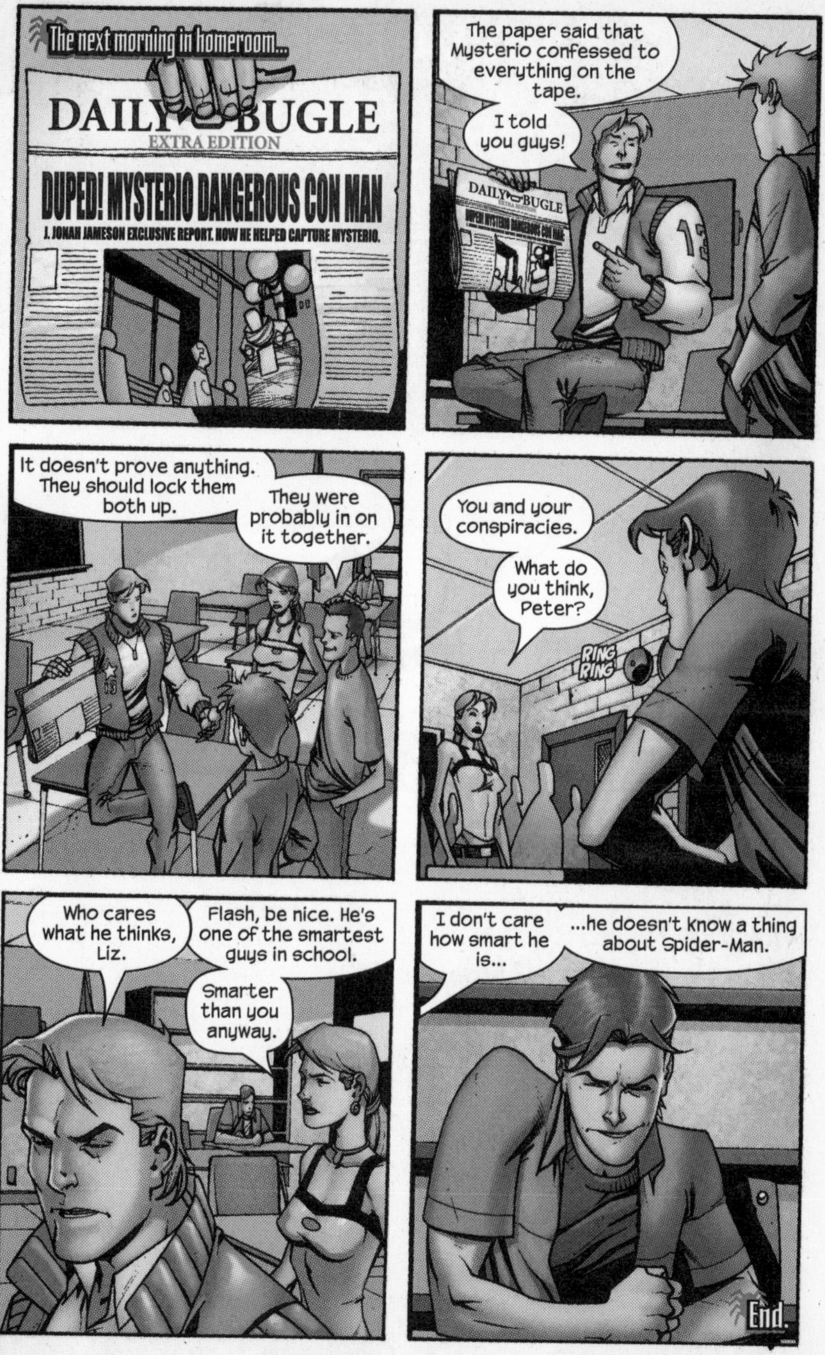
The next morning in homeroom...
DAILY BUGLE
EXTRA EDITION
DUPED! MYSTERIO DANGEROUS CON MAN
J. JONAH JAMESON EXCLUSIVE REPORT. HOW HE HELPED CAPTURE MYSTERIO.
The paper said that Mysterio confessed to everything on the tape.
I told you guys!
It doesn't prove anything. They should lock them both up.
They were probably in on it together.
You and your conspiracies.
What do you think, Peter?
RING RING
Who cares what he thinks, Liz.
Flash, be nice. He's one of the smartest guys in school.
Smarter than you anyway.
I don't care how smart he is...
...he doesn't know a thing about Spider-Man.
End.

Ma
Spider-Man Sketchbook

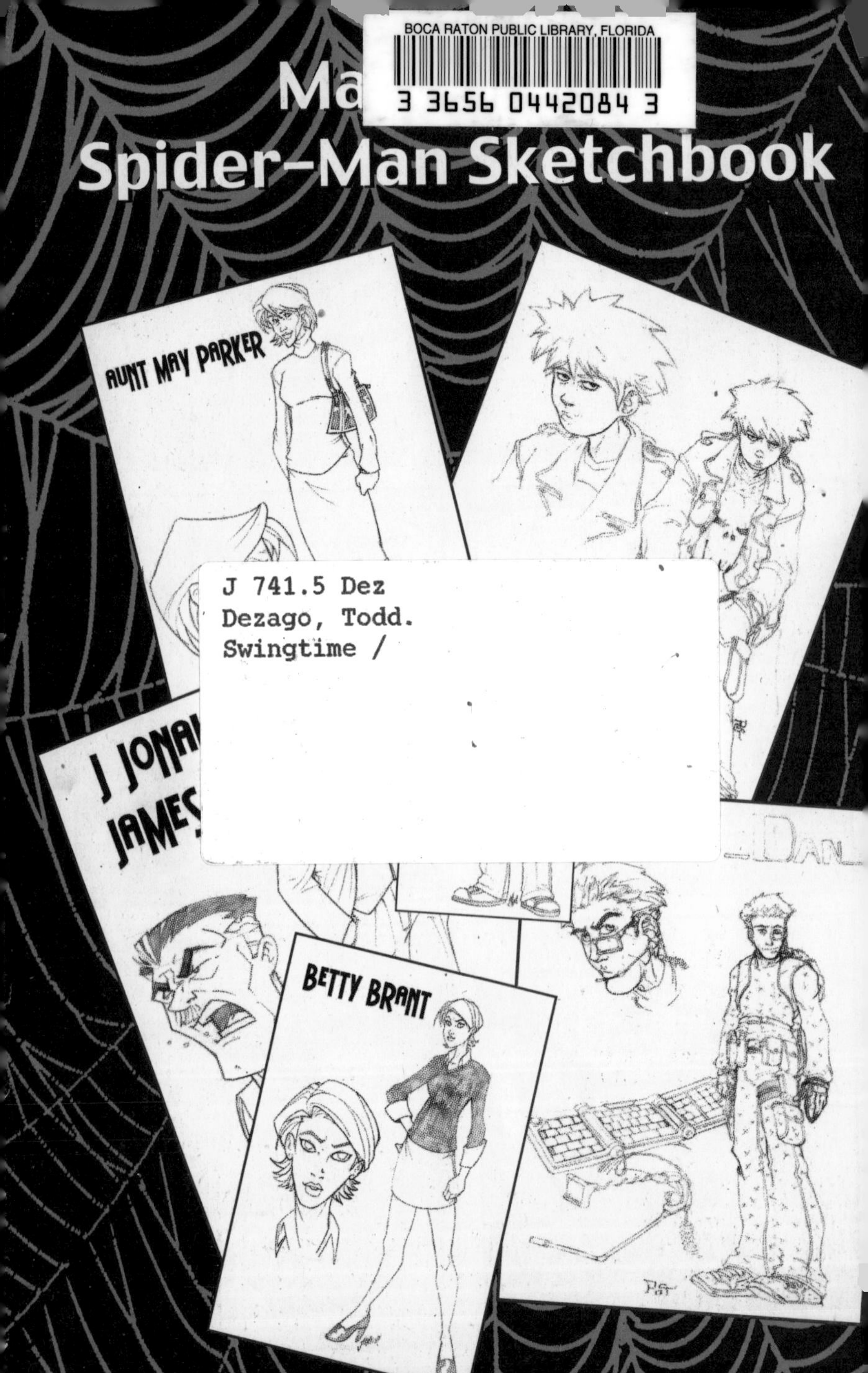
AUNT MAY PARKER
J JONA
JAMES
BETTY BRANT
DAN